EMPLOYMENT,
INCOME DISTRIBUTION
AND
DEVELOPMENT

Employment,
Income Distribution
and
Development

Edited by

FRANCES STEWART

FRANK CASS – LONDON

First published in 1975 in Great Britain by
FRANK CASS AND COMPANY LIMITED
67 Great Russell Street, London WC1B 3BT, England

and in the United States of America by
FRANK CASS AND COMPANY LIMITED
c/o International Scholarly Book Services Inc.
P.O. Box 4347, Portland, Oregon 97208

ISBN 0 7146 3057 8

This collection of essays first appeared in a Special Issue on Employment and Income Distribution of the *Journal of Development Studies*, Volume 11 No. 2, published by Frank Cass and Company Limited.

Printed in Great Britain by
H. E. Warne Ltd., London and St. Austell

Contents

Contents

Introduction

These essays cover diverse topics on questions of employment, unemployment and income distribution in the Third World. The justification for collecting them into a single volume arises from the recent identification of the problem of employment in developing countries with that of income distribution. ILO experts meeting to define un- and underemployment included workers with 'abnormally low earnings' as among the underemployed [*ILO, 1966*;] similarly, Turnham [*1970*], in his review of the employment problem for the OECD, suggested including all those full-time workers whose incomes fell 'below some reference level—say one-third or less of full-time earnings of the employed population'. This approach was developed by the pilot missions on employment of the ILO: 'Poverty therefore emerges as the most compelling aspect of the whole employment problem in Colombia' [*ILO, 1970, para. 217*]. The poverty in question is not simply low absolute standards of living, but low standards *relative* to the average prevailing in the society. Hence it merges into the question of income distribution.

The poverty approach to employment problems is based on a number of factors. In the first place it arose from the difficulties encountered in defining and measuring unemployment in developing countries. The concept of open involuntary unemployment was borrowed from developed countries, where it is fairly easy to measure since the unemployed come forward to claim insurance benefits and to register themselves as seeking work; it is also normally the most significant aspect of excess supply of labour. However, even in developed countries, there are other dimensions of unemployment. Joan Robinson[1] first identified 'disguised unemployment', as those who took inferior jobs when they lost their primary occupations in a depression. Fluctuations in activity rates, with the pressure of demand in the labour market, particularly among married women, also suggest that in developed countries the figures for open unemployment by no means fully cover all those who would be available for work, should jobs materialise. In developing countries the absence of comprehensive unemployment benefits, together with the much more flexible response of the dominant self-employment sector to changes in the supply of labour, means that a major response to failure to find satisfactory employment in the so-called 'modern' sector is to take up some occupation in the self-employment sector.

Open unemployment only captures the tip of the iceberg, in relation to the total numbers who would be available for jobs in the high wage sector, were such jobs available.

In these essays the situation is illustrated for India and Peru, by Krishnamurty and Figueroa. Krishnamurty shows, using National Sample Survey Data, that the urban open unemployment rate (including those working 34 hours or less and willing to undertake additional work) was 2·6 per cent in India in 1966–7, a low rate even by the standards of many developed countries. Moreover, 32 per cent of the workforce in 1964–5 were working long hours (35 hours and more) with very low incomes—monthly per capita expenditure of Rs. 24 or less. Further 'many potential workers prefer to keep out of the labour force rather than actively seek work they know is very hard to get and often very poorly paid' (p.000). Figueroa suggests a remarkably similar (and low) open urban unemployment rate in Peru—2·8 per cent in Lima in 1961 and 4·2 per cent in 1967. But when those working short hours and those earning low incomes are included, the figure rose to 25·6 per cent in 1967.

However, while the argument concerning the inadequacy of the unemployment figures is unexceptionable, it offers no solutions to the problem of identifying and counting the rest of the iceberg. There has been considerable argument about who should be included as underemployed. Much attention has centred around the concept of marginal productivity. Nurkse [1953, Ch. 2] identified the 'disguised unemployed' as those whose marginal product was zero, and who could therefore be employed elsewhere without affecting the level of output in their initial occupation. But the existence of such zero marginal product work has been questioned by many empirical studies showing positive marginal product. Theoretically, Sen [1966] demonstrated that so long as marginal product per hour is constant over the relevant range it need not be zero for the level of output to be unaffected by removal of workers. Others have defined underemployment by the relationship of wage to marginal product. A common definition—used by Fei and Ranis in their essay—is to include as surplus labour all those whose wages or incomes, *exceed* their marginal product. This would of course include those with zero marginal product, but would not necessarily include all the Sen surplus labour. A different approach, adopted by Sabot [1974], is to identify underemployment as arising where marginal productivity of workers in one sector exceeds that in another, and where therefore output could be raised by shifting workers between sectors. This might be termed Pareto-inefficient employment.

None of these suggested definitions need lead to a poverty definition, though it is likely that most of those identified as underemployed according to the marginal product approaches will also be among the poorest in society. The poverty approach is a pragmatic attempt to cut through the theoretical difficulties, and the almost insuperable empirical problem of identifying and measuring marginal product. The poverty approach goes some way to including all those who constitute 'the employment problem' in developing countries. Three different aspects of the employment problem have been identified [ILO, 1970, para. 44]:

  (1) Inefficient use of labour and hence loss of potential output
  (2) Frustration among job-seekers
  (3) Low incomes

Relatively low incomes will tend to characterise each of these categories. Nonetheless the poverty approach has serious drawbacks. First, exactly where the line should be drawn—one-third, one-sixth, or one-tenth of average incomes, for example—is an arbitrary matter. Secondly, lack of income through lack of work, and lack of income through low productivity work are completely different phenomena and analysis and cure may be confused by identifying them. Thirdly, frustration arises at all levels, not simply among those with the lowest incomes trying to secure better jobs, but also the medium income earners seeking high-income jobs, so that poverty only captures a portion of the frustrated. Fourthly, income distribution may be unequal—and hence relative poverty significant—for many reasons besides lack of employment opportunities. Hence the approach may indicate large numbers in relative poverty, despite the fact that they might fairly be described as fully employed.

One must conclude, then, that relative poverty, while clearly an important aspect of employment problems, is neither necessary nor sufficient as a measure of open unemployment, and is only a good measure of *underemployment* if it is taken to be so by definition.

This is not to argue that poverty is unimportant. On the contrary it is the prime problem of developing countries, and should be studied directly. From this point of view, study of employment problems might better be justified for the light shed on poverty, rather than studies of poverty and income distribution justified for the light shed on employment problems.

The last section of this volume includes three essays which have income distribution as their central theme. Each, in a way, supports the general contention that income distribution needs to be studied in large part separately from employment.

Nafziger examines the origins of entrepreneurs in a newly industrialising city in South India and shows that a disproportionate number—particularly among the successful—have their origin in high caste and economically successful families. This is explained by the use of initial privileged status to accumulate further advantages in education, access to capital and government favours, etc., which lead to economic success. Hinchcliffe compares earnings and income differentials in 10 countries at different stages of development. Despite substantial data defects, which he discusses fully, and difficulties in interpretation, some interesting conclusions emerge. In particular, it is shown that the ratio of earnings of the less to the more highly educated is much higher among developing countries than among developed countries. He offers three possible explanations of the phenomenon: differences in the ratios of physical capital per man; differences in relative scarcity; and differences in on-the-job training. The relative scarcity hypothesis relates the differentials most closely to the employment situation. The high educational differential might arise through excess supply of unskilled labour among the less developed countries, and consequently very low relative incomes. According to one study quoted [*Psacharopoulos and Hinchcliffe, 1972*] 35 per cent of the difference in primary/secondary earnings ratio, and 50 per cent of the higher/secondary ratio across countries could be explained by relative stocks of educated manpower. But it must be noted that the concept 'relative stocks of educated manpower' does not subsume relative supplies of uneducated manpower, which is at the heart of the underemployment question. It is interesting to compare Hinchcliffe's ratios (Table 1) between developing countries. For example, the ratios in India and Kenya are pretty similar: yet it is well known that the employment situation, particularly among the educated, was very different at that time, with substantial excess supplies of educated labour of most kinds in India, and deficient supplies in Kenya. It might appear that relative incomes are determined by various institutional and bargaining factors, as much as by the economic factors discussed.

The third essay on income distribution by Douglas Smith discusses the effect of the Green Revolution. Here it is demonstrated that distribution of income depends on technological possibilities, distribution of assets (land) and access to other inputs. It is shown that the distribution of income is a function of social and economic class—via initial distribution of wealth and differing access to inputs. The conclusion is thus similar to that of Nafziger. Some would argue e.g. Griffin [1972] that the technology available is also a function of class, further extending class influence over income distribution.

All three essays thus lend support to the hypothesis that socio-economic class, institutional and bargaining factors are important determinants of income distribution. While none of the essays are directly concerned to test the hypothesis that the balance of supply and demand for different types of labour is the key determinant of income distribution, they do suggest that other factors may be of much greater if not exclusive importance. It is also possible that the distribution of employment opportunities—the balance of demand and supply for labour—is itself determined by more fundamental socio-economic factors. Viewed in this way both relative poverty and maldistribution of employment opportunities may be the effects of the initial inequalities in economic and social status and political power. These hypotheses need testing to establish whether the poverty approach to employment problems is a blind alley which may obfuscate more important issues.

Attention has been mainly directed at *static* measures of un- and underemployment—that is to say quantities at a particular time. Dynamic aspects, showing how such quantities are changing over time, are possibly of greater importance, and also easier to measure, insofar as the arbitrariness of particular static measures, may not matter much, or may cancel each other out, in looking at dynamic trends. There are a number of ways in which the dynamic question may be approached. Three are adopted here.

First, the aggregative approach, illustrated in Figueroa's figures for Peru. Taking figures for population increase, work force increase and rates of migration, it can readily be shown that the 'modern' sector would have to expand at a much faster rate than it has in many countries to absorb the extra supplies of labour, and consequently the employment problem is likely to worsen overtime. The approach may be generalised. Assume the rate of growth of population and work force are the same, at n per cent per annum, the ratio of modern sector to total employment is Qm, then the required rate of growth of modern sector employment to absorb all the extra labour coming on the labour market each year is[2]

$$\bar{e} = n/Qm$$

Since the modern sector in most developing countries forms only a small proportion of the total workforce (varying from 1 to say 30 per cent), employment in the 'modern' sector has to grow correspondingly faster than the total workforce to absorb all the extra labour. In the 'typical' case, where the modern sector forms 10 per cent of the total work force, and the workforce increase is $2 \cdot 5$ per cent per annum the required annual increase in modern sector employment would be 25 per cent per annum. At rates of employment expansion less than this, numbers outside the 'modern' sector would continue to rise. If it is assumed that outside the 'modern' sector there is already chronic underemployment, then additions to numbers there will add to the problem of underemployment, unless there are off setting changes in productive employment opportunities. This approach implicity assumes that additions to employment outside the so-called 'modern' sector add to underemployment rather than to productive activity. It does not, of course, imply that there are no productive opportunities outside this sector—after all most people's means of subsistence are produced in the non-'modern' sector, but it denies that these productive activities are being added to overtime. One of the main purposes of the new approach to the *informal* sector is to challenge this implicit assumption. We shall be discussing this more below.

Two of the essays provide a less aggregative approach to the dynamic question—though they too concentrate on 'modern' sector employment opportunities. Fei and Ranis examine the developmental experience of Korea and Taiwan, paying particular attention to the differing role of agriculture and industry, and the implications for employment. They argue that in both countries an initial import-substituting (I-S) strategy subsequently gave way to export substitution, and that the export substitution policy made for rapid increases in employment, and removed any conflict between employment and output growth. In Korea, a stagnant agricultural sector meant that the initial I-S strategy had to be financed by imported capital. In Taiwan, the agricultural sector provided the export surplus required to finance industrialisation. Export substitution is defined as occurring where labour intensive manufactured exports replace traditional exports as the dominant export items. In both countries, labour surplus (defined as existing where the real wage exceeds the marginal product in agriculture) was exhausted a few years after the export substitution. This is called the commercialisation point. The *switching* point (where numbers in agriculture begin to decline) is expected to occur within 10 years or so of the commercialisation point. The Fei-Ranis model thus suggests that labour surplus is a temporary phenomenon associated particularly with the I-S stage of development. However, the elimination of labour surplus in the two countries occurred only using the Fei-Ranus definition; alternative definitions, e.g. abnormally low earnings, would still reveal some underemployment. Nonetheless the two countries did experience remarkably rapid rates of growth of output and employment. Although there are reasons for believing them to be exceptionally well placed to adopt an export substitution policy successfully, the Fei-Ranis model offers a helpful corrective to overconcentration on the I-S stage of development, in which so many countries seem to be stuck. Fei-Ranis argue that a major reversal of policies was required to move from I-S to export substitution. A major problem in many countries appears to be the difficulties involved in achieving such a reversal, in view of the many vested interests that have developed in the I-S policies. It would be interesting, therefore, to have more information on how the change was achieved so thoroughly in these countries.

Zaidi and Mukhopadhyay use input/output matrices to compare the differing structural links in economies at different stages of development, and in particular the links between primary (food and raw material production and processing) and secondary (other industry) sectors. They hypothesise that underdevelopment is characterised by isolation of the two sectors: as countries develop they may do so on the basis of agriculture providing inputs for industry, or industry providing inputs for agriculture. Which trends are predominant emerge from examination of the input/output matrices. It is shown that in the U.S.A. agriculture consumes the products of industry, but industry makes little use of agricultural output. Japan is seen to be moving in a similar direction. However, it must be noted that the matrices do not allow for the consumption of agricultural products by industrial workers, or the converse. India initially (1959) displays the lack of interdependence believed to characterise underdevelopment. However, since then trends have been towards industrial use of primary products, in contrast to the U.S. and Japan. The pattern of development can have significant employment implications, insofar as employment requirements per unit of output differ between the sectors. Unit labour requirements change over time with technical change, and the net change in employment is the product of changes in sectoral output and in unit labour requirements. In India, it is estimated that, while employment per unit of primary output fell between 1959 and 1970, the rise in total employment (direct and indirect in the primary sector) requirements in industry meant that 'the overall employment potential in the economy has increased considerably' (p.73).

These dynamic approaches are almost exclusively concerned with modern or formal sector employment, treating the rest of the economy as a residual which may absorb additional supplies of labour, or release them, according to the demands of the 'modern' sector, but which offers little in the way of productive economic opportunity. This view has been challenged by recent attention paid to the concept of the informal sector.[3] It is claimed, with some empirical backing, that those outside the recognised 'modern' sector structure are also involved in economic activities, and are not automatically in a state of disguised unemployment or underemployment. At its most extreme this view would mean that everyone who is capable and willing finds as much work (often self-employed rather than employed) as they want, in the informal sector if not the formal sector. Accordingly, concepts of underemployment or disguised unemployment are inapplicable; employment may be allocatively inefficient, and it may be associated with low productivity and low earnings, but it is not deficient in *total* quantity, though there may be fewer opportunities in particular types of activity than the numbers who would like to occupy them.[4]

An obvious criticism of the concept of the 'informal sector', is its lack of clear-cut and widely-accepted definition. Each observer seems to have their own ideas of what it is. Kenneth King here defines the sector as follows: 'their informality derives from their being unrecognised in government employment statistics, and operating in the main out of makeshift shelters on urban wastelands, roadsides and forest fringes' (p.108). While this definition makes the concept precariously dependent on government statistics—would the sector disappear if the government decided to include them in its statistics?—his essay gives vivid empirical flesh to the somewhat amorphous concept. He is concerned to examine training provided in and mainly for the informal sector. 'There are probably greater numbers moving through this level than there are in the whole of the government's technical school and training projects' (p.109). As King shows, the conditions of training, its duration and nature, differ radically from government sponsored or approved training. This suggests that so long as government policy only extends to a portion of economic activity, it is likely to be ineffective.

It may indeed not only be ineffective but actually counter-productive. Stewart and Weeks suggest that the proposed policy of wage reduction to increase employment may suffer in this way. A reduction of wages in the formal sector may increase employment in that sector, but total employment opportunities may decline insofar as the lower wages in the formal sector encourages a shift of economic activity from the more labour intensive low-wage informal sector, to the less labour intensive high-wage formal sector.

Roemer provides a good example of the one sector analysis and prescription. He applies a constant elasticity production function to manufacturing industry in Ghana and concludes that a 25 per cent fall in the wage-rental ratio would result in about 30 per cent more jobs. The methodology involved in the C.E.S. production function approach has been subject to searching criticism for its rigid and unrealistic assumptions [O'Herlihy, 1972]. It has also been shown that results from studies in different countries have been radically different both absolutely and in industry ranking (Morawetz, 1973). The Stewart-Weeks paper suggests that the conclusions may also be defective because of the single sector approach, ignoring the flexible wage sector.

One important and difficult question that arises is how research should be conducted in the informal sector. By its very nature (unrecorded in official statistics and often illegal) many established statistical techniques are inapplicable. Methods of research used in social anthropology may be more appropriate.[5] King uses a sort of halfway house methodology relying on fairly informal chats with fifty or so roadside operators selected, presumably, because they were willing and able to talk. The method throws a good deal of light on this murky area, but does not provide data amenable to econometric techniques. The technique, inevitably, makes generalisation difficult and leaves a lot to the interpretation of the investigator. The informal sector lends itself to informal research techniques, and hence, unavoidably, to informal conclusions.

Elkan is fairly firmly anchored in the formal sector, looking at the employment generated in the tourist industry in Kenya and Tanzania. He shows that facile generalisation is not possible, in the differing conclusions for Kenya (where much demand generated by tourists is met by local supplies) and Tanzania, where it is imported. Hence whether or not tourism is a labour-using industry depends on the country concerned, and also on the nature of the industry. As with much other industry, small scale operations are less capital intensive than large. Apart from psychological effects, which tend to be assessed subjectively, there may also be an effect on employment and income distribution via the effect on products, which is not allowed for in Elkan's essay. Tourism provides a market for high standard Western style products, in terms of food, medical services, hotel accommodation and clothes. Local provision of such commodities often involves relatively capital intensive methods, import and technology intensive. While the initial justification for local production may be tourist demand, the products tend also to be consumed locally, providing the type of consumption goods which give reality to monetary inequality in income. The greater the import content of tourist consumption, the less important this effect is likely to be.

This discussion raises a different aspect of the link between income distribution and employment: income distribution (itself largely a product of the structure of employment) in turn influences that structure via the consumption pattern it generates. Figueroa examines the link between income distribution and employment in Peru, by looking at input/output tables, and derived demand for labour of the consumption of different income groups. He shows that the derived demand for labour increases with income but at a decreasing rate, so that redistribution of income towards a more egalitarian distribution would increase employment opportunities. Similar research elsewhere has produced conflicting results.[6] The labour intensive nature of services, consumed to a greater extent by the rich, has tended to offset the more capital intensive nature of the consumer goods they consume. However, most of the research has failed to examine in detail the nature of the products consumed by each income category, in each industrial category. It has been assumed that the labour intensity of production methods within each industrial category is the same for each income group.[7] Within industrial groups there are very large variations in product characteristics, and labour requirements. For example, housing may use no machinery at all, and only local materials and unskilled labour, or it may be highly import and machine intensive. Similar variations are possible in most industrial categories. In general, it is likely that for any category the lower income groups will consume more labour intensive products than the richer. This is because high income products tend to be those developed in advanced countries using their inputs and capital intensive methods, while poorer products are often those developed locally reflecting the local resource base. Thus in the subsistence sector all products consumed must be highly labour intensive; similarly the urban informal sector makes ingenious use of local labour in the products produced and consumed. There is likely therefore to be an important link between income distribution and labour requirements via product, which is not captured in research using conventional input/output tables, with single technical coefficients for each industry.

The relationship between employment and income distribution is therefore a complex one. Maldistribution of access to inputs leads to unequal distribution of productive employment possibilities, and hence to inequality in income distribution. In this way the distribution of employment opportunities and the distribution of income, and hence poverty, are associated. But this is not to argue that it is the employment situation which *creates* poverty; rather it is a system in which some secure a disproportionate share of the economy's resources—of access to capital, land and technology—which has the effect of producing both maldistribution of employment and of income. The system which produces these effects is itself historically produced, the initially privileged being in a powerful position to reinforce their privilege, as the essays here by Nafziger and Smith show. Technological possibilities are also important. Insofar as advanced country technology is adopted, it leads to the use of capital intensive methods and hence maldistribution of resources in Third World countries. Where technology is locally created much depends on who creates it and for whom; the informal sector is gradually developing its own egalitarian technology.[8] But technology developed for the Third World may also be inegalitarian in effect, as the Green Revolution suggests.

FRANCES STEWART

NOTES

1. 'It is natural to describe the adoption of inferior occupations by dismissed workers as disguised unemployment' [*Robinson, 1937, p.84*].

2. The extra labour supply, $\Delta E = n.N$, where N=total work force, n the % rate of growth. The annual rate of growth of the 'modern' sector required to absorb all these additions

$$\bar{e} = \frac{\Delta E}{M} \quad \text{where M= numbers in the modern sector.}$$

$$M = Qm.N$$

$$\text{so } \bar{e} = \frac{n.N.}{Qm.N} = \frac{n}{Qm}$$

indicating that the required rate of growth of the 'modern' sector is less the lower the rate of growth of the workforce and the larger the 'modern' sector. To allow for some absorption into the non-'modern' sector, one can modify the formula to

$$\bar{e} = \frac{r.n.}{Qm}$$

where r is the proportion of the extra labour force who remain 'productively' in the non-'modern' sector.

3. Keith Hart has done pioneering work in this field [*1971*] and ILO [*1972*].

4. Put like this, the view is similar to that of Ricardo in the early nineteenth century, who claimed in argument with Malthus that there was no overall deficiency of employment opportunities, only short term imbalances in the supply and demand in particular occupations.

5. These are the methods used by Hart [*1971*].

6. These results are summarised by D. Morawetz [*1974, pp.505-6*].

7. With the exception of R. Soligo [*1972*] in West Pakistan, who finds that within each industry group the consumption of the poor tends to be more labour intensive than that of the rich.

8. The relationship between technology and employment is examined in F. Stewart *1974*].

REFERENCES

Griffin, K., 1972, *The Green Revolution: an Economic Analysis*, UNRISD, Geneva.

Hart, K., 1973, 'Informal Income Opportunities and Urban Employment in Ghana', in Jolly *et al.* (eds.), *Third World Employment, Problems and Strategy*.

ILO, 1966, *Measurement of Underemployment, Concepts and Methods*, Geneva: Eleventh International Conference of Labour Statisticians, Report IV.

ILO, 1970, *Toward Full Employment, A Programme for Colombia* prepared by a Geneva: Inter Agency Team organised by the ILO.

ILO, 1972, *Employment, Incomes and Equality: A Strategy for Increasing Productive Employmentin Kenya*, Geneva: ILO Kenya Employment Mission.

Morawetz, D., 1973, *Elasticities of Substitution in Industry: What do we learn from Econometric Estimates?*, Jerusalem: Hebrew University, Economics Department Research Report No. 51.

Morawetz, D., 1974, 'Employment Implications of Industrialisation in Developing Countries: A Survey', *Economic Journal*, pp. 505-6.

Nurkse, R., 1953, *Problems of Capital Formation in Underdeveloped Countries*, Oxford: Blackwell.

O'Herlihy, St. J., C., 1972, 'Capital Labour Substitution and the Developing Countries: A Problem of Measurement', *Bulletin of the Oxford University Institute of Economics and Statistics*.

Psacharopoulos, G., and K. Hinchcliffe, 1972, 'Further Evidence of the Elasticity of Substitution between Different Types of Educated Labour', *Journal of Political Economy*.

Robinson, J., 1937, *Essays in the Theory of Employment*, London: Macmillan.

Sabot, R., 1974, mimeo, Oxford Institute of Economics and Statistics.

Sen, A. K., 1966, 'Peasants and Dualism with or without Surplus Labour', *Journal of Political Economy*.

Soligo, R., 1972, *Factor Intensity of Consumption Patterns, Income Distribution and Employment in West Pakistan*, mimeo, Rice PDS.

Stewart, F., 1974, 'Technology and Employment', *World Development*.

Turnham, D., and I. Jaeger, 1970, *The Employment Problem in Less Developed Countries, A Review of the Evidence*, Paris: OECD.

Some Aspects of Unemployment in Urban India

By J. Krishnamurty*

A careful examination of the information available for the 'sixties suggests rather low urban unemployment rates for India. Using more 'generous' definitions of unemployment makes very little difference and the much higher live register 'estimates' are totally unreliable. Also it is clear that literates up to and including secondaries who are in their twenties face a serious unemployment problem. The problem facing graduates is less serious and it is suggested that an employment policy which puts all the emphasis on eradicating graduate unemployment may in fact aggravate the unemployment problem.

In much of the literature on Indian planning there has been a tendency to overstate the extent of open unemployment in urban areas. This partly arises from the use of the estimates of the 'backlog' of unemployment provided in the earlier Plan documents which, in the case of urban areas, were derived from the numbers reported to be on the live register of the employment exchanges.[1] We attempt below to show why such estimates are unreliable and then use the available National Sample Survey (NSS) data to examine the extent of urban unemployment.

The live register figures relate to job seekers registering at employment exchanges. These include rural registrants (who do not form part of the urban labour force), students (who apply in anticipation of joining the labour force), and employed persons seeking better jobs (the 'unhappily employed'). Not all the unemployed register, while many job seekers register at more than one exchange. By using a set of correction factors obtained from a sample survey of the live register [*Directorate General of Employment and Training, 1969; Dantwala Committee, 1970, Ch. 1*] we can estimate the number of urban unemployed registrants. To obtain the number of urban unemployed we divide this estimate by the proportion, reported by the urban labour force surveys of the NSS, of unemployed persons who register with the employment exchanges. The procedure may be represented as follows:

---

*Fellow in Indian Studies at St. Antony's College, Oxford. This paper originated with my work as technical consultant to the Committee of Experts on Unemployment Estimates appointed by the Indian Planning Commission. I am indebted to the members of the Committee, Professors M. L. Dantwala, K. N. Raj and D. B. Lahiri, and my fellow technical consultants, Dr P. M. Visaria and Mr Sudhir Bhattacharya, for advice and help. Thanks are also due to Professors A. K. Sen and Michael Lipton, and Mrs Frances Stewart for suggesting improvements.

$$U = U_R \; \frac{U'}{U_R'}$$

$$\text{Or,} \;\; U = \frac{U_R}{U_R'} \cdot U'$$

where U represents the new estimate of the number of unemployed persons in urban India; U_R the 'corrected' number of urban unemployed registrants; U' the NSS estimate of the number of unemployed persons and U_R' the NSS estimate of urban unemployed registrants.

The fundamental assumption is that the NSS faithfully records the proportion of the urban unemployed who register, but does not faithfully record the actual number. This implies that the unemployed 'excluded' by the 'narrow' definition of the NSS have the same kind of registering behaviour as those 'included' by the NSS. Since the NSS appears to cover just about one in every three urban unemployed registrants, the assumption of similarity in registration behaviour cannot be accepted unless some evidence is brought forward in its support.

It is sometimes held that the live register data are useful, in that they do indicate the pressure of job seekers on the urban labour market.[2] This is doubtful: coverage is partial, and while adjustments can be made for the increase in the number of exchanges, no correction factors exist for multiple registration—which probably increases with the number of exchanges. Also, in many cases job seekers register when they feel jobs are in the offing. For example, this would account for the sharp increase in the numbers on the live register in the wake of the China war in 1962.[3] One cannot deny however that a very sharp deterioration in the employment situation might show up on the live register. The increase from 3·4 million in 1969 to 5·7 in mid–1972 and 7·6 million in mid–1973 cannot be due solely to multiple registration or expansion of coverage. But, as we shall argue later, more reliable indicators of the job situation exist, in particular the Employment Market Information data, free from the defects of the live register.

An obvious alternative is to estimate urban unemployment directly from the NSS. Yet even in the assessment of the employment performance of the Third Plan, while NSS data were used for the rural sector, urban estimates were obtained from the live register. Right up to the Draft Outline of the Fourth Plan (1966–1971) this practice of depending on the live register was followed, [*Dantwala Committee, 1970, pp.5, 12–13*] presumably on the ground that the NSS urban estimates were too low.

The main criticism of the NSS is that while it has a sophisticated sampling procedure and skilled investigators, its definition of employment is too liberal. This is said to cause an understatement of the number of unemployed persons. According to the NSS:

If a person worked (for however short a period) during the seven days immediately preceding the date of enquiry for salary, wages, remuneration or profit in some gainful occupation or as an unpaid helper in the household enterprise, the person is considered to be 'gainfully employed' or simply 'employed' and 'at work'. [*NSS, 1971, p.4*]

TABLE 1

UNEMPLOYMENT RATES IN RECENT YEARS: NSS DATA FOR URBAN INDIA (PERSONS)

	17th Round 1961–62 (1)	18th Round 1963–64 (2)	19th Round 1964–65 ULF (3)	IHH (4)	20th Round 1965–66 (5)	21st Round 1966–67 (6)
1. Unemployed as percentage of population	0·98	0·63	0·62	1·18 (0·51)	0·61	0·51
2. Unemployed as percentage of labour force	3·05	1·99	1·96	3·51 (1·55)	1·97	1·60
3. percentage of employed population working 34 hours or less and available for additional work	—	2·02	—	—	—	0·98

SOURCES: Computed from Table (S.2) on p. 7 of NSS, 21st Round [*1971*]. Column 4 is taken from NSS. 19th Round [*1969, p.7, Table 5*]. The unemployed who do not seek but are available for work are included in the figures for column (4), but excluded from the unemployed and the labour force in calculating the figures in parenthesis. While the estimates in column (3) were obtained from the Urban Labour Force Survey, those of column (4) were a by-product of canvassing an integrated household schedule.

The NSS definition appears to include anybody who did any work during the reference week, but it does exclude from the employed all those who may have worked for a number of weeks, but did not work during the reference week. What needs to be stressed, however, is that if we accept the NSS estimates of the size of the labour force we can use NSS evidence on the hours worked by the employed population and their availability for additional work to get a variety of unemployment estimates from the same set of basic data. For example, in 1966–7, according to the usual NSS definition 1·6 per cent of the labour force was unemployed. If we deem all persons working 34 hours or less and willing to undertake additional work as 'severely underemployed' and club them with the openly unemployed, we get an unemployment rate of about 2·6 per cent. For 1963-64, the corresponding estimate comes to about 4 per cent [NSS, *1967, pp.29, 49*].

This ability to provide a range of estimates is clearly an advantage. We may be interested in the numbers who seek work or in the numbers willing to undertake work if an offer (under specified conditions) were made to them, or the numbers who need work, irrespective of whether they feel the need or not. The NSS data do make it possible to isolate the category of one's choice and set about estimating the numbers involved. The live register figures do not lend themselves to such procedures.

Even on relatively liberal definitions of unemployment the urban unemployment rates appear rather low, both in relation to rural India— where the *open* unemployment rate was about 4 per cent around 1961—

and in relation to urban rates in other underdeveloped countries [*Turn-ham, 1971, pp.48–50, 53–4, 137–140*]. But three sets of factors must be kept in mind while assessing the urban employment situation.

First, there are many members of the employed population who engage themselves in activities like petty trade or household industry with long hours of work, but little to show in terms of income: they face an income, rather than an employment, problem. For example, in 1964–65, out of all workers with a monthly per capita expenditure of Rs 24 or less, over 80 per cent worked for 35 hours or more per week and such workers formed 32 per cent of the working population [*NSS, 1969, pp.104–5*].

Secondly, many potential workers prefer to keep out of the labour force rather than actively seek work which they know is hard to get and often very poorly paid—they are available for, but do not seek, work. Such persons were deemed unemployed in the NSS urban surveys up to the 15th Round and also in the 19th Round (integrated household schedule only). Even if we accept the 19th Round result, which is probably on the high side, our liberal definitions would give a rate of less than 5 per cent—still well below the corresponding rates for other underdeveloped countries or for rural India.

Finally, the employment situation probably worsened after 1967. While the urban working force grew at over 3 per cent per annum between 1961 and 1971, employment in the organised sector grew linearly between 1967 and 1973 at about 2·4 per cent per annum.[4] During the earlier period 1961 to 1966 organised employment grew much more rapidly, at about 6 per cent per annum linear, *i.e.* at about double the rate of growth of the urban labour force. The relatively low rates of unemployment recorded for 1961 to 1967 no doubt reflect the improved job situation which unfortunately did not last.

We next attempt to identify the different segments of the unemployed population in urban areas. Unfortunately, most of the detailed information currently available relates to the openly unemployed and similar information about the under-employed is not available in a ready form, though it could be obtained through additional tabulations of NSS data.

In Table 2 we present unemployment rates by sex, age and educational level. The rates for illiterates are rather low, indicative perhaps of the ease with which they obtain employment, and their willingness to accept almost any kind of employment. The unemployment rates recorded for the more educated sections of the labour force are probably more meaningful as an educated person may prefer to remain unemployed rather than accept a low intensity or low wage job. Unemployment rates are generally low for the 'literate but below secondary' category, only slightly higher for the 'graduates and above' category and rather high for the 'secondary' category. Also rates are generally higher for females compared with males.

One would expect to find high unemployment rates for each educational level around the average age of initial entry into the labour force: 15–19 for illiterates, 'literates below secondary' and 'secondaries' and between 20 and 24 for 'graduates'. Also it is clear from Table 2 that unemployment rates are low for the labour force aged 30 and over. We therefore concentrate our attention on the labour force aged 20–29 and attempt to gauge the magnitude of their problem.

TABLE 2

UNEMPLOYMENT RATES BY SEX, AGE AND EDUCATIONAL LEVEL, URBAN INDIA, 1966–67

	15–19	20–24	25–29	30–39	40–49	50–59	All Ages
1. Illiterates							
Persons	1·41	1·08	1·02	0·54	0·48	0·47	0·69
Males	1·63	1·18	0·91	0·39	0·36	0·42	0·58
Females	0·91	0·81	1·28	0·92	0·71	0·56	0·77
2. Literate below secondary							
Persons	5·94	3·48	1·44	0·73	0·63	0·67	1·68
	(6·30)	(3·85)	(1·49)	(0·76)	(0·63)	(0·69)	(1·78)
Males	5·95	3·37	1·37	0·65	0·61	0·70	1·45
	(6·17)	(3·69)	(1·41)	(0·67)	(0·62)	(0·71)	(1·52)
Females	5·65	4·46	2·42	2·16	0·64	—	2·61
	(6·51)	(5·92)	(2·92)	(2·36)	(0·64)	—	(3·11)
3. Secondary							
Persons	27·47	8·78	2·19	0·56	0·31	0·21	3·82
	(25·61)	(7·70)	(2·03)	(0·46)	(0·28)	(0·14)	(3·46)
Males	24·91	7·92	1·93	0·51	0·31	0·21	2·82
	(23·23)	(7·02)	(1·85)	(0·44)	(0·31)	(0·15)	(2·56)
Females	34·66	14·14	5·89	1·62	—	—	12·07
	(32·20)	(12·16)	(4·77)	(0·82)	—	—	(10·64)
4. Graduates and above							
Persons	15·12	12·01	2·06	0·21	—	—	2·18
Males	7·63	11·65	1·86	0·18	—	—	1·65
Females	43·97	12·99	4·04	0·69	—	—	5·87
5. Total							
Persons	5·64	4·14	1·48	0·61	0·51	0·52	1·60
Males	5·61	4·06	1·40	0·53	0·47	0·52	1·39
Females	5·71	4·42	1·97	1·15	0·68	0·52	1·84

SOURCES: Calculated from NSS, 21st Round. [1971], Tables (3.1), (3.2), (8.1) and (8.2). The category 'other than graduate, with technical education' was available for the unemployed but not for the labour force. We added it to 'secondary'. The figures in parentheses were obtained by dividing the unemployed in this category equally between categories 2 and 3.

Table 3 highlights the magnitude and intensity of unemployment among those in their twenties. We concentrate on the results for persons, as the results for males and females are much the same. Unemployment rates for the early twenties (i.e. aged 20–24), are generally high and especially so for graduates, but then, as pointed out earlier, this is about the age at which they enter the labour force. About 36 per cent of all unemployed persons were in their early twenties and out of these some 70 per cent were literates up to and including secondaries. Unemployment rates for the late twenties (i.e. aged 25–29) are of course much lower though, significantly, secondaries record a higher unemployment rate than graduates. About 14 per cent of all unemployed persons were in their late twenties and out of these about 60 per cent were literates up to and including secondaries. So about a half of the unemployed population were in their twenties, and literates up to and including secondaries in their twenties accounted for a third of the total unemployed of all ages. If we consider only the educated unemployed (i.e. secondaries and above), we find that about two-thirds of the educated unemployed were in their twenties and of these about 60 per cent were secondaries while about 24 per cent were graduates; of course most of the graduates were in their early twenties facing the initial problems of entry into the labour force.

TABLE 3

SELECTED PERCENTAGES RELATING TO THE URBAN UNEMPLOYED IN 1966–67

	UE Rate %	Share in total UE of specified sex* %	Share in total educated UE of specified sex* %	UE Rate %	Share in total UE of specified sex* %	Share in total educated UE of specified sex* %
		Aged 20–24			Aged 25–29	
Persons						
1. Literate below secondary	3·48	15·01	—	1·44	6·33	—
2. Secondary	8·78	10·68	30·39	2·19	3·12	8·87
3. Graduates	12·01	4·18	11·89	2·06	1·31	3·73
All educational levels	4·14	35·90	51·84	1·48	14·30	14·09
Males						
1. Literate below secondary	3·37	16·96	—	1·37	7·04	—
2. Secondary	7·92	10·58	32·01	1·93	3·35	10·65
3. Graduates	11·65	4·05	12·25	1·86	1·32	4·00
All educational levels	4·06	37·54	53·81	1·40	14·32	15·20
Females						
1. Literate below secondary	4·46	6·38	—	2·42	3·16	—
2. Secondary	14·14	11·15	25·10	5·89	2·08	4·67
3. Graduates	12·99	4·76	10·72	4·04	1·28	2·87
All educational levels	4·42	29·57	45·46	1·97	14·20	10·4͜

*UE Rate=Percentage share of the unemployed in the labour force i.e. of the same sex and education.

SOURCES: Compiled from Tables 2, 4 and 5.

The pattern of unemployment rates observed fits in well with our understanding of the Indian educational system.[5] Graduates do not have to wait long to get employment; secondaries do. The better-off secondaries go ahead to graduation and get ʾobs for which graduation has increased their chances though often not their skills. The remaining second-

aries who cannot go on to graduation—in spite of it being highly subsidised—have to wait long for jobs since they are being competed out by
graduates. This is reflected in the unemployment rates for secondaries:
(1) they are lower than for graduates in the 20–24 age-group, but are still
high considering that many must have left the educational system in their
teens; (2) even for the 25–29 age-group, the secondaries record a slightly
higher unemployment rate than graduates, though they have been in the
market for jobs for a much longer time.

An employment policy which regards graduate unemployment as the
really serious problem and assigns priority to its solution may have un-
fortunate consequences. It would further increase the demand for graduate
education, without in most cases providing additional and relevant skill;
at the same time it would accentuate the difficulties of secondaries who
have not the means to take advantage of subsidised graduate education.

TABLE 4

PERCENTAGE DISTRIBUTION OF THE UNEMPLOYED BY SEX, AGE AND EDUCATION, URBAN
INDIA, 1966–67

	15–19	20–24	25–29	30–39	40–49	50–59	All ages
Persons							
1. I	3·04	2·57	3·02	3·18	2·19	1·42	16·22
2. LBS	15·48	15·01	6·33	5·60	3·39	1·89	48·39
3. S	8·56	10·68	3·12	0·76	0·31	0·04	23·47
4. OGTE	1·33	3·36	0·52	0·46	0·07	0·07	5·83
5. G	0·17	4·18	1·31	0·20	—	—	5·86
6. Total	28·72	35·90	14·30	10·20	5·95	3·42	100·00
7. UE Rate	5·64	4·14	1·48	0·61	0·51	0·52	1·60
Males							
1. I	3·05	2·48	2·25	1·89	1·38	1·02	12·72
2. LBS	17·07	16·96	7·04	5·84	3·98	2·38	53·94
3. S	6·99	10·58	3·35	0·94	0·37	0·05	22·29
4. OGTE	1·06	3·16	0·35	0·37	0·09	0·09	5·11
5. G	0·85	4·05	1·32	0·19	—	—	5·65
6. Total	28·42	37·34	14·32	9·21	5·82	3·49	100·00
7. UE Rate	5·61	4·06	1·40	0·53	0·47	0·52	1·39
Females							
1. I	3·00	2·99	6·40	8·89	5·77	3·12	31·57
2. LBS	8·47	6·38	3·16	4·60	0·77	—	24·01
3. S	15·45	11·15	2·08		—	—	28·67
4. OGTE	2·52	4·28	1·30	0·88	—	—	8·98
5. G	0·53	4·76	1·28	0·21	—	—	6·77
6. Total	29·96	29·57	14·20	14·58	6·53	3·12	100·00
7. UE Rate	5·71	4·42	1·97	1·15	0·68	0·52	1·84

I= Illiterates; LBS=Literate below secondary; S=Secondary; OGTE=Other than
graduates with technical education and G=Graduates. UE Rate=Percentage share of
the unemployed (of a specified sex and age) in the labour force (of the same sex and age).
SOURCES: The same data as in Table 2. Row 7 of the present table corresponds to row 5
of Table 2.

TABLE 5

PERCENTAGE OF DISTRIBUTION OF THE EDUCATED UNEMPLOYED BY SEX, AGE AND EDU-
CATION: URBAN INDIA 1966–67

	15–19	20–24	25–29	30–39	40–49	50–59	All ages
Persons							
1. S	24·35	30·39	8·87	2·17	0·87	0·12	66·75
2. OGTE	3·79	9·57	1·49	1·32	0·20	0·21	16·58
3. G	0·48	11·89	3·73	0·56	—	—	16·67
4. Total	28·62	51·84	14·09	4·04	1·07	0·33	100·00
Males							
1. S	21·16	32·01	10·65	2·83	1·13	0·15	67·45
2. OGTE	3·22	9·55	1·05	1·11	0·26	0·28	15·46
3. G	0·26	12·25	4·00	0·58	—	—	17·10
4. Total	24·63	53·81	15·20	4·53	1·39	0·43	100·00
Females							
1. S	34·77	25·10	4·67	—	—	—	64·54
2. OGTE	5·67	9·64	2·92	1·99	—	—	20·22
3. G	1·19	10·72	2·87	0·47	—	—	15·24
4. Total	41·64	45·46	10·46	2·46	—	—	100·00

SOURCES: The same data as in Table 2. For abbreviations see Table 4. Row 4 relates to
the total educated unemployed of the specified sex and is the sum of rows 1–3.

It is therefore important to realise the largely transitory nature of
graduate unemployment and the seriousness of the problem among
literates up to and including secondaries in their twenties. The latter form a
substantial segment of the 'hard core' urban unemployed and employment
policies must keep this in mind. Regarding illiterates our rates are rather
misleading and their problem is probably poverty rather than open
unemployment. More generally we find rather low employment rates for
urban India which cannot be explained away merely in terms of the
alleged restrictiveness of NSS definitions of unemployment: at any rate,
this does not justify the dependence in the past on the highly unreliable
live register based estimates.

NOTES

1. Until the publication of the Fourth Five Year Plan, Draft, 1969–74, official
documents used employment exchange data to estimate urban unemployment. As the
Committee of Experts on Unemployment Estimates argued this led to an overstatement
of the 'backlog' of unemployment in urban India. See Dantwala Committee [*1970, p.9,
para. 2.6*].

2. This appears to be the position taken by Sen; see Amartya Sen [*1975, especially
p. 134*].

3. The numbers on the live register rose from 1·8 million in December 1961 to 2·4
million in December 1962. There is also the curious business of the absolute decline in
the live register in Uttar Pradesh and West Bengal between 1963 and 1968. It is difficult
to believe that the 15 per cent decline in job seekers in the context of a 16 per cent
increase in the number of exchanges in West Bengal reflected a marked improvement
in the ob situation in the urban sector of that state [see *Dantwala Committee, 1970,*

p. 126, para. 151].

4. Our data for employment growth of the organised sector are those collected by the Directorate of Employment and Training under its Employment Market Information Programme. The estimates we have used for 1961–6 cover all public sector establishments and private establishments employing 25 workers or more outside of agriculture. For 1967–73, our estimates include establishments employing 10 or more workers [see *Dantwala Committee, 1970, Table 47* and *Government of India, 1974, Tables 3.1 and 3.2*]. The EMI figures do provide a good indication of trends in the urban labour market, though an urban-rural breakdown would enhance their value and should be easy to provide. A further advantage with the EMI data is they are collected quarterly and are available with hardly any time lag.

5. For a valuable discussion of these problems see Amartya Sen [*1971*].

REFERENCES

Dantwala Committee, Government of India, 1970, *Report of the Committee of Experts on Unemployment Estimates*, New Delhi.

Directorate General of Employment and Training, Government of India, 1969, *Report on Survey to Ascertain the Proportion of Employed Persons on the Live Register of Employment Exchanges*, mimeo, New Delhi.

India, Government of, 1974, *Economic Survey 1973–4*, New Delhi.

National Sample Survey, 1967, 18th Round, February 1963–January 1964, *Tables with Notes on the Urban Labour Force*, No. 164, Calcutta.

National Sample Survey, 1969, 19th Round, July 1964–June 1965, *Tables with Notes on Employment and Unemployment in Rural and Urban Areas of India*, No. 201, Calcutta.

National Sample Survey, 1971, 21st Round, July 1966–June 1967, *Tables with Notes on the Urban Labour Force*, No. 181, Delhi.

Sen, Amartya, 1971, *The Crisis in Indian Education*, in Chaudhuri, P., (ed.), *Aspects of Indian Economic Development: A Book of Readings*, London.

Sen, Amartya, 1975, *Employment, Technology and Development*, Oxford.

Turnham, David, 1971, *The Employment Problem in Less Developed Countries: A Review of Evidence*, Paris.

Income Distribution, Demand Structure and Employment: The Case of Peru

By Adolfo Figueroa*

The present growth process of Peru is characterized by a relatively low rate of labour absorption in the modern firms (together with growing urbanization and urban under-employment). This fact, which is common in underdeveloped countries, has been usually attributed to factor market imperfections and/or imported technology. This study attempts to estimate empirically the hypothesis that the rate of industrial employment may also be influenced by the demand structure which is associated with the existing income distribution profile in Peru. The result is that income transfers from the rich to the poor would increase industrial employment. This 'redistribution effect' is not remarkably high, however. For example, a 3 per cent increase in industrial employment would require a selective redistribution of 6 per cent of Peru's national income.

I. INTRODUCTION

Income distribution is often considered to be a question of equity. But, from an analytical viewpoint, the way in which national income is distributed has some effects upon other economic magnitudes of an economy and, therefore, income distribution may be regarded as a variable in positive economics as well. As to this second thought, we find an example in the context of growth theory, where some economists have called attention to the role of income distribution in determining the savings ratio of the economy. Our own concern here will be the role of income distribution in influencing the structure of demand for final commodities.

At the same time, our concern will be with a factual phenomenon: the problem of urban unemployment and underemployment in less developed countries. Population growth rates in these countries are quite high, but the growth rates of urban population are even higher. The result is a high demand for jobs in the urban areas, which in reality is a demand for income. Since most of these countries have embarked on an industrialization strategy for growth, it is expected that the modern manufacturing sector should be the one to create enough jobs. However, this is not the case, as we can read in one of the standard references on this issue: 'in the first half of the 1960s a note of concern, often bordering on disillusionment, could be observed among the most ardent industrialization advocates. The dynamic sec or of the economy was not absorbing labour at a satisfactory

---

*Professor of Economics, Catholic University of Peru, (Lima).

rate [*Baer and Hervé, 1966, p. 88–89*]. The consequence of this failure being the increasing allocation of labour in low productivity activities.

Let us take the economy of Peru as an example. The average annual growth rate of labour force from 1950 to 1968 was 2·6 per cent (after 1963 this rate has been 3 per cent and 3·1 per cent). The labour force engaged in the manufacturing sector has grown at the rate of 2·6 per cent, showing that it has maintained its share, while industrial output has shown a growth rate of 7 per cent. Any assessment of the capacity to absorb labour by the manufacturing sector must look at the growth of urban labour force, however. We can now see the failure of this sector, as urban labour force grew at a rate of 4·2 per cent annually. These figures show that the migrants from the rural to the urban areas are being allocated to government, commerce, construction and service sectors.

Some general characteristics about migration seem to be worth mentioning. According to the 1961 national census, 23 per cent of the total population was migrant; from this amount 41 per cent had less than 4 years of residence, 29 per cent had between 5 and 14 years of residence and 23 per cent had more than 15 years living in the place where they were interviewed on the census day. The population of Lima—Peru's capital and by far the the largest city of the country—was 17 per cent of Peru's population in 1961; for 1972 this percentage is around 20 per cent. Also Lima absorbed, in 1961, 40 per cent of the total migrants. These figures indicate the increasing rate at which the migration phenomenon is taking place; moreover, they indicate the permanent nature of migration to the urban areas; on the other hand, as Table 1 shows, 70 per cent of the migrants to Lima were between 15–49 years old, which shows the tremendous impact of migration on the urban labour market.

TABLE 1

PERU: AGE AND SEX STRUCTURE OF THE MIGRANT POPULATION, 1961
(THOUSANDS OF PEROSNS)

Age (Years)	Peru			Lima		
	Total	Men	Women	Total	Men	Women
0–14	490	250	240	147	71	76
15–49	1,538	842	696	648	335	313
50–59	164	89	15	70	36	34
60–	153	76	17	60	29	31
Undecl.	1	—	—	—	—	—
Total	2,346	1,258	1,088	925	471	454

SOURCE: DNEC, *VI Censo Nacional*, p.vii.

Nevertheless, it is important to notice that unemployment rates are not too high compared with developed countries. (The 1961 census showed 2·8 per cent and the 1967 survey of Lima's labour market showed 4·2 per cent.) There exists, however, another type of under-utilization of human resources. This is *underemployment*. Even if a person has a job, because he cannot afford to be unemployed, he may not be 'adequately employed'. Definitions of underemployment are usually based on two criteria. Firstly, abnormally short work-weeks; and secondly, abnormally low incomes. On the basis of such definitions, underemployment in Lima stood at 25·6 per cent in 1967.

In Table 2, differentials in average productivity (net value added per worker) by sectors are presented. Average productivity in the manufacturing, mining and electricity sectors is almost 2 times the average productivity in commerce, government, and transportation; 3 times the average productivity in construction and services, and 10 times the average productivity in agriculture. These differences in average productivity between sectors may not reflect defects in labour allocation alone, since average productivity is also influenced by (1) varying amount of capital with which workers are equipped, and (2) possible differences in the quality of labour between sectors in terms of skills, education, native ability, and other relevant attributes.

TABLE 2

PERU: INCOME ORIGIN[a], EMPLOYMENT[b], AND
AVERAGE PRODUCTIVITY BY SECTORS, 1966

Sectors	Y_i	L_i	Y_i/L_i
Manufacturing	25·3	184	132·0
Electricity	1·2	12	100·6
Mining	8·1	83	97·7
Commerce	20·6	356	54·0
Government	12·7	240	53·0
Transportation	4·9	121	41·0
Construction	5·4	141	38·2
Services	14·3	387	37·0
Agriculture	22·4	12·17	13·2

a. National income by sectors, in billions of soles.
b. Employment, in thousands of persons.

SOURCES: Computed for all sectors, but manufacturing, from Banco Central, *Cuentas Nacionales* [*1966, 1970*]. For the Manufacturing sector from Ministerio de Industria Comercio [*1970, pp. 17, 18*].

Figure 1 shows the same information contained in Table 2; on the vertical axis we measure average productivity and on the horizontal axis we measure labour. Thus the area of each rectangle represents the total income generated in each sector, which must be distributed as wages, rent, taxes. In order to see how much of each sectoral income goes to wages we need to look at the average money wages by sectors.

For the manufacturing sector, the average wages and salaries are 32,500 soles/year [*Ministerio de Industria y Comercio, 1970, pp. 18–19*]. This average may be assigned to mining, and electricity as well.[1] For the remaining non-agricultural sectors we can approximate it at the legal minimum wage (15,600 soles/year), as suggested by a survey [*CISM, 1967, p. 41*].

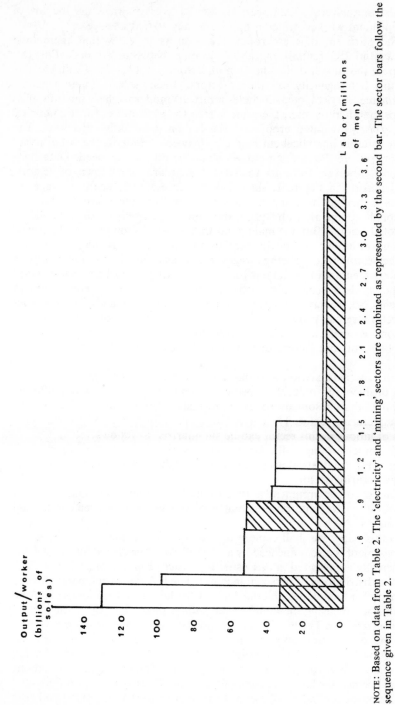

Figure 1.—Peru: Average Productivity by Sectors, 1966

NOTE: Based on data from Table 2. The 'electricity' and 'mining' sectors are combined as represented by the second bar. The sector bars follow the sequence given in Table 2.

In the agricultural sector we take as the average wage the income of independent workers which is approximately 10,000 soles/year.[2]

The purposes of these rough estimates is to show that there exist substantial differentials in labour income between 'sectors'. For this purpose the standard classification of sectors is not the most suitable, due to the heterogeneity of these sectors. Each sector—manufacturing, commerce, services, etc.—includes a mix of 'modern firms', small familial shops, handicrafts, etc.; the same is true for agriculture, for it comprises the export-orientated crops and the Indian community activities. The most suitable analytical cut might be between 'modern' and 'traditional' sectors, where the ranking criteria could be output per head. Data limitations, however, force us to use the standard breakdown of sectors.

Therefore, in Figure 1, shaded areas represent the share of wages in sectoral income; the sum of all shaded areas is the share of wages in national income and, obviously, the sum of the areas of all rectangles is national income. But, the main point that Figure 1 shows is that there exist significant labour income differentials and that labour is mainly allocated in the sectors where average wages and salaries are lower; conversely, a small percentage of the labour force—the privileged workers—are engaged in the 'modern' sector with higher salaries and some other non-pecuniary benefits. So, we have a skewed income distribution. In addition, if salaries reflect marginal productivity values, this allocation of labour among sectors is inefficient. The interrelation between resource allocation, employment, and income distribution is, thus, empirically approximated.

II. INCOME DISTRIBUTION AND DERIVED DEMAND FOR LABOUR

A problem for underdeveloped countries is, therefore, how to reallocate urban human resources so as to increase employment in the modern manufacturing sector. The current arguments for a relatively low absorption of labour in this sector can be summarized as follows:

(1) Imperfections in the factor markets, which create a relatively high wage rate; if industrial wages came down, labour would be shifted to the manufacturing sector.

(2) The other argument is that technology is imported and relatively capital intensive, with no possibilities of substitution between capital and labour.[3]

In this paper we shall explore the possibility that the rate of industrial employment is also influenced by a variable so far neglected, or at least not sufficiently emphasized in this issue: the *structure of demand*, which results from a distribution of personal incomes. The link between the structure of demand for final goods and the demand for labour in the industry may be established by using the familar Marshallian theoretical tool: the *derived demand analysis*. The possible connection between structure of demand and income distribution appears clear, when one recognizes that the consumption bundle of the rich is different from that of the poor; and, finally, the relation between income distribution to the derived demand for labour arises because the labour content of these bundles is likely to be different.

The purpose of what follows in this paper is, to examine empirically the

TABLE 3

DEMAND STRUCTURE (AND INDUSTRIAL LABOUR REQUIREMENTS) ON DOMESTIC AND IMPORTED MANUFACTURING PRODUCTS: LIMA, 1964–1965

Industries	Income Brackets (Soles/Year)					Man-Years/ 1,000 Soles
	3,000	5,000	7,000	9,000	11,000	
Wage Goods	1,093	1,764	2,358	2,663	3,087	—
Food process	929	1,484	1,968	2,149	2,536	·00316
Beverage	74	133	193	257	272	·00273
Chemicals	90	147	197	247	279	·00409
Luxury Goods	336	600	906	1,321	1,614	—
Tobacco	14	18	25	43	59	·00339
Textiles	272	488	721	1,010	1,150	·00587
Furniture	26	48	67	110	153	·01003
Printing	19	36	63	97	148	·00671
Gasoline	—	—	9	32	62	·00072
Mach. & Vehic.	5	10	21	29	42	·00621
Imports	245	411	607	786	975	·00090

SOURCE: Adolfo Figueroa [1972, Table 18].

possible effect of income distribution on the derived demand for labour in a specific sector of the Peruvian economy—manufacturing. The problem at hand is similar to the one that commanded much attention in the 1930s when economists were interested in the effect of income redistribution on aggregate savings, hence GNP and aggregate employment. What is significant in such enquiries is not the difference between the average propensities to save, but rather differences in the *marginal* counterpart. Similarly, turning to labour content, what is significant is the incremental concept. In other words, what is significant are possible differences in the incremental labour requirements between unit expenditure (in value) on various goods with unequal marginal propensities to consume. As long as there are incremental differences the relevance of income distribution to demand for labour follows.

III. PRELIMINARY EMPIRICAL FINDINGS FOR PERU

The demand structure estimates for industrial products in Peru is shown in Table 3 (wage goods are defined as those for which average propensity to consume decreases with income; and luxury goods those whose average propensity increases); also the total—direct and indirect—industrial labour requirements per unit of expenditure are shown. These last coefficients are of the Leontief type and were estimated by *partitioning* an input-output table into 'manufacturing' and the 'rest'; so, these coefficients indicate the *total* increase in employment in the industrial sector as the expenditure in an industrial product increases by one unit. Table 4 shows the derived demand for labour by income brackets.[4] At the bottom of this table we can see that the derived demand for labour increases with income *but at a decreasing rate*. Thus, a redistribution of income would increase demand for industrial labour; the implicit assumption being that a consumer who is moved to another income bracket behaves similarly to the people in that income bracket. As E. Hemingway's famous saying goes: the difference between the rich and the poor is that the former 'has more money'.

These results are preliminary, however. The number of income brackets is relatively small for any statistical analysis; the demand structure refers to one urban city only; although the largest one in the country. The distinction between wage and luxury goods and their labour-content could not escape from some arbitrariness. The input-output table used was not designed—as most input-output tables—with this distinction in mind.

Notwithstanding the preliminary character of the results, let us analyze them in terms of their practical implications. We can take the case when differences in slopes (actually, in increments) are the greatest in the labour demand schedule. This happens in Table 4 when the second and the fifth income brackets are compared.[5] In other words, we can 'simulate' the income redistribution effect in the following way: if we took away 1,000 soles from a family in the fifth income bracket the demand for labour would decrease by ·0033 units. Now, let a family in the second income bracket get those 1,000 soles; this family's demand for labour would increase now by ·0039 units. Thus, for every 1,000 soles of income transfer the net gain in demand for labour would be $\cdot0039 - \cdot0033 = \cdot0006$ units. More generally, the net gain in employment as income is redistributed can be expressed as:

$$\Delta L = (\cdot0006)\ \Delta W \tag{1}$$

where ΔW reflects the total income transfer from the fifth income group to the second one in thousands of soles.

TABLE 4

CROSS-SECTION OF TOTAL (DIRECT AND INDIRECT) DEMAND FOR DOMESTIC INDUSTRIAL LABOUR: LIMA, 1964–1965 (MAN-YEARS)

Industries	Income Brackets				
	3,000	5,000	7,000	9,000	11,000
Wage goods	·003506	·005653	·007552	·008503	·009898
Food processing	·002936	·004689	·006219	·006791	·008014
Beverage	·000202	·000363	·000527	·000702	·000743
Chemicals	·000368	·000601	·000806	·001010	·001141
Luxury goods	·002063	·003711	·005548	·008032	·009785
Tobacco	·000047	·000061	·000085	·000146	·000200
Textiles	·001597	·002865	·004232	·005929	·006751
Furniture	·000261	·000481	·000672	·001103	·001535
Printing	·000127	·000242	·000423	·000651	·000993
Gasoline	—	—	·000006	·000023	·000045
Machin. & vehicles	·000031	·000062	·000130	·000180	·000261
Imports	·000221	·000370	·000546	·000707	·000878
Total demand for labour	·005790	·009734	·013646	·017242	·020561
Increments in labour demand	—	·003944	·003912	·003596	·003319

SOURCE: *Ibid.* [*Table 19*].

If the production and consumption structure of 1963–4 is the same for the following years, we can make some estimates of the influence of income redistribution upon industrial employment in Peru. For instance, if we redistributed 10,000 thousands of soles (6 per cent of 1968 Peru's national income) employment would increase by 6,000 persons (3 per cent of 1968 manufacturing employment). We can do better, however, and show all the possibilities of percentage redistribution of national income and the accompanying percentage increase in employment. Set (1) as the following expression:

$$\frac{\Delta L}{\bar{L}} = (\cdot0006)\ \frac{\Delta W}{\bar{L}} = \frac{\cdot0006}{\bar{L}}\ r\ \bar{I} = \left[\frac{\cdot0006\ \bar{I}}{\bar{L}}\right]\ r \tag{2}$$

where $\bar{I}$, $\bar{L}$ are the national income of a given year and employment in manufacturing of that given year, respectively; and r is the percentage of national income. Clearly, the relation is linear. Therefore, Figure 2 shows, for a given desired level of industrial employment increase, the 'right amount of income and the right people' for redistributing income. For instance, a redistribution of 10 per cent of national income would increase employment 5 per cent.[6]

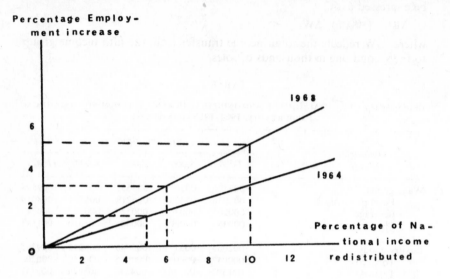

Figure 2 – Income Distribution Elasticity of Industrial Employment.

We could also show the effect of any transfer from any income group upon employment. As explained above, the marginal value is usually assigned to the midpoint of an interval, so that we have 4 income groups with which we can form a 4 by 4 matrix showing the 16 possibilities of income transfers (see Table 5). Because redistribution within the same group will have no effect on employment, the diagonal elements are zero. An income transfer from group III to group II would increase labour slightly; whereas the greatest effect is obtained when the income is transferred from the fifth group to the second, which is shown in Figure 2 as well; above the diagonal all elements are negative and except for this change in sign the matrix is symmetrical. Also Table 5 helps to determine linear combinations of income transfers and employment.

TABLE 5

PERU: A SIMULATION MATRIX OF THE EFFECT OF FIVE PER CENT OF NATIONAL INCOME REDISTRIBUTION UPON INDUSTRIAL EMPLOYMENT (THOUSANDS OF WORKERS)

Income groups (thousand soles)	From	To II	III	IV	V
3–5	II	0	—0·3	—3·5	—6·3
5–7	III	0·3	0	—3·2	—5·9
7–9	IV	3·5	3·2	0	—2·8
9–11	V	6·3	5·9	2·8	0

The origin of this paper was to explain a particular problem: the labour demand in the industrial sector of Peru. Given the national income and labour employed in the manufacturing sector for 1964, we can also 'simulate' the redistribution effect upon employment in that year. For instance, had income been 4,000 thousand soles (5 per cent of 1964 national income) greater for low income groups and 4,000 thousand soles lower for higher income classes, employment would have been 2,400 persons greater (1·5 per cent of 1964 manufacturing employment). All the possible outcomes for different income distribution shares are shown in Figure 2 by the lower line labelled 1964. The difference in the height of both lines reflects the fact that national income of 1968 increased much more than industrial employment.

The empirical result shows, therefore, that the demand for labour depends on whose income goes up relatively. In our analysis of two income groups only—the second and the fifth—we know that employment rises according to the income increase of each group and their respective income effects; i.e.:

$$\Delta L = \frac{dL_2}{dI_2}\, \Delta I_2 \; + \; \frac{dL_5}{dI_5}\, \Delta I_5 \qquad\qquad (3)$$

Then, if the increase in national income goes mainly to higher income groups, the increase in the demand for labour would not be as high as where the increase in national income had been distributed more evenly. That is, the distribution effect can be utilized for a given *level* of national income and for a given *increase* in it. In both cases the analysis is the same, the variables to consider are the same, and the result is the same.

Studies about trends of income distribution in Peru indicate a tendency to increase inequality [*Figueroa 1972, pp. 29–37*]. Thus one can conclude that a relatively low increase in industrial labour demand is explained, but only in part, given the small employment effect of income redistribution, by the fact that *additional national income has been regressively distributed.*

A stronger conclusion we may draw from the results, however, is that there is no trade-off between more equal income distribution and industrial employment. In other words, if the target is income redistribution, this can be accomplished without jeoperdizing the increase in employment or, to put it even more conclusively, without decreasing demand for labour.

IV. GROWTH AND DISTRIBUTION

The secondary effects of industrial employment creation, i.e., employment multipliers—have not been considered in this study. Nor have the effects of changes in the demand for industrial goods on employment on other non-manufacturing sectors been taken into account. Our main interest has been with the industrial sector only and with the initial employment impact. Any empirical assessment of employment effects of income redistribution upon other sectors of the economy needs better quality data on direct-labour-coefficients; besides the underemployment in agriculture, service, and other sectors weakens the estimate of these coefficients, as compared with the modern manufacturing sector.

The other dynamic aspect we need to discuss in the light of our model is economic growth. Suppose income is redistributed to the lower income classes and, thus, industrial employment increased. What would be the effect of this redistribution on the economic growth of the economy? By economic growth we mean increase in the productive capacity of the economy, mainly investment.

The relationship between income distribution and growth in the context of growth theories is well known [*Kaldor 1960, pp. 228–30*]. One should —according to this theory—expect a trade-off between income distribution and growth. So, if we redistribute income, growth may be jeopardized because the savings ratio of the economy depends on the income distribution. Thus, investment will also depend on income distribution.

There are two qualifications to this argument, however. First, this theory is true under a full-employment situation. If all resources are utilized, the more of our national product is devoted to consumption, the less resources would be available for producing capital goods. But in developing countries where some resources are underutilized, there is a possibility for both investment *and* consumption expansion. As some theories of investment have suggested, investment may be *induced* by a high consumption level. Of course, this short-run expansion might result in a balance of payments problem. But income redistribution will affect both the mix of consumption goods (not only its level) and the overall capital-output ratio which will, in turn, alter import requirements. Thus, any assessment of the effect of income redistribution policies on growth requires empirical knowledge concerning the magnitude and the direction of these changes. In addition, accompanying policies, such as import-substitution or non-traditional exports promotion, may tend to attenuate the external constraint.

Secondly, the main argument for a relation between income distribution and savings is: 'The fact that the bulk of *profits* accrues in the form of company profits and a high proportion of companies' marginal profits is put to reserve' [*Kaldor, 1960, pp. 229*]. Thus, the relevant distinction is between what proportion of national income is in the form of profits. If we subtract undistributed profits (savings of firms) from national income, we get *personal income*. (Our estimates of the structure of demand referred to personal income which is also the magnitude to be redistributed.) So, if the redistribution of personal income in our model changes savings, this means that personal marginal propensities to save are different between income brackets and this is a quite different proposition from Kaldor's, which requires further investigation. In any case, for Peru, at least, it is the firms' savings which are the most important (almost 70 per cent of total gross saving.) Therefore, we may redistribute personal income and expect that their influence on savings and growth will be very small. This is, of course, only a conjecture, and further investigation—theoretical and empirical—is badly needed.

NOTES

1. For 1968, the average wage and salary for industry was 43,046 soles/year [*Min. Ind. y Com., Estadistica Industrial, 1970*]; for mining and electricity this average was 46,879 soles [*Min. Energia y Minas, p. 115*].

2. This amount includes payments in kind also [see *Banco Central del Peru, 1966, Table 3, n. 2*].

3. See Clague [*1969*] where strikingly low elasticities of substitution in eleven manufacturing industries of Peru are reported.

4. The methodology used is presented in Figueroa [*1972, Chapter IV*].

5. Since increments are usually assigned to the midpoint of the intervals considered—as we do in drawing marginal costs, for example, we are left with four income brackets, which for convenience we number from II to V.

6. Since the top population decile gets 50 per cent of national income to transfer only 5 per cent of income to the lower income group would imply a reduction of 10 per cent in the income of the top population decile. One can then imagine the practical difficulty of redistributing 10 per cent of national income. This shows the small employment effect of income redistribution.

REFERENCES

Baer, W. and Hervé, M., 1966, 'Employment and Industrialization in Developing Countries', *Quarterly Journal of Economics*.

Banco Central del Peru, 1966, 1970, *Cuentas Nacionales*, Lima.

CISM, 1967, *Poblacion Economicamente Activa de Lima Metropolitana*, Lima: SERH.

Clague, C., 1969, 'Capital-Labor Substitution in Manufacturing in Developing Countries', *Econometrica*, 37.

Figueroa, A., 1972, 'Income Distribution, Employment and Development: The Case of Peru', unpublished PhD Dissertation, Vanderbilt University, Tennessee.

Kaldor, N., 1960, *Essays on Value and Distribution*, London: Duckworth.

Ministerio de Industria y Comercio, 1970, *Boletin Estadistico de Industria y Comercio*, No. 1, Lima.

Ministerio Energia y Minas, 1970, *Anuario Minero del Peru*, Lima.

A Model of Growth and Employment in the Open Dualistic Economy :

The Cases of Korea and Taiwan

By John C. H. Fei and Gustav Ranis*

In this paper, the pressing problem of unemployment in the contemporary developing world is studied from an historical perspective of transition growth, i.e. the process representing the termination of economic colonialism and the initiation of modern growth. This problem is investigated for a particular type of LDC, namely, the open dualistic labour surplus economy. The post-war (1950–70) experience of Taiwan and Korea were analyzed from this viewpoint—emphasizing the fine differences as well as the family resemblance among these countries. As ex-Japanese colonies, both these countries shared a relatively strong agricultural infrastructure and the open dualistic and labour surplus characteristic at the beginning of the transition in the 1950s. However, as we show, Taiwan had an initially more favourable set of institutional and economic conditions in agriculture.

In the post-war decade, we indicate that both countries experienced two sub-phases of transition: an import substitution sub-phase followed by an export substitution sub-phase. In the former, entrepreneurial experience was accumulated along with a further strengthening of the rural infrastructure, e.g. by land reform. In the latter, both countries rapidly developed labour intensive manufacturing exports to the world market. It was this latter development that contributed substantially to the solution of the unemployment problem and permitted the labour surplus condition to be gradually terminated. This major 'turning point', as well as other turning points related to the historical role of the agricultural sector, are deduced theoretically in the paper as well as verified empirically.

The overall experience of the '50s and '60s seems to indicate a worsening of the unemployment or underemployment problem in the developing world, even where per capita income growth has been quite satisfactory. When this experience is then projected forward, given the knowledge that

*Economic Growth Center, Yale University. The authors wish to acknowledge the substantial contributions of Professor Sung Hwan Jo of Sogang University, Korea and Professor Chi-Mu Huang of National University, Taiwan to this paper, especially its empirical portions. Portions of this research were financed by funds provided by the Agency for International Development under contract CSD/2492. However, the views expressed in this paper do not necessarily reflect those of AID.

even the most successful population control programmes cannot affect labour force size for some 15 years to come, the gloom thickens. Something has to be done for employment—even if it means sacrificing the GNP growth rate.

The purpose of this paper is to demonstrate, with the help of a theoretical framework applicable to at least one type of LDC, that the necessity of contemplating a trade-off between employment and GNP may, in fact, be illusory and based on a misinterpretation of the historical record. The model presented 'opens up' the traditional closed dualistic model of development [*Lewis, 1954*], based on the notion that the full potential complementarity between growth and employment is best demonstrated when the focus of analysis is broadened from the process of domestic 'labour' reallocation within the closed dualistic setting, to include the possibility of labour reallocation through trade. While we believe that the solution of the employment problem in the context of growth, as demonstrated by the model, applies to all but the very large (and therefore domestically-oriented) labour surplus LDCs, our empirical test is concentrated on Korea and Taiwan.

In historical perspective, the post–war performance of most LDCs is a transition between a long epoch of colonialism and a long epoch of modern growth.[1] Korea and Taiwan share the colonial heritage of a heavy dependence on traditional land–based production and exports, moving gradually to a non-traditional labour-based output mix as they successfully solve their employment problem, mainly through trade.

We shall accept the 'initial' period of transition as 1952-4 for Taiwan and 1953-7 for Korea,[2] with the 'terminal' period as 1968-70, in both cases. In Section I we present a comparative static model, with statistical evidence, to examine the initial and terminal structural characteristics of the two countries under observation. Section II identifies several important turning-points during the transition process. In Section III we present our conclusions and the implications of our analysis for employment and output policy in labour-surplus LDCs.

I.   COMPARATIVE STATIC ANALYSIS

The basic purpose of our comparative static analysis is to identify the structural change within the economy between the initial and terminal years. In the open dualistic labour surplus economy this structure can be described by a set of indices such as shown in Table 1, including production, consumption, saving, investment, trade, labour allocation, each of which has its place in the context of the model we intend to develop in the course of this section.

Since countries of this particular type are overwhelmingly agricultural, at least at the initial point, we begin our analysis with relations focussing on agricultural productivity, the allocation of labour between sectors, and trade in agricultural goods. The labour surplus condition is eliminated by the reallocation of unemployed or inefficiently employed (underemployed) workers from the subsistence to the commercialized sectors, where they

TABLE 1

COMPARATIVE STATIC ANALYSIS*

(1)		Initial Period		(4) Parity	Terminal Period		(7) Parity
	(2) Taiwan 1952–54 a	(3) Korea 1955–57 b		b/a	(5) Taiwan 1967–69 c	(6) Korea 1968–70 d	d/c
1. v — agricultural labour productivity	$273·4	$198·5		·73	$668·0	$386·8	·57
2. θ — labour allocation ratio	42·3%	32·0%		·76	58·0%	49·5%	·84
3. $E\Delta$ — 'per capita' agricultural net exports	$ 19·4	$—8·3		—	$ 9·3	—38·9	—
4. C_a^Δ — 'per capita' consumption of agricultural goods	$138·5	$142·4		1·04	$263·2	$223·14	·77
4a. GDP/X — 'per capita' GDP	$131·2	$83·4		·64	$276·8	$150·5	·54
5. w_a — agricultural real wage	303·8	195·4		·64	472·5	$317·3	·67
6. w_i — industrial real wage	$313·9	$219·0		·69	$529·2	$367·8	·69
7. — internal terms of trade Pa/Pi	95·5%	96·1%		1·0	96·5%	119·7%	1·24
8. C_i^Δ — 'per capita' consumption of industrial goods	$221·0	$139·5		·63	$416·1	$240·0	·57
9. $K^* = K/W$ — industrial capital-labour ratio	$2543.0	$4508·0		1·77	$2372·0	$3051·0	1·28
10. $q = Y/W$ — industrial labour productivity	$659·6	$541·3		·82	$1442·9	$906·2	·62
11. $Y\Delta = Y/P$ — 'per capita' industrial output	$279·1	$169·9		·61	$837·5	$453·0	1·84
12. E_i^Δ — 'per capita' industrial exports	$ 16·0	$6·8		·43	$223·5	$110·0	·49

No.	Symbol	Description	Taiwan (1)	Taiwan (2)	Taiwan coef.	Korea (1)	Korea (2)	Korea coef.
13.	E/GDP	export ratio	11·2%	27·6%	·37	4·1%	25·4%	·92
14.	$E_\triangle$	'per capita' exports	$43·8	$251·9	·25	$11·0	$123·0	·48
15.	E_i/E	industrial share of exports	37·2%	88·5%	1·65	61·6%	89·8%	1·01
16.	E_a/Q	agricultural export ratio	12·2%	3·3%	·25	3·1%	6·9%	2·09
17.	M_c/C_d	import substitution potential index	8·5%	10·2%	·76	6·5%	6·5%	·63
18.	M_c/M	industrial consumer goods share of imports	23·0%	15·9%	·57	13·3%	7·5%	·47
19.	$M_a(M_a+Q)$	agricultural import fraction	5·1%	6·4%	1·58	8·1%	21·3%	3·32
20.	$(S_a+S_i)/GDP$	domestic saving rate	10·0%	34·4%		−4·1%	18·5%	
21.	I/GDP	investment rate	17·2%	33·0%		15·4%	35·4%	
22.	S_a/I	agricultural saving contribution	18·5%	23·5%		15·2%	2·1%	
23.	S_i/I	industrial saving contribution	40·0%	80·7%		−43·5%	49·5%	
24.	S_f/I	foreign saving contribution	41·0%	−4·4%		128·3%	48·2%	
25.	X	population	8·438 mil.	13·313 mil.		22·263 mil.	32·056 mil.	
26.	P	labour force	2·828 mil.	4·926 mil.		6·924 mil.	9·886 mil.	

Cumulative Contribution to Investment During Transition

	Taiwan	Korea
agricultural saving $\Sigma S_a/\Sigma I$	25·9%	8·6%
industrial saving $\Sigma S_i/\Sigma I$	68·6%	29·7%
foreign saving $\Sigma S_f/\Sigma I$	5·7%	61·6%

*See Appendix for data sources.

U.S. $ figures for Korea are in 1965 constant prices, and those for Taiwan, in 1964 constant prices.

are efficiently or competitively employed.[3] In the early phase of the transition growth, 'this' is the heart of the employment problem.

Suppose the economy's total initial labour force (P) is divided into an agricultural labour force (L) and a non-agricultural labour force (W), i.e. $P = W + L$. Let us denote $\theta = W/P$ as the fraction of the total labour force in the non-agricultural sector (i.e. $1 - \theta = L/P$ is the fraction in the agricultural sector). Suppose the total output of agricultural goods is Q and the average productivity of agricultural labour is $v = Q/L$. Then the demand and supply of agricultural goods is

$$Lv = Q = C_a + E_a \qquad\qquad (1)$$
(supply) (demand)

where the demand for agricultural goods is either for domestic consumption (C_a) or for export (E_a)—as is typical in the colonial pattern. Dividing throughout by total population (and letting $x^\triangle = x/P$, i.e. per capita x), we have

$$(1 - \theta)v = Q^\triangle = C_{\underset{a}{\triangle}} + E_{\underset{a}{\triangle}} \quad \text{or} \qquad (2a)$$
$$v = (E_{\underset{a}{\triangle}} + C_{\underset{a}{\triangle}}) / (1 - \theta) \qquad\qquad (2b)$$

From (2b) we can see that a higher agricultural productivity (v) can lead to a combination of a higher consumption standard of agricultural goods ($C_{\underset{a}{\triangle}}$), a higher per capita export level ($E_{\underset{a}{\triangle}}$), and a higher fraction of the labour force already allocated to industry (θ).

Let us assume that land and labour are the only important traditional factors of production in agriculture.[4] If the supply of land is approximately fixed, the total productivity of labour, say for Taiwan, in the initial year, may be represented by the Q_T-curve in Figure 1a (i.e. the agricultural labour force L_T is measured on the horizontal axis to the left). If the total population is represented by a point 'P' in Figure 1a, the industrial labour force is PL_T, while the agricultural labour force is OL_T, leading to an initial agricultural labour productivity v_T represented by the slope of the straight line Oa_T in Figure 1a. In Figure 1b (below 1a) with the same fixed initial population P, the per capita output for the economy as a whole is represented by the $Q_{\underset{T}{\triangle}}$ curve (i.e. $Q_{\underset{T}{\triangle}} = Q_T/P$). The initial supply of agricultural output per head for Taiwan is then equal to $L_T b_T$ as indicated in Figure 1b. For the case of Korea, in a similar way, the initial agricultural output (Q_K-curve in Figure 2a), output per head ($Q_{\underset{K}{\triangle}}$ curve in Figure 2b) and labour allocation point (L_K) are shown.

What we have just portrayed is a realistic comparative picture of the agricultural condition of the two countries at the initial point. Taiwan inherited a more favourable agricultural infrastructure, reflected in a higher initial productivity of agricultural workers (slope of Oa_T in Figure 1a > slope of Oa_K in Figure 2a).[5] As indicated in Table 1, row 1, Korea's initial agricultural labour productivity was only 70 per cent of that of Taiwan. However, possibly due to their common colonial experience, the agricultural consumption standard ($C_a^\triangle$) in both countries is seen to be

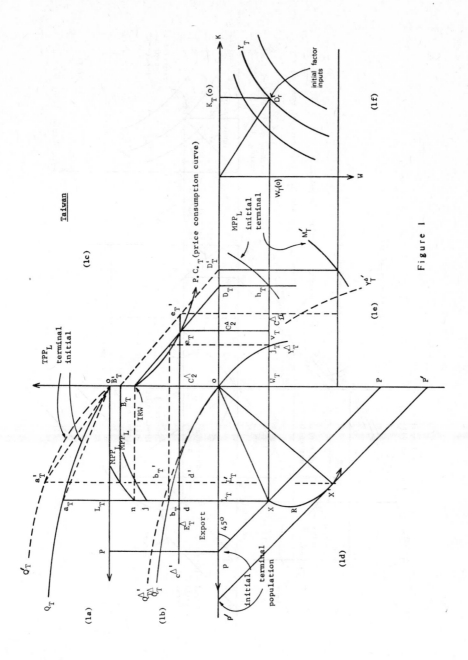

Figure 1

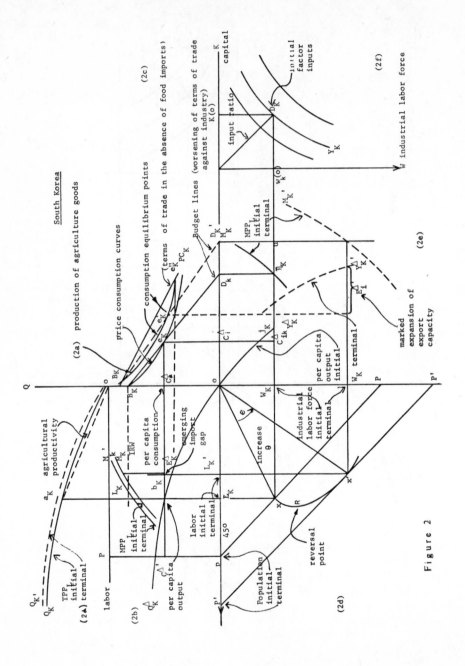

Figure 2

approximately the same (Table 1, row 4). Moreover, Table 1, row 2, indicates that initially Taiwan had already allocated 42 per cent of her labour force to non-agriculture, in sharp contrast to Korea with only 32 per cent. Thus, using equation (2b), the higher productivity in Taiwan led to *both* a higher fraction of labour in the non-agricultural sector (θ) *and* a higher level of agricultural exports on a per capita basis.

Even more startling is the contrast summarized in row 3. While Korea was initially already a net importer of agricultural goods, Taiwan exported a hefty $19 per capita and thus provided capacity to import capital goods and raw materials for the growing non-agricultural sectors.[6] This means that, from the very beginning, the agricultural sector in Taiwan played a much more positive role in fuelling the expansion of the industrial activities than Korea, in which the relative backward agricultural sector constituted a burden for industrialization. In the case of Korea, the agricultural sector was 'pulled along' by a dynamic non-agricultural sector rather than an important 'push' for industrialization, as in the case of Taiwan.

Since the individual worker consumes two kinds of commodities (agricultural goods, measured on the vertical axis of Figure 1c, and non-agricultural goods, measured on the horizontal axis), the agricultural real wage level for a typical Taiwanese worker may be represented by the budget line $B_T D_T$ (in Figure 1c). In other words, OB_T, (OD_T) is the level of the real wage in terms of agricultural (non-agricultural) goods, while the slope of the budget line represents the initial terms of trade. In a similar fashion, the budget line for Korea may be shown as $B_K D_K$ in Figure 2c. $B_K D_K$ is meant to lie below $B_T D_T$ since Korea's initial real wage in terms of agricultural goods, OB_K, is lower than Taiwan's, OB_T (see row 5), as well as in terms of industrial goods (row 6). Since the wage parity in terms of both conditions are approximately the same ('·64' and '·69', column 4) the internal terms of trade are approximately the same for the two countries (row 7). This means that, in the context of an open economy, the possibility of the import of agricultural goods in Korea compensated for her relatively backward condition in agriculture and that, initially the internal terms of trade in both countries are governed by a common international terms of trade in the Japanese market.[7]

In the context of a labour surplus dualistic economy, the real wage in terms of agricultural goods (e.g. OB_T in Figure 1c for Taiwan) may be thought of as the institutional real wage (IRW) which is determined by the institutional forces prevailing in the agricultural sector. In such an economy the IRW is likely to be above agricultural labour's marginal product (MPP_L), signifying the existence of surplus labour in the economy.[8] During the transition process, the IRW, moreover, is likely to increase only moderately, certainly less than the MPP_L, as long as $IRW > MPP_L$. However, once the labour surplus is exhausted and labour becomes scarce, $IRW = MPP_L$, and we can expect the wage to follow the MPP_L thereafter.

In Figure 1c, given the fixed IRW at level OB_T, the price-consumption curve PC_T, for Taiwan, is shown.[9] Where this curve intersects the typical worker's budget line (B_TD_T), *i.e.* at point e_T, locates the initial consumption equilibrium point for Taiwan (OC_2^A units of agricultural goods and OC_i^A of non-agricultural goods). Similarly, for Korea, the price-consumption curve PC_K may be drawn in Figure 2c. As we have noted earlier, virtually the same OC_a^A, is seen to prevail in both Korea and Taiwan initially. Thus, in the case of Taiwan, we can show (see row 3) the existence of a substantial agricultural export surplus per head ($E_T^A = b_Td$ in Figure 1b), while in the case of Korea, there exists a need to import agricultural goods at the outset.[10] Since Korea's budget line (B_KD_K in Figure 2c) is lower than Taiwan's (B_TD_T in Figure 1c) the fact that the two countries consume about the same amount of agricultural goods per capita, implies, moreover, that Korea's farmers initially consume substantially less non-agricultural goods on a per capita basis. This is confirmed by the data in row 8, columns 2 and 3.

Let us turn next to the production of and demand for non-agricultural (or, in shorthand, industrial) output. With respect to industrial output, there are two factors which differentiate the industrial from the agricultural sectors: first, the primary factors of production are now labour (W) and capital (K); and second, the industrial sector is assumed to be commercialized in that the real wage (in terms of industrial goods) may now be equated with the marginal productivity of labour. In Figures 1f and 2f, with labour (W) and capital (K) being measured on the vertical and horizontal axes, respectively, the production contour map, for Taiwan and Korea, for the initial period, is represented by the solid production contour maps indexed by Y_T and Y_K. Given the initial capital stock, e.g. ($K_T(o)$) for Taiwan, the MPP_L-curve is represented by the solid M_T-curve in Figure 1e, 'below' 1f. To show the consistent equilibrium position for the case of Taiwan, let the 45-degree line PP be drawn in Figure 1d with the aid of which the initial industrial labour force P_T^L (in Figure 1b) can be projected as OW_T on the vertical axis (downward). Since the initial non-agricultural real wage in Taiwan is OD_T,[11] the MPP_L-curve (i.e. the M_T-curve) passes through the point h_T in Figure 1e, indicating that OW_T units of labour are demanded at the real industrial wage OD_T. Similarly, for Korea, with capital stock $K_K(o)$ in Figure 2f, the MPP_L-curve is represented by the M_K-curve in Figure 2e, with an employment equilibrium point at h_K —indicating that OW_K units of workers are demanded at the industrial real wage OD_K.

A possible important initial difference in the state of industrial technology in Korea and Taiwan should be noted. From the theoretical standpoint, if the initial production functions of the two countries were exactly the same, then the higher level of the industrial real wage in Taiwan would imply that Taiwan also has (1) a higher industrial capital-labour ratio ($K^* = K/W$) and (2) a higher average productivity of industrial labour ($q = \dfrac{Y}{W}$). However, the empirical evidence (rows 9 and 10) indicates otherwise. Korea has an initially higher industrial capital-labour ratio than Taiwan—in spite of the lower Korean real wage level—and nevertheless sports a lower level of labour productivity—than Taiwan.[12] The cause of this difference may be traced once again to the Japanese colonial heritage; while the Japanese lavished relatively more attention on agricultural infrastructure in Taiwan, they pushed industrialization more heavily in Korea, which probably led to a more capital intensive, less innovative industrial structure. [13]

With respect to the demand and supply of ind`strial goods a formula symmetrical to (2a) is

$$\theta \, q = Y^{\triangle} = C^{\triangle} + E_i^{\triangle} \qquad (3)$$
$$\text{(supply)} \quad \text{(demand)}$$

where $Y^{\triangle}$ ($= Y/P$) is the per capita output of industrial goods and q is industrial labour productivity. From row 11, we see that the initial $Y^{\triangle}$ is much higher in Taiwan than in Korea (the parity is ·61) in spite of a much smaller gap in q (row 10 with a parity of ·82), simply because a larger proportion of the population has already been allocated to the non-agricultural sector (see row 2). On the demand side, a much larger fraction of Korea's non-agricultural output is exported at the outset—i.e. the percentage E_i/E is 50 per cent larger in Korea than in Taiwan (see row 15)—even though the actual magnitudes are small in both cases (see row 12).

Let us turn next to the overall magnitude and structure of international trade in the initial years in both countries. As far as the volume of total trade is concerned, given the already established fact that per capita GDP (row 4a) was higher in Taiwan initially, we would expect foreign trade to be quantitatively more important in Taiwan. Two indicators—exports as a fraction of GDP (row 13) and exports per capita (row 14)—are shown to corroborate this fact.

The contrast in the structure of the two countries' trade is even more dramatic than the difference in external orientation. While the initial export pattern of Taiwan was dominated by agricultural goods, Korea's modest exports were dominated by non-agricultural commodities (row 15). In fact, Taiwan inititally exported nearly 12 per cent of her agriculural output while Korea exported only 3 per cent of hers (row 16).

On the import side, during the initial years of transition growth total imports (M) consisted of imported industrial consumer goods (M_i) and producers' goods (M_p), i.e. capital goods and/or raw materials destined as productive inputs into the industrial sector ($M = M_i + M_p$). This breakdown will be seen to be significant for any analysis of the phenomenon of *import substitution (I-S) growth* which often characterizes the initial phase of transition.

By I-S growth we shall mean a sub-phase dominated by the development of the indigenous consumer goods industry with tradiional consumer goods imports (M_i) gradually being replaced. In order to build up these import substituting industries the LDC, however, usually needs to import more raw materials and capital goods M_p. Bearing this in mind, rows 17 and 18 attempt to describe the initial potential for I-S growth. Row 17, for example, shows that, while Taiwan initially imported 8.5

per cent of her total requirements for industrial consumer goods, the corresponding figure for Korea was $6\cdot5$ per cent. In the case of Taiwan, moreover, the imported industrial consumer goods accounted for $23\cdot0$ per cent of her total imports while the corresponding figure for Korea was only $13\cdot3$ per cent (row 18). Thus, both from the viewpoint of the domestic market and from the viewpoint of the allocation of foreign exchange, the importation of industrial consumer goods was more important in Taiwan than in Korea in the initial period under observation—allowing more scope for I-S growth.

The above description of the structure of trade reveals a contrasting pattern during the early phase of transition growth in the two countries under examination. In the case of Taiwan, there is in evidence a pattern of triangularism, i.e. the agricultural sector produces an exportable surplus which, in turn, provides the import capacity used for two types of industrial imports, consumer goods and producers' goods. The same agricultural exports, moreover, generate the incomes and demand for the larger volume of industrial consumer goods now produced at home. In this manner, agriculture fuels I-S growth as M_p imports permit the continued building up of the domestic import substituting capacity that gradually replaces M_i imports.

In the case of Korea, on the other hand, the growth dynamics represent more of a bilateral interaction between industry and the foreign sector as agriculture remains relatively stagnant. The industrial sector in consequence has to be depended upon to produce an exportable surplus which, together with the provision of capital from abroad, is used to import the capital goods and raw materials needed by the import substitution process. Moreover, as we shall see below, and especially during the later subphase of transition, the industrial sector, instead of being supported by agricultural exports, is saddled with the responsibility of diverting a part of the import capacity it generates for the purchase of food abroad.

The case of Taiwan is described in Figure 1e in which the $Y_T^\triangle$ curve is shown. The initial value of per capita output is seen to be $W_T j_T$, while the initial value of the per capita demand for consumer goods $C_i^\triangle$ is $W_T Ci_T^\triangle$ $(=OG^\triangle)$.[14] Thus, there exists a shortage of $j_T Ci_T^\triangle$ units of industrial goods which must be imported. Since, from Figure 1b, the initial per capita agricultural export is seen to be $E_T^\triangle$ $(=b_T d)$, at the initial terms of trade, the import capacity generated by these agricultural exports is $C_i^\triangle v_T$ (Figure 1e). The other portion of industrial goods required (i.e. $v_T j_T$ units on a per capita basis) is financed by foreign capital.

In the case of Korea, in Figure 2, the inital $Y^\triangle$-curve is labelled $Y_K^\triangle$ leading to an initial per capita output of $W_K j_K$ units. This output is actually higher than domestic demand $W_K Ci_K^\triangle$, signifying that Korea's industrial sector is already producing an exportable surplus, to finance its own import needs. The agricultural sector, on the other hand, is not involved in the financing process; in fact, to the extent that there is a food deficit, it is already drawing on the import capacity provided by industrial exports and foreign capital inflow.

The above presents a fairly accurate picture of the comparative structural conditions of the two countries under observation at the initial point in time. The purpose of comparative structural analysis is to contrast these initial characteristics with those obtaining in the terminal periods. The forces that brought on the marked structural change observable in columns 5–7 of Table 1 include (1) capital accumulation, (2) population growth, and (3) technology change in both the agricultural and non-agricultural sectors.

Let us first concentrate on capital accumulation. The saving fund available to these entrepreneurs, in both the public and private sectors, was composed of three sources: foreign capital (S_f), the reinvestment of industrial profits (S_i), and agricultural saving (S_a), i.e.[15]

$$I = S_a + S_i + S_f \tag{4}$$

Turning once again to Table 1, we have indicated the relative contribution to the total investment fund of the three sources of saving, both for the initial and terminal period—in rows 22–24. In the same table, moreover, we have presented the cumulative contribution of each between the initial and terminal period. In terms of these cumulative figures, the dramatic differences between Taiwan and Korea during the transition period is demonstrated by the fact that foreign capital financed 61·6 per cent of total investment in Korea and only 5·7 per cent in Taiwan. Agricultural saving contributed about three times as much to a higher investment rate in Taiwan than in Korea. This lack of domestic saving capacity, especially in agriculture, to finance her own investment needs and the heavy continued reliance on foreign capital, remains the most serious problem facing Korea's development.

Other evidence of marked structural change can be analyzed in terms of a comparison of (1) the role of agriculture; (2) the behaviour of wages and consumption; (3) the progress of industrial technology and the structure of international trade. While there continues to exist a marked family similarity between these two countries, differences in observed structural change are also instructive for the understanding of the employment problem.

The Role of the Agricultural Sector

To begin with the non-agricultural sector in both countries has grown rapidly enough to absorb the unemployed and underemployed in agriculture in spite of substantial population increase. Thus the centre of gravity of both economies, in terms of the allocation of labour between the two sectors, has shifted markedly. Returning to Figures 1d and 2d, the growth of population may be represented by the parallel and outward shift of the population lines PP to P'P'. At the same time the allocation points have shifted from L_T (L_K for Korea) to L_T^1 (L_K^1 for Korea), representing an increase in θ for both countries, as indicated. Rows 25 and 26 of Table 1 yield an average annual rate of growth between the initial and terminal period of 2·9 per cent in population and 3·7 per cent in the labour force for Taiwan, and 2·5 per cent and 2·7 per cent, respectively, for Korea. In spite of this, as we can see from row 2, Taiwan registered an increase in θ from 42 to 58 per cent and Korea from 32 to 49 per cent. This demonstrates the rapidity of the growth and industrial sector labour absorption process in both countries.

Associated with this marked structural change in terms of labour reallocation, is a markedly different role played by the agricultural sector. In the case of Taiwan, the initially more favourable agricultural infrastructure, and the encouraging policies led to dramatic advances in technology and agricultural labour productivity. This is depicted by the upward shift of the total output curve from Q_T to Q_T^1 (in Figure 1a) and of the per capita output curve from $Q_T^\triangle$ to $Q_T^{\triangle 1}$ (in Figure 1b). Coupled with the labour reallocation effect, agricultural labour productivity has thus advanced from the slope of Oa_T in Figure 1a to the slope of Oa_T'.[16] The exportable per capita agricultural surplus in the terminal period is now $d'b_T'$, in Figure 1b, compared with db_T earlier.

From row 1 we see that agricultural labour productivity in Taiwan advanced by more than 244 per cent. As a result, in spite of substantial gains in the per capita consumption of agricultural goods (row 4) agricultural exports, even on a net per capita basis, could be sustained at a high level (row 3). All this in the face of the fact (row 2) that the agricultural labour force is now a much smaller fraction of the total labour force than in the initial period, and, in fact, declined absolutely after a point.

In the case of Korea, the initially relatively unfavourable agricultural infra-structure, reinforced by the relative government neglect over time thereafter, has led to a situation of comparative agricultural stagnation. Agricultural productivity here also registered some gains. But, as seen from row 1, the gains were more modest leading to a further substantial decline in the relative position of the two agricultural sectors (see row 1, columns 4 and 7). Consequently, the increase in Korea's agricultural consumption standard is modest (row 4—note especially the decline in the parity ratio) from domestic sources; instead, increasing volumes of food imports have been required (see row 3).

To obtain a clear picture of the contrast we can look at the net import or export figure for food only over the relevant period. While Taiwan has been continuously exporting food during the entire transition period, Korea's food deficit problem has been steadily worsening, with more than $300,000 annually being spent on net food imports in recent years. The contrast is best summarized in Figure 3, showing food imports as a percentage of total food consumption in Korea and food exports as a percentage of total food consumption in Taiwan.

Thus, in the case of Taiwan, rapid growth, industrialization and labour reallocation were financed in considerable part by gains in agricultural productivity. In the case of Korea, on the other hand, rapid industrialization, growth and labour reallocation were financed in large part by the inflow of foreign capital. In the case of Korea the agricultural sector was 'pulled along' by a dynamic non-agricultural sector rather than providing an important 'push' for industrialization, as in the case of Taiwan. This contrast was also demonstrated vividly by our earlier analysis of the comparative cumulative sources of finance during the transition.

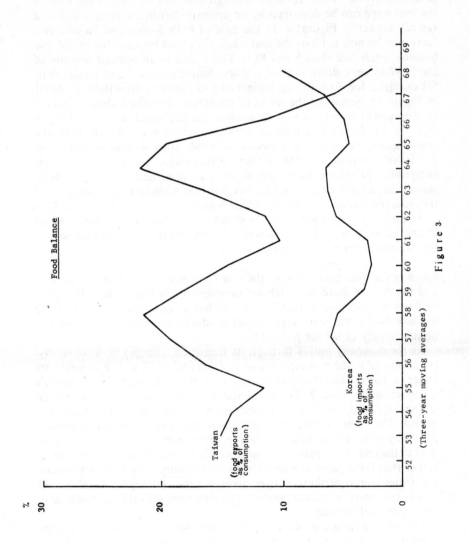

Food Balance

Taiwan
(food exports
as % of
consumption)

Korea
(food imports
as % of
consumption)

(Three-year moving averages)

Figure 3.

Real Wage and Welfare

From the viewpoint of welfare, the impact of economic development may be examined in terms of an economy's (1) consumption level, (2) saving capacity and/or (3) the distribution of income between labour and property-owning classes. All these dimensions are in turn closely related to the behaviour of the real wage through time. An increase in the level of the real wage can be described by an upward shift in the budget line of a typical worker in Figure 1c. In the case of both Korea and Taiwan two facts may be noted. First, the real wage did go up between the initial and terminal years (see rows 5 and 6).[17] This is due to an upward revision of the IRW in agriculture as productivity change occurs[18] and means that, for example, for Taiwan, the budget line has shifted, from $B_T D_T$ to $B_T^1 D_T^1$ in Figure 1c. Secondly, the terms of trade have remained about constant in Korea, but worsened slightly against the industrial sector in Taiwan (see row 7). As far as the consumption standard is concerned, both the consumption per head of agricultural goods (row 8) and of industrial goods (row 9) rises with the increase in real wage. Accordingly, the consumption equilibrium point moves from e_T to e_T^1 and e_K to e_K^1 in both cases. Large food imports made this possible without a deterioration of the industrial sector's terms of trade in Korea.

As far as income distribution is concerned, labour's distributive share in any sector is $\emptyset = (Lxw)/z$ where 'z' is the total output of that sector. Consequently the rate of increase of $\emptyset$ is

$$\eta_\emptyset = \eta_w - \eta_{z/L} \tag{5}$$

which is the difference between the rate of increase of the real wage (η_w) and the rate of increase of labour productivity in that sector. Thus, for each sector, the distribution of income moves against labour when the increase in the real wage lags behind productivity gains during the unlimited supply of labour phase.[19]

As the company moves through its transition, changes in income distribution and in the participation of medium and small scale entrepreneurs under a more market-oriented policy setting, enhance the economy's saving capacity. Row 2, Table 1, indicates that Taiwan's gross domestic saving rate had, in fact, increased spectacularly during the transition period. The same is true of Korea where negative saving rates initially gave way to a very satisfactory saving performance at the $18 \cdot 5$ per cent level at the end of the period. From rows 22, 23, and 24 we may, moreover, gather that these gains in domestic saving capacity were largely based on the increasing contribution over time of the non-agricultural sector which, especially in Taiwan, replaced foreign capital as the main source of developmental finance.

The relative failure of Korea's agricultural sector also resulted in a less dramatic increase in her domestic saving capacity as we have already noted (row 20). In fact, rows 22–24 permit us to see precisely how the agricultural sector's contribution to the economy's total investment fund declined dramatically during the transition period. Consequently, even in the terminal period, foreign capital still had to be relied on for close to 50 per cent of Korea's total investment fund. Thus, while the saving capacity of the industrial sector increased dramatically, the gap left by the failure of agriculture's contribution had to be filled largely by foreign capital.

Industrial Sector and International Trade

Turning, finally, to a brief examination of the non-agricultural sector in the same comparative static setting, we should, first of all, note that it is the performance of this sector that has marked off the path of both Korea and Taiwan from that of other contemporary open dualistic economies, Recalling equation (3), we see that the dramatic increase in θ (proportion of the population already efficiently allocated or employed) and in q (non-agricultural labour productivity) has led to a large increase in the per capita output of industrial goods $Y^\triangle$. Although there has been some increase in the domestic use of that industrial output, the most conspicuous result of this development has been in the spurt of industrial exports.

Referring to row 11, the availability of industrial output per head ($Y^\triangle$) sustained an annual rate of increase of 8·0 per cent in Taiwan and 7·5 per cent in Korea during the transition period. This high rate of increase followed from both the increase in θ (row 2) and the increase in q (row 10). The spectacular change in the extent of external orientation of both countries' rapidly growing non-agricultural sectors is summarized in row 12. In Taiwan (Korea), industrial exports per head grew at the remarkable rate of 19·3 per cent (24·0 per cent) annually, yielding a 14-fold (16-fold) increase during the transition period.[20]

This dramatic increase in the external orientation of the industrial sector brought with it a corresponding change in the structure of foreign trade. First of all, in terms of the overall involvement in trade, as measured by the export ratio (row 13), while Korea participated much less in trade at the outset, the export ratio rose substantially in both countries so that, by the terminal year, more than 25 per cent of GDP was exported in both cases. Furthermore, as seen from row 15, in the case of Taiwan, the initial dominance of the agricultural sector in exports was completely reversed so that in the terminal year almost 90 per cent of exports are seen to be non-agricultural. In the case of Korea which had a relatively much more industrial orientation (including exports) to start with, exports are now also almost exclusively industrial in origin. The fact that agricultural exports lagged along with agricultural output is further confirmed in row 16, i.e. the fraction of agricultural goods exported remains small in Korea and substantial in Taiwan.

II. LANDMARKS IN THE TRANSITION PROCESS

We have thus tried to compare and contrast the economic structure of the two countries under observation during both the initial and terminal periods of the transition process to obtain two flashlight exposures. But it is inadequate in the sense that we are still lacking a picture of the process of continuous change over more than a decade which, of course, brought about the structural changes observed. In this section we will attempt to describe the highlights of this process, in terms of the turning points by

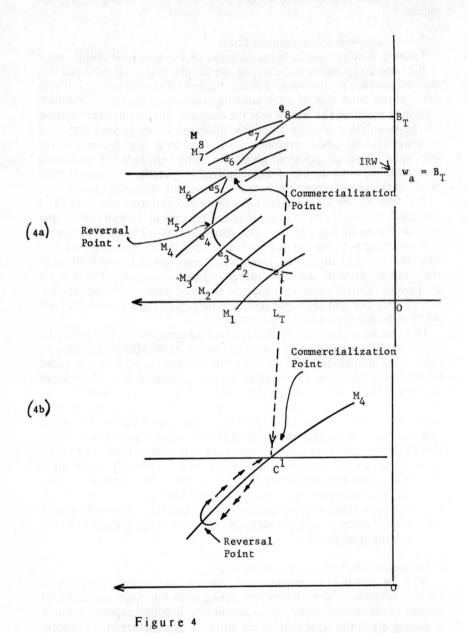

Figure 4

which the sub-phases of the transition process can be marked off.[21] In what follows we shall explore the economic significance of four turning points:

Turning Points	Taiwan	Korea
(a) Commercialization point	65–66	66–67
(b) Reversal point	64–65	66–67
(c) Export substitution point	60	64
(d) Switching point	75 (?)	80 (?)

For a closed labour surplus dualistic economy, the *commercialization point* indicates the termination of the labour surplus condition.[22] From this point on, real wage in the agricultural sector is equated with the marginal productivity of labour (i.e. determined by 'commercial principle' rather than 'institutional forces') which signifies that labour now becomes a scarce factor (from the economic standpoint) and tends to increase rapidly. This concept can be applied to an open dualistic economy.

In the case of Taiwan the causes of the arrival of the commercialization point must be found in a combination of the 'push' effects of continuous technology change in agriculture combined with the 'pull' of industrial demand for labour in a balanced fashion. In Figure 4, which 'blows up' Figure 1b, we indicate the changing marginal product of labour curves M_i as technological change takes place in agriculture. Thus the movement from M_1 (i.e. the MPP_L curve of 1b) to M_8 (the MPP_L' curve of 1b) is replicated in Figure 4. The dynamic process of labour reallocation may then be depicted by a sequence of points e_i which, consistent with a continuously rising θ, or a relative decline in the size of the agricultural population, show, first, an absolute increase in agricultural population (e_1 to e_4), followed by an absolute decrease (from e_4 onward).[23] The commercialization point is reached at e_6.[23] Thus the commercialization point arrives earlier, the faster the upward shift of the MPP_L curve, the slower the rate of population growth, the slower the upward creep of the institutional real wage and the faster the demand for labour increases in the industrial sector.[24]

The above thesis is supported by the actual long-term behaviour of the real wage in the two countries under observation. As shown in Figure 5, the real wage in both countries shows only a minor upward creep until very recently (i.e. after 1965). It thus appears that the commercialization point may have been reached in both Korea and Taiwan[25] towards the end of the '60s—with agricultural 'push' forces contributing much more in Taiwan, and industrial 'pull', fuelled by foreign capital, much more in Korea.[26] If so, we can also expect a further acceleration of real wage increases to characterize their development in the '70s.

The increase of real wages has a profound impact on income distribution, on saving capacity and on the economy's consumption pattern. As income distribution within each sector now shifts in favour of labour, any decline in the propensity to save will be accompanied by a more sustained expansion of the domestic market for consumer goods. In other words, the commercialization point heralds an end to the relative natural austerity typical of the 'unlimited supply of labour' condition. After the commercial-

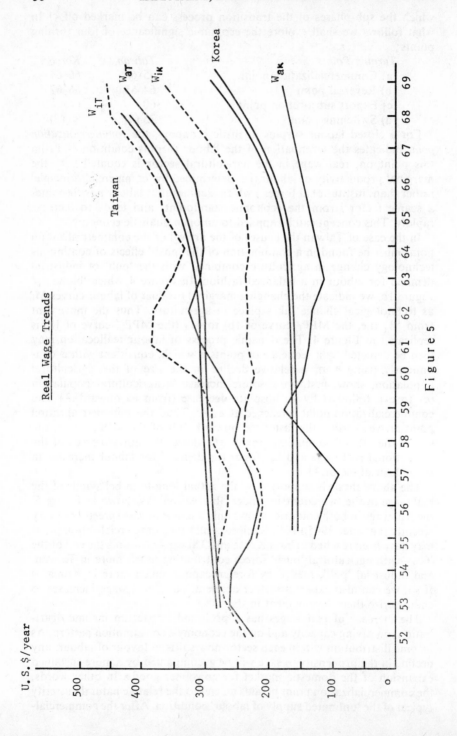

Real Wage Trends

U. S. $/year

Figure 5

ization point, *ceteris paribus*, we can expect the saving rate and the GDP growth rates to level off. Furthermore, in an open dualistic labour surplus economy the commercialization point is also likely to usher in changes in the structure of international trade. The external orientation of the industrial sector, which was previously based on the continuation of maturing entrepreneurs taking advantage of cheap labour,[27] now gives way gradually, to the incorporation of skills and capital goods as the basis for exports. Simultaneously we can expect a shift in the orientation of the industrial sector in the direction of satisfying the growing domestic market for industrial consumer goods, including more durable consumer goods.

The second turning point is the *reversal point* signifying an absolute decline in the agricultural population or labour force. It can be shown that when the rate of increase of the industrial labour force (η_w) is sustained long enough at a level higher than the growth rate of the total labour force ($\eta_w > \eta_p$), not only does θ ($=W/P$) increase continuously, as we have already observed, but a reversal point is reached after some time, when an absolute increase of the agricultural labour force gives way to an absolute decline. In Figure 1d, associated with an increase of the total population or labour force from OP to OP', the initial labour allocation point X changes to X' in the terminal years, representing an increase of θ (slope of OX' > slope of OX) as well as an absolute decline of the agricultural labour force. The movement of the labour allocation point through time is depicted by the locus XRX' in Figure 1d, where R is the reversal point. The same reversal point R can be observed in Figure 4. In the case of the two specific countries under observation here, our data indicate that the reversal point was reached in Taiwan a couple of years before commercialization, while in Korea both seem to have arrived more or less simultaneously, i.e. near the end of the '60s.[28]

When the supply of land is, for all practical purposes, fixed, the arrival of a reversal point signifies that the law of diminishing returns is beginning to work in a reverse direction, as both marginal and average productivities of labour begin to increase even when technology is stagnant. For Taiwan, this implies that the pressure is beginning to appear for the adoption of labour-saving technology (e.g. mechanization) in agriculture—as there is now an absolute shortage of manpower under the old technology. For Korea, this means that it is *possible* to solve the problem of agricultural stagnation by a strategy of 'pulling' this sector up by rapid industrial development. Whether or not this strategy will be successful remains to be seen.[29]

The third turning point is the *export substitution point*. During the long period of growth under colonialism, prior to transition growth, the economy was clearly a land based economy fuelled by primary product exports. During the import substitution sub-phase, which characterizes the initial period of transition growth, the system continued to rely on land based exports, to build up its import substitution industries. The meaning of 'export substitution' is that labour intensive manufacture export (e.g. textile) replaces (i.e. 'substitutes for') the traditional exports (e.g. rice and sugar in Taiwan and the traditional exports in Korea) as the dominant export items of the economy.

Turning to time series in our effort to identify sub-phases in the transition we see that the potential for primary (i.e. consumer goods) import substitution (measured by the share of total industrial consumer goods which is imported, M_c/C_d is initially higher in Taiwan than Korea (see the M_c/C_d curves in Figure 6). Moreover, this potential is being steadily explored (and thus reduced) unt'l around 1960 in Taiwan and 1964 in Korea after which point these curves turn up. Similarly, if we trace the share of consumer goods imports to total imports (M_c/M curves in Figure 6) we see the same turning points 1960 and 1964, respectively, occurring in the two countries. What lies behind these statistical results was the import substitution strategy adopted by the government (high tariff protection for domestic import substituting industries, overvalued domestic currency in the world market by the official exchange rate, artificially low domestic interest rates, etc.) to encourage the use of foreign exchange receipts (earnings by traditional exports) to build up import substitution industries.

When the domestic markets for industrial consumer goods is supplied almost exclusively by the new import substituting industries, the import substitution phase comes to an end (i.e. exhausted). In the case of a relatively small labour surplus economy, the natural development is the emergence of the export substitution phase—i.e. selling labour intensive manufacturing exports in the world market. This transition was facilitated by a change in government policy to promote exports (e.g. realistic foreign exchange rate or even undervaluation of domestic currency) based on labour efficiency (e.g. adoption of realistic interest rate through interest reform to eliminate the artificial 'capital cheapening' condition under the import substitution phase). The results are seen in Figure 7 which shows a marked shift in the composition of exports—with industrial exports as a fraction of total, shooting up in Taiwan after 1960 and a few years later in the case of Korea.[30] The change in export structure is nothing less than spectacular.

For a small labour surplus economy with a colonial heritage of primary product export, the emergence of the export substitution phase, replacing the import substitution phase is a highly significant phenomenon.[31] In respect to the unemployment problem, the import substitution phase was not a period conducive to full employment leading to the, by now popular, slogan of a 'necessary' conflict between 'employment and growth'. In reality, there is no such conflict when the export substitution phase arrives. For the embodiment of labour service in export to the world market is conducive to both rapid growth and full employment—as the country has, for the first time, found a way to make full use of her abundant labour supply. As this process continues it leads to both the 'commercialization point' and the 'switching point' signifying the termination of the labour surplus condition in the economy as a whole as well as in the agriculture sector in particular. For this reason, the export substitution point precedes the other turning point in both countries just mentioned.[32]

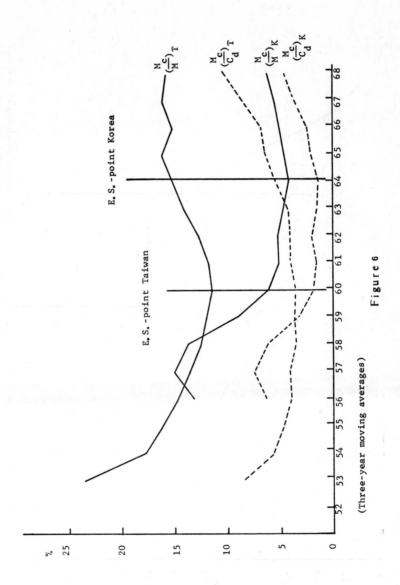

Import Substitution and Export Substitution

Figure 6

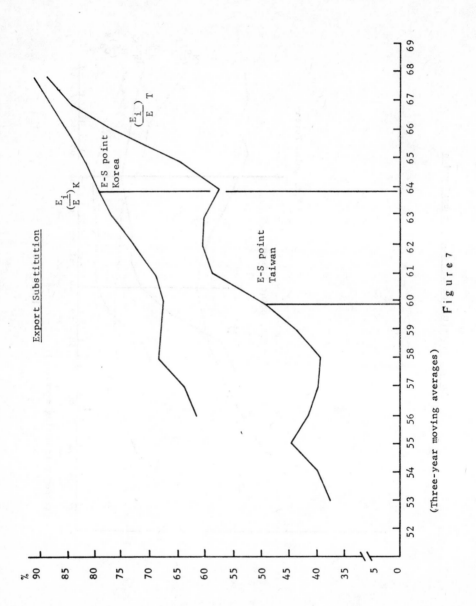

Figure 7

Another turning point in the transition of the open dualistic economy is the *switching point*. It is based on the notion that countries which are basically natural resources poor will at some point in their history have to become net importers of agricultural goods. This is as true of Korea and Taiwan as of historical Japan which became a net importer of agricultural goods from her colonies around the turn of the century.[33] Taiwan's agricultural sector, in spite of its superior performance, through the application of land reform, non-traditional inputs, etc., is, as we have already observed, reaching its natural limits—witness the determination of her industrial sector's terms of trade and the declining level of per capita agricultural exports (rows 3 and 7).[34] Korea, on the other hand, as we have also noted, became a net importer of agricultural goods virtually from the beginning of the transition period; her agriculture sector, we feel, has not fulfilled its historical mission.

The phenomenon of land-based exports at the beginning of the transition must be viewed as a temporary phenomenon in long run historical perspective. A 'switch' from an agricultural exporting to importing position is bound to occur at some stage in the development process in the future. But *when* it occurs and on the basis of *what* kind of agricultural performance remains an all important issue. It matters greatly for Korea whether or not existing reserves of agricultural productivity have been harnessed *en route* to the successful solution of the LDC employment problem. The alternatives may well be failure of the total effort—true for many contemporary LDCs of the type under discussion—or an unacceptably heavy reliance on foreign capital, as in the case of Korea.

III. CONCLUSION AND IMPLICATIONS FOR POLICIES

In the transition process of a labour surplus open dualistic economy, the solution of the unemployment problem may be identified with the arrival of the commercialization point which signifies the termination of the labour surplus condition inherited from the colonial epoch. After commercialization, we can expect to observe a sustained increase in real wage; the 'unemployment problem' will then be of a different type.

The increase in real wage is expected to be accompanied by some reduction in the savings rate, a relative decline in the importance of trade and a shift toward a more skill and capital intensive technology and output mix—an increased concern with the provision of an adequate supply of high talented manpower. These are the major development issues confronted by Taiwan (and to a lesser extent Korea) at the present time and for the near future.

On the road to commercialization, the most important landmark is the export substitution point based on labour intensive export. There will no longer be a sharp conflict between growth and employment objectives— as was the case under import substitution growth. The arrival of the export substitution point 'facilitates' the arrival of the commercial point that terminates the labour surplus condition.

The whole array of government policy measures (e.g. high protective tariffs, exchange controls, low interest rates, overvalued currencies, price inflation) adopted to facilitate the import substitution process—via the exclusion of foreign competition and the augmentation of the profits of the domestic industrialists—are, of course, subject to changes. Both Taiwan and Korea, did, in fact, effect major changes in their policy environment around 1960 and 1963, respectively, to facilitate transitions to export substitution. Stabilization plus dismantling of the various existing direct control measures, on trade, interest rate and foreign exchange rates, thereby created a more market orientated economy most conducive to access for large numbers of domestic entrepreneurs seeking efficient utilization of the economy's relatively abundant resources via embodiment in labour-intensive industrial exports. The experience of Taiwan and Korea teaches us that unemployment problems can be solved through growth in 'this' way.

At some point during its life cycle, the open dualistic labour surplus economy is, moreover, likely to move from the successful exploitation of its agricultural potential to its 'natural' long term position as an importer of agricultural goods. The arrival of such a switching point signifies that the country will ultimately have to accelerate its industrial exports to acquire the needed food and raw materials—a phenomenon which may occur before commercialization point, as in historical Japan, or after commercialization point, as in Taiwan, or Korea in the future.

Finally, given the rates of population growth, a reversal point indicating an absolute decline in the size of the agricultural labour force is likely to occur before the switching point. Thus the policy focus may shift to labour saving techniques in agriculture in order to prolong labour using techniques in industry, while the economy gets ready for the skill and capital intensive phase. At the present time, this is precisely the central policy issue in Taiwan. In the case of Korea, however, due to its neglect of agriculture in the past, the country is still faced with the problem of first building up its rural infrastructure and utilizing the still unexploited slack in agricultural productivity—a process likely to release additional supplies of labour without the need to resort to extensive mechanization.

In Taiwan, the agricultural sector has already fulfilled its historical mission during the early phase of transition. In the case of Korea the story is quite different as it cannot be denied that Korea's agricultural sector has been relatively stagnant.[35] Consequently, throughout the import substitution sub-phase, while industrial entrepreneurial maturation took place, much of the potential domestic fuel for further growth was never generated. Consequently, after the export substitution point had been reached, a tremendous burden fell upon the industrial sector, fuelled largely by foreign capital, to continue to 'pull' the agricultural sector along with it, including the continuous 'pulling out' of agricultural workers.

The rather heavier burden which Korea's non-agricultural sector has consequently had to carry has, in turn, led to certain distortions in that sector. For example, industrial exports have undoubtedly been pushed, at least in some areas, beyond the point of efficiency, and that a good deal of 'premature' backward linkage type of import substitution has consequently taken place[36] (especially since 1968, with the help of a large assortment of special subsidies and other incentives). The simple reason is that, with agriculture's push not forthcoming,[37] industrial exports have had to 'run' ever faster, with the consequence that some fairly technology and capital intensive sub-sectors have been expanded, ahead of what the, admittedly changing, endowment picture would call for. Moreover, Korea was consequently forced to admit an unusually heavy flow of foreign aid, more recently private investment, to keep the process going.

As far as the future is concerned, it is, of course, 'mathematically' conceivable that the present trends continue during the decade ahead—until the non-agricultural sector and the non-agricultural labour force become so predominant that the Korean economy begins to operate something like the city-states of Hong Kong and Singapore, i.e. importing virtually all needed agricultural goods and depending entirely on her industrial exporting sector. Such a strategy is, however, not likely to be successful as a practical choice. Korea's agricultural sector and population remain too large relative to the total economy to permit the hinterland to be 'dragged along' into modernity in this fashion. It is difficult to conceive of trade able to expand fast enough in a competitive fashion; it is equally difficult to conceive of foreign capital as continuing to flow in at the rates required. The increasing import intensity of industrial exports, the heavy foreign debt structure, the growing food gap are all symptoms of difficulties ahead. Whether or not the commercialization point has already been reached, Korea will clearly have to reconsider its policy of agricultural neglect by pursuing a more balanced growth strategy in the years ahead.

APPENDIX 1

In Figure 8bcde, we reproduce the initial equilibrium position of Taiwan described in Figure 1bcde. In Figure 3b, out of a total labour force OP, the agricultural labour force is OL_T producing a per capita output of $L_T b_T$. Total agricultural output is represented by the area OPab. With respect to the allocation of this output, we see that, since the real wage in terms of agricultural goods is OB_T, labour's share is $OB_T cL_T$ ($=B_1+B_2+B_3$).[38] Let us assume that wage earners do not save; then the consumption by farmers of food is B_1 (at the consumption standard for agricultural goods Oe), while the income exchanged by farmers for industrial consumer goods is B_2+B_3. To see the magnitude of the landlord or rent share, let the auxiliary straight line dc be drawn; then from point 'e' let a straight line parallel to cd be constructed, thus obtaining point 'f'. The area B_4 ($=$dhgf) then equals B_2+B_3 by construction.[39] Since the wage share is B_1+B_4 ($=B_1+B_2+B_3$), the remaining total output or rent share is $B_2+B_5+B_6$. Under the assumption that all rental incomes are saved, this constitutes agricultural saving (S_a).

The total output of agriculture is thus allocated in the following way: B_1 is consumed by agricultural workers; B_2+B_5 is exported (hB_T being per capita exports); the remaining output B_4+B_6 is destined for consumption by workers in the industrial sector. The latter two types of shipments summarize the contribution that agriculture makes to non-agricultural development, first in providing import capacity (B_2+B_5) and second in providing food for industrial workers (B_4+B_6).

Let us turn now to the industrial sector (in Figure 8e), where the equilibrium is established at point h_T, i.e. where the M_T-curve intersects the real wage level in terms of industrial goods, OD_T. With a given labour force (OW_T), the total industrial output is then divided into the wage share ($A_1+A_2+A_3$) and the profit share (A_4), the latter constituting industrial saving (S_j). Out of the total wage share, A_1 is consumed by industrial workers, while A_2+A_3 is exchanged for agricultural goods for purposes of consumption. At the given terms of trade (slope of $B_T D_T$) the exchange value of A_2+

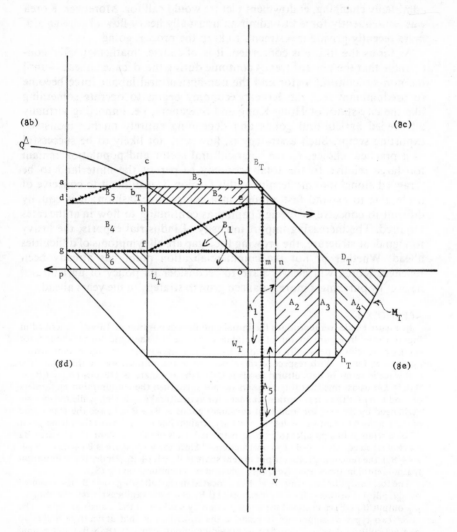

Figure 8

A_3 is B_4+B_6. Notice that A_2 comprises industrial consumer goods exchanged for B_4 units of agricultural goods delivered by the farmers; A_3, on the other hand, represents investment goods exchanged for the landlord's agricultural saving B_6. Notice also that total agricultural export proceeds (B_2+B_3) which accrue to the owners of the agricultural surplus, enable the system to import A_5 (=mnuv) units of investment goods. [40] Thus the total domestic investment fund is $A_3+A_4+A_5$ and financed in the following way:

$$(A1) \quad \underset{(A_3+A_4+A_5)}{I} = \underset{(A_5+A_3)}{S_a} + \underset{(A_4)}{S_i}$$

Since, in addition, there exist also inflows of foreign capital (S_f), the finance equation may be slightly modified to obtain (4). [41]

What we have just presented is pertinent to the case of Taiwan and would have to be modified in a by now predictable fashion to capture realistically the case of Korea. As we indicated in the context of our discussion of Figures 1 and 2, the essential differences are (1) the agricultural contribution to the saving fund here is much lower because of the low level of agricultural productivity; (2) whatever contribution the agricultural sector does make to industrial finance is through the 'domestic route', i.e. inter-sectoral finance; (3) foreign capital plays a much larger role in the financing of domestic capital formation.

APPENDIX 2

Data Sources: (Korea)

(a) *National Income Statistical Yearbook* 1968, 1969 (The Bank of Korea)

(b) *Korea Statistical Yearbook* (1960–69) (Economic Planning Board, Republic of Korea).

(c) *Annual Economic Review* 1955–1959 (The Bank of Korea)

(d) *Economic Statistical Yearbook* 1960–71 (The Bank of Korea).

(e) *Inter-Industry Relations Tables* 1960, 1963, 1966, 1968 (The Bank of Korea).

(f) *Price Statistical Summary* 1961, 1964, 1966, 1968 (The Bank of Korea).

(g) *Yearbook of Agriculture and Forestry* 1964, 1968, 1969 (Ministry of Agriculture and Forestry, Republic of Korea).

(h) *Foreign Trade of Korea* 1964–69 (Ministry of Finance, Republic of Korea).

(i) *Monthly Economic Review* (The Korea Development Bank).

(j) *Agricultural Cooperative Monthly Survey* (National Agricultural Cooperative Federation, Korea).

(k) *Estimates of Korean Capital and Inventory Coefficients in 1968* (by Kee Chun Han, Yonsei University).

(l) *Analysis of Household Spending-Saving Behaviour in Korea*, 1970 (by Sung-Hwan Jo, Sogang University).

Data Sources: (Taiwan)

(a) *National Income of the Republic of China*, 1951-1970 (Directorate-General of Budgets, Accounts and Statistics, Executive Yuan).

(b) *Industry of Free China* (CIECD), 1970

(c) *Commodity-Price Statistics Monthly, Taiwan District*, 1971 (Directorate-General of Budgets, Accounts and Statistics, Executive Yuan).

(d) *Monthly Statistics of the Republic of China* (Directorate-General of Budgets, Accounts and Statistics, Executive Yuan).

(e) *Input-Output Table* (CIECD), 1961, 1964, 1966.

(f) *Taiwan Agricultural Year Book*, 1962-1970 (Department of Agriculture and Forestry, Provincial Government of Taiwan).

(g) *Taiwan Economic Statistics* (CIECD).

(h) *Taiwan Statistical Data Book* (CIECD), 1970.

(i) 'Household Registration' of Provincial Department of Civil Affairs.

(j) *Taiwan Area Report on the Year-End Household Check and Population Registration Statistics* (of Provincial Department of Civil Affairs).

(k) *Export and Import Foreign Exchange Settlements Statistics*, 1970 (Foreign Exchange Department, the Central Bank of Taiwan.)

(l) *The Republic of China, Taiwan Industrial Production Statistics Monthly* (Ministry of Economic Affairs).

(m) *Quarterly Report on the Labour Force Survey in Taiwan*, 1963–69, (Labour Force Survey and Research Institute).

(n) *Taiwan Agricultural Price Monthly* (Department of Agriculture and Forestry, Provincial Government of Taiwan).

(o) *Monthly Statistics on Price Received and Price Paid by Farmer in Taiwan* (Bureau of Accounting and Statistics Provincial Government of Taiwan, Republic of China).

(p) *The Republic of China, Report on Industrial and Commercial Surveys*, 1954, 1962, 1966 (Ministry of Economic Affairs).

(q) *Taiwan Food Statistics Book*, 1970 (Taiwan Provincial Food Bureau)

NOTES

1. S. Kuznets [*1966*]; see also Fei and Ranis [*1969*]. This process, linked to the achievement of political independence, began earlier in Latin America.

2. These dates, coming a few years after the move from the Chinese Mainland, in the first instance, and after the Korean War, in the second, are commonly accepted as appropriate base years.

3. We recognize the incompleteness of the mapping between agriculture and subsistence, on the one hand, and non-agriculture and commercialized, on the other 'Agriculture' is viewed as a proxy for sectors in which wages or income exceed the marginal product and are institutionally determined, and 'non-agriculture' as a proxy for sectors where there is an approximation to a competitive solution. The statistical problem remains and has not been solved in the context of this paper. It would require a careful disaggregation of the services sector, as well as of agriculture and even industry, into their commercialized and non-commercialized components.

4. If desirable, capital can be combined with land.

5. The reasons for this are complicated, but related to the greater attention paid by the Japanese to irrigation and organizational infrastructure in colonial Taiwan where a cash crop, sugar, was to be promoted, along with the staples.

6. In a predominantly agricultural economy, we would expect the relationship in relative agricultural productivities between the two countries to also be reflected in their relative per capita GDP levels. This is borne out by the parity calculations in Table 1, row 4a, column 4.

7. Thus, in column 7 of the statistical table, the internal terms of trade reflect the common international terms of trade.

8. This is shown by the distance nj in Figure 1b.

9. The absolute fixity of the IRW is, of course, only an approximation to reality The model could easily be amended to incorporate a more realistic upward 'creep' in the IRW level. The price-consumption curve (PC_T) is derived by taking the typical worker's income at OB_T and determining his consumption of agricultural and non-agricultural goods at different terms of trade, i.e. it is the locus of tangencies between the worker's indifference map and a 'swivelling' budget line anchored at point B_T.

10. Given Korea's lower level of agricultural productivity (v) approximately the same level of per capita consumption of agricultural goods ($C_{\frac{1}{a}}$) and plus more people still in agriculture, if follows that $E_{\frac{\Delta}{a}}$ must be smaller here (see equation 2b). This is not shown clearly in Figure 2b because the net export is negligible.

11. In the absence of a wage gap between the agricultural worker's real wage in terms of industrial goods and the industrial worker's real wage in terms of industrial goods. The existence, realistically, of a wage gap can be easily accommodated.

12. Suppose the production functions of the two countries were the same. Given the higher input ratio (at D_K, Figure 2f) for Korea than for Taiwan (at D_T, Figure 1f), the equilibrium point for Korea (h_K, Figure 2e) would have implied a higher level of both the marginal and average productivities of labour. For example, the Korean MPP_K-curve would have passed through a higher point such as 'u' in Figure 2e. Compared with such a point, the actual point 'h_K' indicates the presence of 'labour saving innovations' in Korea as compared with Taiwan.

13. Our understanding of the precise causes of such differences in colonial heritage

a phenomenon which must be traced to profit maximization under colonialism, given differential resource endowments in the two colonies—is clearly incomplete at this point. [see, however, *Samuel Ho 1971*].

14. The domestic demand for industrial goods which includes not only consumption but also industrial demands is actually higher than this (i.e. a certain multiple of $W_T C_i^{\triangle}$) We have, however, for simplicity's sake, assumed that $W_T C_i^{\triangle}$ represents the total per capita demand for industrial goods.

15. The forces that determine these contributions to the total saving fund may be traced to the distribution of income as well as to the rules governing intersectoral exchange in the context of our analytical framework. The theory of determination of savings in an open dualistic economy will be explained in Appendix 1.

16. While technological progress (i.e. the upward shift of the Q-curve) increases average labour productivity, the labour allocation effect itself will also increase labour productivity if the agricultural labour force declines absolutely. We shall examine this issue briefly below.

17. While agricultural productivity in Taiwan, for example, increases by 130 per cent during the period, agricultural real wages increased only 50 per cent (rows 1 and 5). The existence of labour surplus is indicated in Figure 1b, by point 'n' (corresponding to the IRW) lying above point 'j' (indicating MPP_L) in the initial year. This signifies the existence of disguised unemployment during much of the transition. In the case of Korea, agricultural real wages lag much less behind productivity gain. This signifies the more rapid 'pulling out' of agricultural labour with the help of foreign capital inflow and the earlier termination of disguised unemployment. We will return to both these points in the next section.

18. And/or, once the more realistic possibility of a wage gap (between agricultural and industrial workers) is admitted, due to a change in the size of that gap.

19. Nevertheless, for the economy as a whole, the distribution of income may well improve for labour, as a consequence of the existence of a wage gap between the two sectors and the shift of the economy's centre of gravity from one to the other. The full analysis of income distribution in the two-sector world under discussion is a complicated one and really beyond the scope of this paper.

20. In recent years, total industrial exports have been rising at close to 35 per cent annually in both countries.

21. In this paper we are not concerned with the formulation of a truly deterministic dynamic theory. Our analysis, it is hoped, can provide some guidelines as to how such a theory should be formulated and tested by time series.

22. For a fuller discussion of commercialization point, see Fei and Ranis [*1964*].

23. Before 'e_6' there exists disguised unemployment in agriculture as the MPP_L is below the institutional wage w_a; after 'e_6' the labour surplus condition terminates as the wage now follows the MPP_L, signifying the fact that the reservoir of the unemployed has been 'mopped up' and wages are henceforth determined according to neo-classical rules. If, more realistically, the IRW itself rises, from B_T to B_T^1 the commercialization point does not occur until productivity level M_8 (leading to point e_8) has been reached.

In the absence of technology change in agriculture, only a major absolute decline in the agricultural population could permit the commercialization point to be reached, i.e. by moving along a constant MPP_L curve.

24. This is traced, in turn, to the rate of capital accumulation and the degree of labour using bias in the industrial sector.

25. This, in fact, has definitely been occurring in Taiwan. The question of whether or not the commercialization point and a condition of labour shortage has really been reached in Korea or whether the recent rise in real wages may be due to a short run deterioration of the industrial sector's terms of trade (as agricultural stagnation continues and P.L. 480 imports are becoming more expensive) is still not entirely clear and the subject of continuing investigation by the authors. One thing is clear, however, i.e. that, if the commercialization point has, in fact, already been reached in Korea it is more by moving upward along given M curves, while in Taiwan there was more of an upward shift in the M curve itself. On this general subject, see also Roger Sedjo (*1971*).

26. A similar pattern of the behaviour of real wages can be observed for historical Japan whose earlier experience as an open labour surplus economy is relevant here.

Here also the pattern of real wage increases shows a modest upward creep in the nine-teenth century followed by a substantial acceleration after World War One [see *Fei and Ranis, 1971*].

27. See the discussion of the 'Export Substitution Point'.

28. In historical Japan the reversal point occurred during the last decade of the nine-teenth century, thus preceding the commercialization point by at least several decades. It is also quite possible for the reversal point to occur after the commercialization point. A systematic investigation of the sequential order of all the turning points is the purpose of a more formal dynamically determistic theory yet to be developed.

29. The crucial factors are (1) the population growth rate (2) the relative size of the labour force in the agricultural sector, (3) the population size relative to the demand for the products of this country in the world market. Hong Kong can solve her 'agricultural problem' by this strategy because all these factors are favourable. There is a serious doubt in our mind that this strategy can be successful in Korea.

30. It should be noted that Korea's E_i/E ratio is substantially higher from the very beginning, as a consequence of the economy's relatively weak agricultural base from the outset. Export substitution here means, in part, a shift from traditional non-agricultural exports (e.g. mining) to non-traditional non-agricultural exports (e.g. labour intensive textiles and electronics). The small differences in determining the E-S point from the import and export sides (in Figures 6 and 7) should not surprise us. 'Nature does not make jumps' and we are really talking about turning ranges rather than turning points. The change in trend and in the structure of the two economies is clearly established. In the case of Korea, there is more of an over lapping between the end of I-S and the beginning of E-S growth.

31. Many theoretical issues and interpretations can be raised, but not elaborated, in this paper. The phenomenon may be approached from the viewpoint of international trade and comparative advantage which emphasized the inefficiency of import substitution (see, for example, Little, Scitovsky and Scott [*1970*] which would view the emergence of export substitution phase essentially as correcting the mistakes of the import substitution strategy). On the other hand, from the growth theoretical point of view the import sub-stitution phase may be viewed as an essential pre-requisite of the export substitution phase (see Paauw and Fei [*1973*] for a full exposition of this view; also see Ranis [*1972*] for an international comparison).

32. Again, these issues can only be explored with further study by dynamic models.

33. Before that point was reached, however, i.e. during the three decades following the Meiji Restoration in 1868, she had been very successful in generating substantial agricultural productivity increases. [see, for example, *Johnston, 1952; Ranis 1959; Ohkawa and Rosovsky, 1960*].

34. A full exploration of the relation between the 'international terms of trade' and the 'internal terms of trade' between agriculture and non-agriculture goods requires an understanding of whether 'free trade' prevailed in these countries and whether they are small countries. We feel that initially, 'free trade' prevailed in these two countries so that the internal terms of trade reflected the common international terms of trade. However, in the process of development in the last 20 years, internal terms of trade gradually diverged from the international terms of trade—a theoretical observation which needs to be investigated further.

35. While there admittedly exist important differences in the soil, climate and other elements of the natural endowment as between Korea and Taiwan—and no one is suggesting that every country has equal reserves of agricultural productivity ready for activation—there is ample evidence that much of the relative failure of Korea's agri-culture to date is man-made. We know, for example, that the Japanese left a relatively inferior agricultural infrastructure in Korea, not only in terms of irrigation facilities, but also, and probably more important, in terms of organizational infrastructure. It is our distinct impression—though admittedly, it is risky to be categorical on this point—that much more could have been done to repair this differential. To cite one example, Korea's rural organization (the NACF) represents an attempt to do too many things in agriculture, including the provision of information, of inputs, as well as the power to tax. It is but a pale reflection of Taiwan's Farmers' Associations, hooked up with the JCRR structure, which farmers could view more as their own instrument. Moreover, agri-

cultural price policies in Korea are directed much more towards income redistribution objectives *after* production decisions have already been made rather than providing *ex ante* incentives for increased productivity, as in Taiwan. There seems, in short, to be a substantial consensus among agricultural economists and agronomists that while the 'Green Revolution' potential of Korea may be below that of Taiwan, the actual performance of Korea's farmers also remains substantially below that potential.

36. Research on this issue is currently under way. For the current use of a variety of special incentives ranging from tariff and tax reductions, to linkage systems, import wastage allowances, deposit rate preferences, differential interest, electricity and freight rates, see Kim Kwang Suk [*1971*].

37. Worse, with industry having to help pay for net agricultural imports.

38. $B_1 = oL_The$; $B_2 = hebb_T$; $B_3 = bb_TcB_T$. $B_1, B_2 \ldots B_6$ are rectangular areas.

39. hf/he = ch/dh. This means hfxdh = chxhe.

40. In Figure 8e total domestic output of the industrial sector is $A_1 + A_2 + A_3 + A_4$, with an output capacity for consumer goods of $A_1 + A_2$. For Taiwan, in fact, the domestic consumer goods production capacity is less than the domestic demand $(A_1 + A_2)$ or the capacity for investment goods production is greater than $A_3 + A_4$. In that situation, a part of imports takes the form of industrial consumer goods.

41. When foreign capital inflows are admitted, the magnitudes of 'investment', 'supply of industrial goods', 'industrial imports' are all augmented by the value of 'S_f'.

REFERENCES

Fei, J. C. H. and G. Ranis, 1964, *Development of the Labour Surplus Economy: Theory and Policy*, Homewood, Ill.: Richard D. Irwin.

Fei, J. C. H. and G. Ranis, 1969, 'Economic Development in Historical Perspective', *American Economic Review*, May.

Fei ,J. C. H. and G. Ranis, 1971. 'On the Empirical Relevancy of the Fei-Ranis Model of Economic Development: A Reply', *American Economic Review*, September.

Ho, S., 1971, *The Development Policy of the Japanese Colonial Government in Taiwan, 1895–1945*, in G. Ranis (ed.), *Government and Economic Development*, New Haven: Yale University Press.

Johnston, B. F., 1952, 'Agricultural Productivity and Economic Development of Japan', *Journal of Political Economy*, 7: 2.

Kim, Kwang Suk, 1971. *Export Promotion and Industrial Incentive Policy in Korea*.

Kuznets, S., 1966, *Modern Economic Growth: Rate Structure and Spread*, New Haven: Yale University Press.

Lewis, W. A., 1954, *Development with Unlimited Supplies of Labour*, Manchester School of Economics and Social Studies.

Little, I., T. Scitovsky and M. Scott, 1970, *Industry and Trade in Some Developing Countries—A Comparative Study*, London: Oxford University Press.

Ohkawa, K. and H. Rosovsky, 1960, 'The Role of Agriculture in Modern Japanese Economic Development', *Economic Development and Cultural Change*, 9: 1, Part 2, October.

Paauw and Fei, 1975, *Development of the Open Dualistic Economy*, New Haven: Yale University Press.

Ranis, G., 1959, 'Financing Economic Development', *Economic History Review*, March.

Ranis, G., 1972, *Relative Prices in Planning for Economic Development*, in D. J. Daly (ed.), *International Comparisons of Prices and Output*, NBER, Columbia University Press.

Sedjo, R., 1971, 'The Turning Point in Korea', paper presented to the ILCORK Conference, Seoul, Korea, August 22–27.

Economic Development, Structural Change and Employment Potential

By Mahmood A. Zaidi* and Sudhin K. Mukhopadhyay**

Economic development is accompanied with changes in the inter-sectoral flows of intermediate goods. This structural change assumes certain patterns depending on the stage and nature of development of the economy. This paper examines such possible patterns and their implications on the basis of input-output analysis for the USA, Japan and India and suggests that the form of interaction between sectors is unilateral—the matrix is either lower or upper triangular signifying the structure of the economy. It also measures the extent of structural change of the three countries and considers the employment implications of such change.

I

Aggregative studies of economic development are concerned mainly with movements of national income or output over time or space. Behind these movements, there takes place an almost continual change in the flows of output between the different sectors of the economy that constitute the subject matter of structural change. An attempt has been made in this paper to examine the nature and implications of the patterns of structural change that accompany economic development. The open static input-output technique has been used to present an inter-temporal and international comparison of structures of development. In Section II the possible patterns of input-output matrices have been outlined with their respective implications for economic development and in Section III some empirical observations have been presented. Section IV has been used to measure and explore the changes in economic structure in the context of an international comparison. Section V presents a discussion and a measure of the employment implications of structural transformation.

———————————

* Professor, Industrial Relations Center, University of Minnesota, Minneapolis, Minnesota, **Lecturer in Economics, University of Kalyani, India. A version of this paper was presented at the European Meeting of the Econometric Society, Budapest, 1972. We are indebted to Professors Mario F. Bognanno, James M. Henderson, Vernon W. Ruttan, Calvin D. Siebert, Shuntaro Shishido and Lance Taylor for comments, encouragement and material support in the preparation of this paper. The comments of the participants in the Budapest meeting of the Econometric Society and the Referee on an earlier version of this paper are also gratefully acknowledged. We alone are responsible for the errors that might remain. This study was supported partly by the AID through the Economic Development Center, and partly by the Industrial Relations Center.

II

The history of economic development suggests that the lack of inter-dependence among sectors is a common feature of underdevelopment. Economic activities at this stage are mostly isolated, self-sufficient and orientated to meeting final demand. Very little of the outputs pass through the processing of intermediate activities leading to zero or near-zero entries in the input-output tables [*Peacock and Dosser, 1957*]. In some countries final consumption may be sustained mostly by imports. There may also be sizeable exports that consist mostly of raw materials the extraction of which has not yet been able to generate sufficient interrelated economic activity in the domestic economy. The input-output matrices of these countries also have very few significant entries.

Economic development is usually accompanied by the gradual replace-ment of zero by positive entries in the input-output tables of countries. But the pattern and magnitude of entries will depend on a number of factors, e.g., the level of aggregation, the natural endowments of the economy, the pattern of final demand, etc. For a given level of aggregation, block-diagonality and triangularity are the chief characteristics of these input-output matrices [*Carter, 1967; Leontief, 1963; Simpson and Tsukui, 1965*].

The implication of a prominent diagonal in an input-output table is that the sectors identified do use intermediate outputs to produce final products, but are confined, by and large, to processing their own intermediate outputs. Economic development continues to transform such economies by bringing out possibilities of technical change that makes use of inputs across the sector-boundaries. Following Karl Fox [*1963*], it is contended here that a useful sector classification of an economy may be made into two complexes:[1] *primary complex*, consisting of farming, forestry, livestock and food and fibre processing industries, and *secondary complex* consisting of all other industries. The classification is such that it will generate a strong diagonal because of the possibility of a large intra-sectoral use of intermediate outputs. Nonetheless, there would still be plenty of technical opportunities for flows of inputs across the sector-borders. Activities in the primary complex (e.g. food grains) make use of inputs produced in the secondary complex (farm machinery, fertilizer, storage and transporta-tion equipment, etc.). On the other hand, there are activities in the secon-dary complex that may use significant amounts of inputs from the primary complex. Examples are, chemicals, paints, construction, etc. These technical possibilities give rise to the transformation of the input-output matrix from a predominantly diagonal into a quasi-triangular one.

There are two types of triangularities that the matrix might assume: (1) *quasi-lower-triangular*, where the primary complex uses inputs from the secondary complex but the latter does not use much input from the former, and (2) *quasi-upper-triangular*, where the secondary complex receives inputs from the primary complex but the latter uses little or no inputs from the secondary complex. The first may be characterized as 'industrialization of agriculture'. On the other hand, economic development may take place through the growth of activities that use a large quantity of natural and primary-sector outputs and with a small proportion of man-made or artificial inputs. For example, a good portion of inputs into construction, transport and chemical industries may come either from the primary complex or from within the secondary complex. It is conceivable that an economy with a large primary sector and at its initial stages of growth might move toward the growth of industries that are based relatively heavily on primary sector's outputs. These industries may consist of both food and fibre processing and other industrial activities mentioned above. This feature may be designated as 'development through agriculturized industries'. Economic development may also affect the nature of triangularity through the pattern of foreign trade. A relatively high degree of imported raw materials for both sectors should account for rather low entries for the off-diagonal elements. If a country proceeds to substitute by domestic production, imports of secondary input for its primary complex at a higher rate than primary inputs for its secondary complex, it will move toward a lower-triangular matrix. And the reverse will lead to an upper-triangular matrix.

As economic development proceeds, two forces are set in motion that might tend to influence the input-output matrix. First, for a viable agriculture and other primary complex activities that can move along with the secondary complex providing inputs for the latter, the lead for intersectoral input supply is gradually taken over from agriculture by industry. On the other hand, the secondary complex makes more use of man-made and industrial inputs (e.g., construction using a larger proportion of metallic inputs) thereby pushing down the rate of inflow of agricultural inputs. Thus the quasi-upper-triangular matrix is gradually replaced by a quasi-lower-triangular matrix or a balanced input-output structure might result from the forces influencing the technical transformation of the economy. The tentative hypothesis suggested here is that efforts at development of an economy in the early stages generates and strengthens interaction between sectors. Depending on the stage and nature of economic development, several structural patterns may be discerned in the intersectoral relations of the economy:

Pattern I: The input-output matrix is characterized by a dominant diagonal with off-diagonal elements insignificant or zero. This usually implies a lack of interdependence and the sectors are isolated and self-sufficient, characteristics of a low level of development.

Pattern II: With economic development and increasing inter-sectoral flows the off-diagonal elements begin to assume importance. But the interaction is unilateral such that the growth of the secondary complex takes place through inputs provided by the primary complex resulting in a quasi-upper-triangular matrix. This is likely for most less developed economies with relatively large primary complex, where initial industrialization is mostly through activities around primary complex. Such a flow is usually sustained by government or private investment in the secondary complex and/or by the inter-sectoral terms of trade being in favour of the secondary complex.

Pattern III: The nature of the economy may be such that the primary sector is relatively less important in size than the secondary complex. Here economic development may occur through the transformation of the primary sector by using more inputs from the secondary sector. This leads to a quasi-lower triangular matrix. An economy may assume this pattern both at the beginning of industrialization or at a later stage succeeding pattern II. In the first case there is usually external investment in agriculture that stimulates the flow of industrial inputs there, while in the later case agriculture through pattern II, is able to generate enough surplus for reinvestment in transforming its structure.

There may also be a pattern with the different sectors maintaining a balance in the flows of intermediate products leading to a symmetric matrix. In reality such a balance is unlikely except during a transition. It is important to bring out the difference between these types of triangularities, because they not only signify different economic structures with different corresponding input requirements and factor demands, but are also useful for economic policy formulation.

III

The objective of this section is to provide some empirical support for the hypothesis presented above. For this purpose, seven input-output tables for 3 countries[2]—USA (2 tables), Japan (2 tables), and India (3 tables)—have been aggregated into 2 sector matrices (*viz.*, primary complex and secondary complex) at constant prices and their input-coefficient matrices and Leontief inverses have been calculated.[3]

Examining the input-output matrix for USA, in 1947, Karl Fox observed that the input-coefficient and Leontief inverses are quasi-lower-triangular. This is illustrated in Table 1 on the 1947 matrix for USA at 1963 prices.

TABLE 1

COEFFICIENT MATRICES AND INVERSE, USA: 1947, 1963
(AT 1963 PRICES)

	1947		1963	
	Primary Complex	Secondary Complex	Primary Complex	Secondary Complex
	Coefficient Matrices (A)			
Primary complex	·4323	·0186	·4083	·0246
Secondary complex	·1223	·3839	·1799	·4186
	Inverse Matrices $(I-A)^{-1}$			
Primary complex	1·7729	·0535	1·7120	·0724
Secondary complex	·3519	1·6337	·5297	1·7423

The implication of this kind of matrix, as mentioned earlier, is that in the USA, the agricultural complex consumes industrial outputs substantially, but industry in its turn does not use much of input from the agricultural complex. Fox has suggested that the US economy would show a sharper quasi-lower-triangular coefficient matrix over time because with economic growth there would be increasing substitution of man-made materials for primary inputs. However, as Table 1 shows, although the US input-output relations continue to be quasi-lower-triangular in character, the upper right hand block has not diminished relative to others. It appears from the Leontief inverses that an increase in final demand for one dollar worth of primary complex outputs created a demand for ·53 dollars in 1963. Similarly, the increased requirement for primary complex outputs to meet the increase in final demand for secondary complex goods worth one dollar rose from ·05 dollars in 1947 to ·07 dollars in 1963. By and large, therefore, the US economy did not experience substantial reduction in the use of primary complex inputs in the secondary complex relative to the use of secondary complex inputs in the primary complex and the matrix has remained quasi-lower-triangular.

With her remarkable industrialization in the past two decades, Japan should provide us with some useful illustrations of the transformation of input-output relations. Table 2 below on the input-output relations for Japan in 1951 shows a quasi-lower-triangular character with a prominent diagonal. By 1965, however, Japan's input-coefficient became distinctly quasi-lower-triangular. The increase in the demand for industrial inputs as a result of rise in final demand for primary complex output almost doubled to ·61 yen in 1965 from goods worth ·31 yen in 1951. On the other hand, it seems that Japan developed substitutes for primary complex inputs for

TABLE 2

COEFFICIENT MATRICES AND INVERSES: JAPAN, 1951, 1965
(AT 1965 PRICES)

	1951		1965	
	Primary Complex	Secondary Complex	Primary Complex	Secondary Complex
	Coefficient Matrices (A)			
Primary complex	·4066	·0845	·4213	·0498
Secondary complex	·1072	·4133	·1974	·4301
	Inverse Matrices $(I-A)^{-1}$			
Primary complex	1·7299	·2514	1·7809	·1556
Secondary complex	·3215	1·7494	·6168	1·8084

her secondary complex so that the need for primary inputs for meeting increased demand for secondary outputs declined. Thus the substantial transformation of the inter-sectoral relationships in Japan during 1951–65 served the increased industrial base for Japanese agriculture relative to her agriculture meeting the needs of industries.

Beginning at a considerably lower level of development and endowed with a distinctly different economic base, as compared with the USA and Japan, the Indian economy has been subjected to deliberate development through planning. An examination of India's input-output relationships should, therefore, be particularly instructive. Table 3 below shows the input-output relationships in India in 1959, 1964–65 and 1970–71 [4] respectively. It appears that the economic structure of India changed very little

TABLE 3

COEFFICIENT MATRICES AND INVERSES: INDIA, 1959, 1964–65, 1970–71
(AT 1960 PRICES)

	1959		1964–65		1970–71	
	Primary Complex	Secondary Complex	Primary Complex	Secondary Complex	Primary Complex	Secondary Complex
Coefficient Matrices (A)						
Primary complex	·3028	·0608	·2679	·0618	·2683	·1060
Secondary complex	·0275	·2808	·0270	·3468	·0608	·6700
Inverse Matrices $(I-A)^{-1}$						
Primary complex	1·4473	·1223	1·3708	·1296	1·4036	·4508
Secondary complex	·0553	1·4030	·0566	1·5364	·2586	3·1122

during 1959/1964–65, and the matrices had relatively dominant diagonals indicating low levels of interaction. For both 1959 and 1964–65, however, the overall character of the coefficient matrices and Leontief inverses are quasi-upper-triangular. Not only is this feature retained but it becomes even more visible in the 1970–71 matrix. For example, increases in the final demand for primary complex output worth one rupee led to an increase in the requirement of secondary complex output worth Rs. ·05 in 1959/1964–65, the figure rose to ·26 in 1970–71. As far as the increase in the final demand for industrial output is concerned, it led to an increase in primary output worth Rs. ·13 in 1959/1964–65 and Rs. ·45 in 1970–71. This indicates that while the input-output relation in India became increasingly quasi-upper-triangular during 1959/1970–71, the rate of increase of the upper right hand entry has been less than that of the lower left hand coefficient. This period has witnessed the use of the new agricultural technology in India, i.e., the Green Revolution, which involved an increased use of non-agricultural inputs in the agricultural complex. While this might have influenced the input-output matrix toward lower-triangularity, in reality the adoption of the new technology seems to have been quite limited on the economy level. However, if this tendency continues, the nature of the matrix might eventually change.

The analysis does not take into account imports and exports and is based on the current transactions of domestic inputs and outputs between sectors. The substitution of inputs from the domestic primary complex by imported and/or man-made inputs would reduce the upper-right coefficient. In the USA a highly developed industrial complex, and in Japan the existence of a large foreign trade sector might to some extent account for the quasi-lower-triangular matrix. It is conceivable that in India there was higher import-substitution in the primary inputs for secondary complex than in the secondary inputs for primary complex. Besides, in India the relative proportion of certain industries in the secondary complex and the technology used by them seem to explain a quasi-upper-triangular matrix. The growing importance of such activities as construction, equipment, chemicals, drugs, paints, etc., and their dependence on inputs from timber, forest products, paper, rubber, vegetable oils, etc., are more pronounced in India than in the USA and Japan. Thus the differences in the role of imports, and the structure of industries and the use of technologies associated with them might explain the contrast between input-output matrices of the USA and Japan on the one hand and India on the other. It appears that the ranking of sectors in the hierarchy of triangulated input-output matrices [*Leontief, 1963*] may not necessarily be identical for countries. India's input-output matrix might be made quasi-lower-triangular if the arrangement of sectors were the reverse of that of the USA and Japan.

IV

The transformation of inter-industry relations presented in the preceding section is the manifestation of changes in the structures of individual sectors. Changes in the production structures may be usefully measured comparing the input-coefficient matrices columnwise at two points and computing the weighted average changes in the input coefficients of the different sectors. Such changes in input-coefficient may be due to many factors, not all of which refer to technological change, *viz.*, product mix, levels of aggregation of the sectors (which involve effects of both changing product mix leading to changing coefficients and combining substitutes leading to increased stability), extent of non-proportionality, scale of operation, etc. [*Sevaldson, 1970; Vaccara, 1970*]. Since our analysis is highly aggregative our results may be subject to all these factors. However, our modest aim here is simply to measure the extent of change without attempting to attribute it to specific causes.

We presented two sets of indices of structural change[5] in Table 4 below. It appears that in the USA and India it has been the secondary complex that led the structural change while in Japan the primary complex has been the leading sector. However, it should be noted that since this index measures net change in input structures, it would be lower in absolute value if the changes in input-coefficients in the two sectors have opposite signs. For example, the agricultural complex in the USA used less inputs from itself per unit of output in 1963 than in 1947, whereas it increased its

TABLE 4

INDEX OF STRUCTURAL CHANGE: USA, JAPAN, INDIA

	USA (1947–1963)	Japan (1951–1965)	India (1959–1970–71)
	Rasmussen Index		
Primary complex	·0629	·2228	·0063
Secondary complex	·0976	—·0587	·7792
	Alternative Index		
Primary complex	·1460	·2228	·2128
Secondary complex	·0976	·0591	·7792

input-output ratio for industrial inputs, and thus the index of structural change of the primary complex was pushed down. The secondary complex used more inputs per unit of output in both the sectors in 1963 over 1947.

In Japan during 1951–65 the primary complex shows larger absolute change than the secondary complex. However, here the secondary complex seems to have economized on the use of input from the primary complex to such an extent that its weighted impact reversed the sign of the index of structural change for this sector. For the primary complex, the input-coefficients increased with respect to both sectors. The relative effects of the changes in inputs from the two sectors may be illustrated by the fact that if there were no change in the coefficient with respect to inputs from the primary complex, then the indices of structural change would be ·6024 and ·0002 for the primary and secondary complexes respectively. On the other hand, if the input-coefficient with respect to the secondary complex inputs remained unchanged, the indices would have been ·0353 and —·5253 respectively for the primary and secondary complexes. This may explain the sharp transformation of the Japanese input-output matrix into a quasi-lower-triangular one in 1965.

For India the most notable feature is the extent of structural change in the secondary complex. The primary complex shows almost negligible change in its structure. This is due to the fact that there took place almost equal but opposite changes in the input coefficients of the primary complex during this period—the per unit use of primary inputs went down and that of industrial inputs went up. Had the input-coefficient for primary complex inputs in the primary complex itself remained the same over the period, the index of structural change would have jumped to ·7542 from the mere ·0063 for the primary complex and to ·8186 from ·7792 for the secondary complex. On the other hand, had the input coefficient with respect to the secondary complex remained unchanged, the indices of structural change would have been —·1208 and ·5418 for the primary and secondary complexes respectively. Sengupta's estimates on the basis of the same formula showed that there was negligible change in the Indian economic structure during 1952–60 [Sengupta, 1963]. If we break up the period under our review, it seems that during 1959–65, the primary complex used less of inputs from both sectors per unit of its output, while the secondary complex recorded moderate change in its structure. During 1965–71 the primary complex reversed the direction of its change while the secondary complex went straight ahead in the process of structural change. The nature of the predominant change in the structure of the secondary complex here is consistent with the quasi-upper-triangular feature of the Indian input-output matrix.

For the purpose of measuring structural change as an indicator of the dynamism of the sectors we have prepared an alternative index ignoring the signs of the differences in input-coefficients. From these measures two observations may be made: (1) industry has been the leading sector in structural change in India while the primary complex has led the structural change in the USA and Japan; and (2) the extent of change has been much more in India (particularly in the secondary complex) than in the USA or Japan. The first is in contrast with the Rasmussen index where the leading sectors are the secondary complex for the USA and India, and primary complex for Japan. The relatively high index of structural change in India is consistent with its rather recent industrialization. Parenthetically, this index of structural change for the 2 sectors follows the same ordering as the sectoral hierarchy required for a lower-triangular matrix noted in Section III.

V

Due to its sheer urgency, the creation of employment opportunities has come to be regarded as an explicit goal of economic policy. An economic policy can be more effective if there is a clear understanding of the employment implications of structural change. This section seeks to highlight this point briefly and to offer a measure for the employment implications of structural change. Due to shortage of time, our efforts here are confined to India only. Later we hope to present comparable results on the USA and Japan.

An economic activity has implications for employment, first, through the direct employment of labour to produce the output in the given sector, and second, indirectly through creating demand for intermediate output from other sectors. Thus changes in the input composition of a sector have implications for employment generation in the economy. One of the goals of economic policy is to encourage through various means the adoption of an input mix consistent with the supply of labour. As seen in the preceding section, structural changes in any one sector may result in either an increase or a decrease in the input coefficient associated with each supplying sector. Thus the net effect on employment potential caused by a structural change depends on both the degree and direction of change in each input coefficient and the corresponding employment potential of each sector.

The employment potentials of the primary and secondary complexes in India are respectively 786·8 and 339·7 per unit of final demand for the respective complexes.[6] On the basis of the changes in the input coefficients of the primary complex with respect to both the sectors, we have estimated[7] that the total employment generated has fallen by about 5·5 units per unit of primary complex outputs during 1959/1970–71. On the other hand, total employment per unit of output in the industrial complex has increased by 154·2. Thus although structural change in India has reduced the employment potential in the primary complex, the overall employment potential in the economy has increased considerably. It seems in India agriculture is playing its ancient role of releasing labour for employment in the industrial sector.

NOTES

1. The purpose of this classification and its description is mostly illustrative, to explore the possibilities of divergent patterns of structure that might accompany economic development. It is, however, possible to pursue the exercise with further disaggregation and rearrangement of sectors.

2. The study is being extended to a larger number of countries. Preliminary results support the findings of this paper.

3. International comparisons of input-output tables are subject to the well known limitations, most important of which is the differences in relative price structures. For some ingenious methods to render international comparison of input-output tables possible, see Augustinovics [1970].

4. The 1959 Table was prepared by the Economic Division of Planning Commission, Government of India in Mathur and Bharadwaj [1965]; and the 1964–65 and 1970–71 tables are from Government of India [1966].

5. The first index is computed according to the formula developed by Rasmussen [1956], which gives structural change in sector j as:

$$T \cdot_j = \frac{1}{\frac{1}{2} \sum_i (X'_{ij} + X_{ij})} \sum_i \frac{A'_{ij} - A_{ij}}{A'_{ij} + A_{ij}} (X_{ij} + X_{ij})$$

$$J = 1, 2, \ldots n$$

Where X''s and X's are respectively inter-industry transactions at the two points in time and A's are input coefficients. The alternative index is computed by the above formula with $|A'_{ij} - A_{ij}|$ replacing $(A'_{ij} - A_{ij})$ in the numerator.

6. Estimated on the basis of weighted average of the employment potentials of the component sectors calculated by Hazari and Krishnamurty [1970].

7. Change in the total employment potential of the jth sector has been measured by:

$$\sum_{i=i}^{n} (L'_{ij} - L_{ij}) \; Ni,$$ where Ni = employment potential in the ith sector and L_{ij} and L'_{ij} are the elements in the Leontief Inverse in 1959 and 1970–71 respectively.

REFERENCES

Augustinovics, Maria, 1970, 'Methods of International and Intertemporal Comparisons of Structure' in Carter and Brody [1970 : vol.1].

Barna, Tibor, (ed.), 1963, *Structural Interdependence and Economic Development*, New York : Macmillan.

Carter, A. P., 1967, 'Changes in the Structure of the American Economy, 1947–1958 and 1962', *Review of Economics and Statistics*.

Carter, A. P. and A. Brody, (eds.), 1970, *Contributions of Input-Output Analysis*, Amsterdam : North-Holland, 2 vols.

Fox, Karl A., 1963, 'The Food and Agricultural Sectors in Advanced Economies' in Barna [1963].

Government of India, 1966 *Draft Fourth Plan : Material and Financial Balances*, India.

Hazari, Bharat R. and J. Krishnamurty, 1970, 'Employment Implications of India's Industrialization : Analysis in an Input-Output Framework', *Review of Economics and Statistics*.

Leontief, W. W., 1963, 'The Structure of Development', *Scientific American.*

Mathur, P. N. and R. Bharadwaj, (eds.), 1965, *Economic Analysis in Input-Framework*, Poona.

Peacock, A. T. and D. M. Dosser, 1957, 'Input-Output Analysis in an Underdeveloped Country', *Review of Economic Studies*, 25.

Rasmussen, P. N., 1956, *Inter-Sectoral Relations*, Amsterdam : North-Holland.

Sengupta, J. K., 1963, 'Models of Agriculture and Industry in Less Developed Economies' in Barna [*1963*].

Sevaldson, Per, 1970, 'The Stability of Input-Output Coefficients' in Carter and Brody [*1970 : vol. 2*].

Simpson, David, and Jinkichi Tsukui, 1965, 'The Fundamental Structure of Input-Output Tables : an International Comparison', *Review of Economics and Statistics.*

Vaccara, Beatrice N., 1970, 'Changes over Time in Input-Output Coefficients for the United States' in Carter and Brody [*1970*].

The Neoclassical Employment Model Applied to Ghanaian Manufacturing

By Michael Roemer*

The neoclassical framework is applied to analyze employment generating policies for Ghanaian industry. Elasticities of substitution clustering around 1·0 were found for five industries. However, as guides to employment policy, such econometric measurements of the CES function measure the wrong concept of elasticity, may contain serious upward biases, and miss some important features of LDC industry. Although these shortcomings suggest less scope for intra-industry labour-capital substitution, changes in output mix promise sufficient additional substitutability to justify neo classical policy prescriptions. Ghana's recent experience indicates the feasibility of reducing the wage-rental ratio significantly. If part of the change is borne by lower real wages, then under Ghanaian conditions a 25 per cent fall in the wage-rental ratio could, over 5 years, create 30 per cent more jobs in manufacturing than if no change occurs.

INTRODUCTION

A large and growing volume of literature on industrial employment policy advises the developing countries to work within a neoclassical framework to maximize both output and employment. The basic elements of this policy prescription are, first, the probability of substantial scope for factor substitution within any production activity; second, the need and potential for restructuring a country's output mix to emphasize industries which use abundant factors, especially labour, most intensively; and, third, the effectiveness of suitably manipulated market prices in allocating resources to achieve factor substitution and economic restructuring.

This paper is an attempt to apply the neoclassical framework to employment policy for Ghanaian industry. The first section deals with factor substitution within industries, reporting the results and limitations of a standard constant-elasticity-of-substitution (CES) production function measurement. The second section briefly discusses the potential for labour-capital substitution by varying the output mix of the manufacturing sector. A third section explores the behaviour of relative factor prices in Ghana since 1960, and this is followed by a simple model which is used to gauge

* Institute for International Development, Harvard University. The paper has benefited substantially from comments by Clark Leith, John Odling-Smee, William Raduchel, Max Steuer, Lance Taylor, Edward Vickery and Gordon Winston. The arguments presented here, as well as any remaining errors, are solely the responsibility of the author and should not be taken as reflecting the views of the Harvard Institute for International Development.

the potential employment creation which may be induced by adjusting factor prices. The income distribution effects of feasible employment-creating policies are discussed briefly and a final section sums up the conclusions for economic policy.

INTRA-INDUSTRY FACTOR SUBSTITUTION

In order to measure the potential for intra-industry factor substitution in Ghana, industrial census data covering the seven years, 1962 to 1968, were collected for seven industries which had four or more firms[1] and this pooled set of inter-firm and inter-temporal data was used to estimate the elasticity of substitution from CES production functions for each of the 7 industries.[2]

Taking the CES production function of the firm with constant returns to scale,

$$Q = A \, [\delta L^{\rho} + (1 - \delta) \, K^{\rho}]^{1/\rho} \tag{1}$$

and assuming that firms adjust their inputs so that, in the long run, the marginal product of labour equals the real wage, we can derive the familiar equation,

$$\text{Log } q^* = C^1 + \sigma \, \text{Log } w + u \tag{2}$$

Q is value added; K and L are capital and labour services, respectively; A, δ and ρ are the usual CES parameters; q^* is labour productivity, Q/L, once long-run equilibrium has been established; w is the prevailing real wage; σ is the elasticity of substitution, equal to $1/(1-\rho)$; C^1 is a constant incorporating A, δ and ρ; and u is a disturbance term. As the industrial census returns have virtually no useful information on capital stock or services, equation (2) was the basic relationship used to estimate σ.

Equation (2) describes a long-run equilibrium after firms have adjusted to the prevailing wage rate, but no firm is likely to be observed in that situation. To obtain a more realistic estimating equation, assume that firms adjust to the prevailing real wage such that if the desired long-run productivity changes by 1 per cent in any period, then firms adjust factor proportions sufficiently to change productivity by π per cent in that period, or

$$\text{Log } (q_t/q_{t-1}) = \pi \, \text{Log } (q^*/q_{t-1}) + v_t \tag{3}$$

where q_t and q_{t-1} are the observed values of labour productivity in the current and previous years, respectively; π is the adjustment factor, a number between 0 and 1; and v_t is a disturbance term. Using expression (2) for Log q^* and rearranging, we get

$$\text{Log } q_t = \pi C^1 + \pi \sigma \quad \text{Log } w + (1 - \pi) \quad \text{Log } q_t + x_t \tag{4}$$

where $x_t = \pi u + v_t$. The coefficient, $\pi \sigma$, can be interpreted as the short-run (one-period) elasticity of substitution, while σ is the long-run elasticity.

Two different proxies were used for the 'prevailing' wage in equation (4): the current wage, w_t, and a lagged wage, w_{t-1}.[3] Also, the possibility of Hicks-neutral technological change at the annual rate, τ, was accommodated by assuming $A = A_0 e^{\tau t}$, which changes the constant, $\pi C'$, to $C + (1 - \sigma) \pi \tau t$. Since each regression involves several firms in an industry, we introduce the subscript, i, to refer to a firm. With these changes, equation (4) can be rewritten in two forms:

$$\text{Log } q_{it} = C + \pi\sigma \ \text{Log } w_{it} + (1-\pi) \ \text{Log } q_{i,\,t-1} + (1-\sigma)\pi\tau t + x_{it}$$
$$\text{(5a)}$$

$$\text{Log } q_{it} = C + \pi\sigma \ \text{Log } w_{i,\,t-1} + (1-\pi) \ \text{Log } q_{i,\,t-1} + (1-\sigma)\pi\tau t + x_{it}$$
$$\text{(5b)}$$

Finally, as a concession to the sometimes erratic data, productivity was defined both as value added per worker and as gross output per worker, and equations (5a) and (5b) estimated for both definitions.

To use these equations to estimate the CES and adjustment parameters for firms within each industry, it is necessary to make several assumptions:

(a) at all times, firms are adjusting towards a position along their production frontiers;

(b) labour markets are competitive;

(c) labour is a homogeneous factor of production;

(d) production is homogeneous, so that firms in the same industry produce the same output mix; and

(e) there are no economies of scale.

Assumption (a) implies that all managements are equally effective, which is unlikely. If deviations from the production frontier are not correlated with productivity, then differences in efficiency would not bias the estimate of σ. However, if higher productivities are generally due to more efficient management, and if such managements are willing to pay higher wages because they are more profitable, then higher productivity would be the *cause* of higher wages, not the result. Because the estimating equation cannot distinguish between these two different phenomena, it attributes both to higher elasticities and overestimates σ. Assumption (b) is likely to hold in all but one of the industries studied (diamond mining), but assumption (c) may be violated. If firms have work forces with varying skills, then some of the productivity-wage correlation should be due to differing skill mixes rather than to labour substitution, imparting another upward bias to estimates of σ. Differing production mixes should not be a serious problem for the narrowly defined industries in the sample. It seems unlikely that at least 5 of the 7 industries face substantial scale economies and in any case the other 2 (diamond mining and power generation) yielded only one significant estimate of σ.

The elasticity of substitution was estimated for seven industries, each with four or more firms: diamond mining (4 firms, 26 observations), baking (11,74), clothing manufacture (7, 38), saw-milling (13, 77), printing

TABLE 1
REGRESSION RESULTS

Industry	Estimate	Coefficients (t-ratios) for						Cor. R^2	DW	Estimates for		
		C	$\text{Log } w_{i,t}$	$\text{Log } w_{i,t-1}$	$\text{Log } q_{i,t-1}$ Gross Output	Value Added	t			π	σ^*	τ
Diamond mines	1	−·100 (−·35)†	·192 (·98)†		·848 (5·99)		−·009 (−·19)†	·95	1·69	·15	—	—
	2	−·107 (−·35)†	·188 (·96)†			·845 (5·94)	−·008 (−·15)†	·94	1·52	·15	—	—
	3	−·040 (−·13)†		·830 (·44)†	·923 (6·76)		−·003 (·06)†	·95	1·79	·08	—	—
	4	−·042 (−·13)†		·079 (·41)†		·920 (6·65)	−·006 (·12)†	·94	1·62	·08	—	—
Bakeries	1	·223 (·92)†	·412 (2·88)		·679 (6·37)		·010 (·30)†	·90	2·37	·32	1·28 (0·86)	—
	2	·232 (·77)†	·488 (3·37)			·512 (4·12)	·100 (2·19)	·83	2·32	·49	1·00 (0·53)	0
	3	·233 (·92)†		·349 (2·41)	·730 (6·94)		·002 (·05)†	·90	2·37	·27	1·29 (1·02)	—
	4	·192 (·64)†		·521 (3·78)		·503 (4·35)	·088 (1·99)	·83	2·12	·50	1·05 (0·51)	−3·6
Clothing	1	−·009 (−·07)†	·777 (4·30)		·415 (3·23)		·023 (·53)†	·98	2·10	·59	1·33 (0·59)	—
	2	·011 (·07)†	·916 (4·80)			·137 (·85)†	·165 (2·75)	·95	2·07	—	0·9‡ (0·2)	—
	3	·040 (·26)†		·487 (1·93)	·608 (3·38)		·052 (·97)†	·96	2·47	·38	1·27 (1·19)	—
	4	·042 (·23)†		·760 (3·41)		·253 (1·34)†	·181 (·65)	·93	2·51	—	0·8‡ (0·2)	—
Sawmills	1	0·010 (−·07)	·450 (3·59)		·595 (6·32)		·088 (2·67)	·95	2·27	·41	1·11 (0·56)	−2·0

2	·004 (·02)†	·663 (5·06)	—	·614 (5·69)	·379 (3·73)	·091 (2·02)	·89	2·13	·62	1·07 (0·38)	—2·2
3	·029 (·20)†	—	·386 (2·92)	—	·357 (3·20)	·127 (3·70)	·95	2·38	·39	1·00 (0·61)	0
4	—·022 (—·12)†	—	·629 (4·73)	—	—	·151 (3·45)	·89	2·20	·64	0·98 (0·37)	11·7
Printing 1	·051 (·20)†	·191 (1·93)	—	—	—	—·019 (—·73)†	·93	1·78	·16	1·21 (1·18)	—
2	·103 (·32)†	·355 (2·64)	—	·842 (10·84)	·688 (6·31)	—·037 (—·92)†	·83	1·86	·31	1·14 (0·81)	—
3	·058 (·28)†	—	·178 (1·77)	·850 (10·78)	·700 (6·39)	—·015 (—·51)†	·93	1·80	·15	1·19 (1·27)	—
4	·114 (·36)†	—	·336 (2·49)	—	—	—·030 (—·74)†	·82	1·89	·30	1·12 (0·83)	—
Blocks 1	·556 (·87)†	·992 (2·95)	—	—	—	—·023 (—·33)†	·76	2·31	—	1·0‡ (0·3)	—
2	·216 (·30)†	·939 (2·69)	—	·152 (·58)†	·133 (·49)†	—·008 (—·11)†	·66	1·81	—	0·9‡ (0·3)	—
3	·557 (·80)†	—	·710 (1·94)	·365 (1·31)†	·304 (1·16)†	—·014 (—·18)†	·71	2·30	—	0·7‡ (0·4)	—
4	·307 (·41)†	—	·727 (2·14)	—	—	—·007 (—·09)†	·63	1·85	—	0·7‡ (0·3)	—
Electricity 1	—·032 (—·18)†	·178 (1·49)†	—	—	—	·115 (1·56)†	·92	2·16	·21	—	—
2	—·032 (—·17)†	·263 (2·18)	—	·795 (8·89)	·746 (7·93)	·024 (·31)†	·90	1·88	·25	1·04 (0·84)	—
3	—·005 (—·03)†	—	·092 (·81)†	·850 (9·55)	·807 (8·36)	·142 (2·00)	·92	2·29	·15	—	—
4	·014 (—·07)†	—	·166 (1·40)†	—	—	·062 (·80)†	·90	2·02	·19	—	—

* Asymptotic standard error in parenthesis. The asymptotic variance, V_σ, is given by $V_\sigma = (1/\pi^2)(V_w - 2\sigma V_{wq} + \sigma^2 V_q)$, where V_w is the variance of the coefficient of Log w, V_q the variance of the coefficient of Log q, and V_{wq} the covariance between the two coefficients. Note that V_σ increases rapidly as the adjustment parameter, π, declines.

† Not significant at the 10 per cent level.

‡ Lower limit estimate, based on $\pi = 1\cdot00$, since the coefficient of Log q is insignificant at the 10 per cent level and may therefore be zero. For these cases, the standard error given is that for the coefficient of Log w.

(10, 68), concrete block manufacture (4, 28) and electricity generation (19, 74).[4] These industries represented 28 per cent of value added in mining, manufacturing and utilities in 1969. Data on gross output, value added, total wages and average number of employees were collected for the years 1962–8. Output price indices for each industry except printing were used to deflate productivity and average wage data.

The regression results are summarized in Table 1. For all industries except concrete blocks, corrected R-squares were between 82 and 98 per cent. Durbin-Watson statistics do not indicate serial correlation. Because of insignificant coefficients, diamond mining yielded no estimates of σ and electricity yielded only one. The five manufacturing industries gave estimates of σ that clustered around $1 \cdot 0$, with a range of $0 \cdot 7$ to $1 \cdot 3$. In most cases the estimate for σ is at least 70 per cent larger than its asymptotic standard error, implying significance at the 10 per cent level or better. But for 8 observations (bakeries, equations 1 and 3; clothing, 3; all of printing; and electricity, 3) the asymptotic standard error approaches (and in one case exceeds) the estimate of σ. In these cases, more reliance should be placed on the estimate of the short-run elasticity, $\pi\sigma$, the coefficient of the wage term. Where it could be estimated, the adjustment coefficient, π, for these 5 industries ranged from 15 to 64 per cent of the remaining adjustment being made each year; for diamond mining and electricity the adjustment was generally slower, ranging from 8 to 25 per cent a year. Very few estimates of the rate of technological change were possible, but of the 6 estimates, 5 were either zero or negative. The gross output measure of productivity gives somewhat higher estimates than the value added measure in most cases. If this difference is taken seriously, it implies, not unreasonably, that labour is more substitutable against capital and raw materials combined than against capital alone. There is little to choose between the current and lagged wage formulations.

These results lend support to elasticity optimists, especially since they derive from narrowly defined industries and include very little substitutability due to changing product mixes. However, 3 serious limitations inherent in this methodology invite reflection.[5] First, for the purpose of predicting employment creation due to changes in factor prices, it is necessary to measure elasticity along the technological production frontier, which is probably relevant to near-future investment decisions. Yet econometric estimates of the elasticity measure a production function defined by existing firms producing with different vintages of technology, the wrong concept for this purpose. Second, as explained above, the assumption of uniformly competent managements may mask an upward bias to measurements of the elasticity. It would be more realistic to recognize the varying quality of managements, but the problems of defining and measuring management as a separate factor of production have so far been insoluble.

The third problem is an internal contradiction peculiar to inter-firm estimates confined to one economy. For 6 of the 7 industries the inter-firm effects seem to be more important in determining the regression coefficients than the intertemporal effects. To show this, the standard deviations of two variables were calculated for each industry: average wages across all firms in each year (WT) and average wages over all years for each firm (WF). Only for clothing was WT greater than WF (15 per cent greater); for the others, WT varied from 20 to 56 per cent of WF, indicating at least twice as much variation between firms as overtime. Thus a good deal of the estimated substitutability of labour for other inputs depends on differing wages among firms. Yet the assumptions of labour homogeneity and competitive labour markets rule out such differences unless they can be explained by locations and workers' tastes, which seems unlikely.

The complexity of the real world and the limitations of econometrics seem to preclude reliable measurements of the CES parameters. But is the CES function an adequate representation of production technology in the first place? Neoclassical production functions miss some of the most important characteristics of industries which typically dominate during the early, import-substituting stages of industrialization. First, the most important single factor cost is usually material inputs and the bulk of these is typically imported. In Ghana, for example, material inputs represent almost half of gross output in manufacturing and about three-quarters of these are imported. Yet neoclassical representations of the production process normally concentrate on value added and neglect material inputs. Second, it seems likely that there is greater scope for saving raw materials by using more capital than by using more labour. Although some industries may be able to add labourers to improve raw material handling or to collect waste materials for recycling, examples of adding more sophisticated equipment come to mind more readily: storage facilities with controlled environments that reduce spoilage, materials handling apparatus which reduces breakage or spillage, electronically controlled equipment which applies or mixes components within much reduced deviations from optimum, and so forth. Yet the CES production function assumes all substitution elasticities are equal, so it cannot represent the potentially important advantage of capital over labour in reducing material costs.[6]

Third, it may be that labour—intensive processes require fewer management skills than do capital—intensive ones. Running capital equipment involves competent mechanics and technical managers whose skills are routinely learned by citizens and easily acquired overseas in the interim. Managing labour to obtain high productivity requires a combination of local knowledge and sophisticated approaches to work incentives and employee relations. Foreign managers may not be good substitutes for astute local managers, especially at the middle or lower levels. Furthermore, it seems at least plausible that more managers are required per unit of output for labour—intensive than for capital—intensive processes. This complementarity of scarce management skills with labour makes the latter a more costly input than our traditional models allow. If these three suggested features—substantial material inputs, capital the more important substitute for materials, and management more complementary to labour than to capital—were introduced into our production functions, the revised model is likely to indicate less scope for labour-capital substitution than neoclassical estimates have shown.[7]

The econometric and theoretical limitations of production function estimates leave serious doubts about the usefulness of the tools which have been in vogue among economists for several years. Our knowledge of LDC industry and our advice to LDC policy makers might both be improved if we retreat to the less elegant and more tedious engineering estimates of production possibilities. This approach would probably lead to complex programming solutions which contain alternative techniques for each step of production in any single industry. Although neoclassical measurements may overestimate the scope for intra-industry labour-capital substitution, it seems likely that engineers, once sensitized to the needs of LDCs, would still leave ample scope for factor substitution. [8]

VARYING THE OUTPUT MIX

Even if industry production functions turn out to have low elasticities of substitution, there can be considerable room for substitution by varying the manufacturing output mix. A policy of low wages relative to capital costs can, over time, induce consumers to substitute cheaper labour—intensive goods for capital—intensive ones; encourage modernized handicraft industries to compete with modern, capital—intensive producers; and make it more profitable to import-substitute for and export goods which are labour intensive. The last is likely to be the most important mechanism and it will be especially effective for smaller countries which maintain open economies.

In Ghana there has been considerable scope during the past few years for varying the manufacturing mix to create employment. A compilation of 40 investments proposed for some form of tax relief from 1969 to 1971 shows a range of capital intensities from $1,000 per employee at full capacity (furniture parts for export) to $30,000 per employee (lubricant mixing). [9] Some of the contrasts are interesting. Simple agriculture-based industries, such as cassava processing for export and poultry feed mixing, for which there are large potential markets, show capital-labour ratios of about $3,000 per man; compared to a ratio of about $18,000 per man for two breweries which were constructed to satisfy unmet domestic demand (imports are banned). More sophisticated knitting and zipper factories used twice the capital per worker as firms making simple garments from cloth. And a firm making woodwool slabs, which would effectively substitute for cement in house construction, showed a ratio of $13,500 per worker, versus only $1,700 for 2 plants manufacturing furniture parts for export. So long as Ghana will, even after considerable development, have a trade ratio not far below the present 20 per cent, it has considerable choice among industries like these.

However, the strategy of changing the output mix by making labour relatively cheap is difficult for policy makers to accept, because it involves the apparent contradiction that capital must be made relatively more expensive even though a country is encouraging investment. It is especially difficult when a substantial change from existing factor prices is required, because this may discourage pending investments which were planned under the old price regime without promising alternative, labour—intensive investments for some time.

RELATIVE FACTOR PRICES

The third element of a neoclassical employment policy is the manipulation of relative factor prices to reflect real scarcities in the economy. The typical import-substituting pattern of developing countries—keeping capital costs low to encourage investment while labour unions and legislation tend to raise wages above market-determined levels—is precisely the opposite of the neoclassical prescription.[10] If Ghana's experience is any guide, however, a neoclassical factor price policy may be within reach. Even though Ghana has followed the import substitution path, it has kept the wage-rental ratio from rising during most of the 1960s and then introduced policies which reduced it during 1970 and 1971.

TABLE 2

INDEXES FOR THE WAGE-RENTAL RATIO AND ITS COMPONENTS:
GHANAIAN MANUFACTURING, 1960–1970
(1960 = 100)

	1963	1966	1967	1969	1970
A. *Without Profit Tax*					
1. Wages in manufacturing (W)[a]	122	155	159	191	210
2. Cost of domestic financing (A_d)[b]	100	105	104	105	105
3. Cost of foreign financing (A_f)[c]	97	108	106	113	111
4. Cost of factory construction (P_c)[d]	98	122	122	135	141
5. Price of capital equipment in cedis, c.i.f. Ghana (P_e^1)[e]	105	114	164	157	170
(i) Foreign wholesale price index for industrial goods[f]	104	112	113	118	125
(ii) Official exchange rate[f]	101	101	145	134	138
6. Tariff factor (T)[g]	100	100	100	105	145
7. Rental (R)[h]	100	125	160	176	239
8. Wage-rental ratio (W/R)	121	124	99	111	90
B. *With Profit Tax*					
1. Effective tax rate (not an index) on:					
(i) Repatriated profits (·40 in 1960) (t_f)	·65	·65	·58	·50	·50
(ii) Unrepatriated profits (·40 in 1960) (t_d)	·45	·45	·45	·50	·50
2. Rental (R_t)[i]	107	138	170	182	245
3. Wage-rental ratio (W/R_t)	114	112	94	105	86

[a] Ghana Central Bureau of Statistics (CBS), earnings of male African employees in firms of 10 or more employees, 1960 to 1969; estimated 10 per cent increase for 1970.

[b] Based on 10-year annuity factor computed from Bank of Ghana data on domestic interest rates.

[c] Based on 10-year annuity factor computed from weighted average of short- and long-term rates for West Germany, U.K. and U.S. as reported in *International Financial Statistics* (IFS); weights are explained in Note e.

[d] CBS, construction price index.

[e] $P_e^1 = ·54\,P_kF_k + ·28\,P_gF_g + ·18\,P_sF_s$, where P = industrial wholesale price index from *IFS*: k, g, and s refer to U.K., W. Germany and U.S., respectively; and F is the cedi-pound, -mark, or -dollar rate. The weights (also used to find A_f—see Note c) are based on the three countries' shares of exports to Ghana of machinery and transport equipment (SITC 7); together, these three suppliers account for two-thirds of Ghana's imports under SITC 7.

f These indexes were computed as follows:

$$P = \cdot 54P_k + \cdot 28P_g + \cdot 18P_s,$$
$$F = \cdot 54F_k + \cdot 28F_g + \cdot 18F_s$$

and are shown only to indicate the contribution of foreign market prices and exchange rate adjustments; they were not used directly in subsequent calculations.

g Defined as $T = 1 + t$, where t is the ad valorem tax on imports of capital equipment.

h $R = A_d[a\ P_c + (1 - a)\ P_e^1\ (T - 1)] + A_f\ (1 - a)\ P_{fe}^1$

The share of construction in total manufacturing investment, a, is 30 per cent in Ghana. R is an index of the cost of using capital in Ghana.

i $R_t = A\ (i_{td}, 10)\ [a\ P_c + (1 - a)\ P_e^1\ (T - 1)] + A\ (i_{tf}, 10)\ [(1 - a)\ P_e^1]$

where A (i, 10) is the 10-year annuity factor;

$$i_{td} = (1 + \frac{etd}{1 - t_d})\ i_d, \text{ and similarly for } i_{tf};$$

i_d and i_f are the foreign and domestic interest rates, respectively, used to calculate A_d and A_f; and e is the share of equity financing in the total, taken as 33 per cent. This formulation requires two assumptions:

(1) the after-tax return on equity is equal to the interest rate on borrowed funds, and
(2) the depreciation rate for tax purposes is the same as the 'natural' rate used by investors.

Both assumptions are wrong, but they are necessitated by lack of data and the resulting errors tend to cancel.

Table 2 shows the trend from 1960 to 1970 in the wage-rental ratio relevant to Ghanaian manufacturing, along with the components of the ratio. The note to Table 2 explains how each component index was derived.[11] The capital rental index assumes that costs of imported equipment, c.i.f. Ghana, are financed in the markets from which the equipment is imported and other costs (including duties paid on equipment) are financed in Ghana. Other possible permutations on the sources of finance give similar results. In order to account for the effects of profit taxes (called the company tax in Ghana), it was necessary to make assumptions about the share of equity financing, the relation between the return on equity and the cost of borrowed funds, and the relationship between 'natural' rates of depreciation based on investment life and rates permissible for tax purposes; these are explained in note i to the table. Because the resulting wage-rental index (item B3) is so heavily laden with unsubstantiated assumptions, the table also shows a wage-rental index which ignores profits taxes and is based more solidly on available data (item A8).

The years shown in Table 2 were selected to highlight the policy changes which affected the wage-rental index most. The trend during the Nkrumah period, which ended in February 1966, was a rising wage-rental ratio, due primarily to briskly rising wages (7·6 per cent a year) in the face of more gentle rises in the cost of financing and of capital equipment. Abstracting from profit taxes, the ratio rose by 24 per cent over the first six years of the decade, but a substantial increase in tax rates on repatriated profits ameliorated the rise to 12 per cent. The first major break in the trend came with the devaluation of 1967, which caused the wage-rental index (with profit taxes) to fall from 112 to 94. Rising wages (10 per cent a year) dominated again for the next two years, but in 1970 a 40 per cent surcharge was added to the 5 per cent duty on capital goods and the wage-rental index fell to 86, a drop of 23 per cent from the 1966 level. (The ratio without profit taxes fell by 29 per cent.)

There followed a hectic succession of policy changes, beginning with the July 1971 budget and culminating in the military coup in January 1972,[12] which had the ultimate effect of (1) raising domestic interest rates from a 7–10 per cent range to one of 11–15 per cent; (2) devaluing the cedi by a weighted average 35 per cent (in local currency terms); (3) removing the 40 per cent surcharge on capital equipment; and (4) raising the minimum wage by one-third. Assuming the latter would have caused the average wage in manufacturing to rise 15 per cent and assuming all components not affected by policy changes retain their 1970 levels, these policies would have raised the index (with profit taxes) to 94 in early 1972, a drop of 16 per cent since the high of 1966. (Without profit taxes, the early 1972 index would stand at 101.)[13]

Ghana's experience during the 1960s was typical of small LDCs: political pressures act to raise wages more rapidly than domestic and foreign market forces raise the cost of capital. However, policy changes which are often advisable on other grounds, such as higher interest rates to attract savings into organized financial markets and exchange rate devaluations to help break chronic foreign exchange constraints, work to correct market trends and twist relative factor prices in favour of labour—intensive investments. Exchange rate adjustments or tariff increases are the most powerful instruments for factor price adjustment. As governments try increasingly to reduce unemployment without sacrificing growth, the reinforcing relationship between policies to improve the balance of payments or increase savings, on the one hand, and policies to accelerate employment creation, on the other, needs to be re-emphasized.

EMPLOYMENT CREATION

How much job creation can the economist promise through factor price adjustments? Although the question ought to have an empirical answer, there are not adequate data in Ghana to answer it, and for most LDCs it would probably be extremely difficult econometrically to sort out the effect of relative factor price shifts from the various forces impinging on employment creation. Instead, a simple model using plausible parameters can give a rough estimate of the potential employment-creating impact of factor price changes.

Consider a one-time drop in the wage-rental ratio, w, which changes relative factor prices from $(w/r)_0$ to $(w/r)_1$, and convinces investors that the new relative factor prices are permanent. This changes the cost-minimizing capital-labour ratio from k_0 to k_1, the ratio which will be realized on future investments. Assume, conservatively, that there are no adjustments to factor proportions with existing capital stock, so the only change comes through future investment for additional capacity and replacement. Further assume that the fall in real wages and the rise in real rentals, with the price of output as the common deflator, have no income effect. That is, investors will plan for the same additional output as before the price change, but will substitute labour for capital along the isoquant relevant to their original investment plans.[14] Because there are no income effects, manufacturing output continues to grow at the previous rate, g_0. For convenience, we ignore technological change and assume capital stock has also been growing at g_0.[15] During the first period (say a year) after the factor price shift, capital stock will grow at a slower rate than output, because investors will produce the same increment to output as previously planned, but with more labour and less capital. After that, investment in additional capacity (but not capital stock) will resume the same growth rate as output.

To find a relationship between the long-run growth rate of output and capital stock, g_0, and the first-period disequilibrium growth rate of capital stock, g_1, the following relationships can be used:

(1) Along the isoquant, Q, which refers to increases in output, either

$$Q = (\delta L_0^\rho + (1 - \delta) I_0^\rho)^{1/\rho} = (\delta L_1^\rho + (1 - \delta) I_1^\rho)^{1/\rho} \qquad (1a)$$

where δ and ρ are the CES distributive and elasticity parameters, respectively, and the elasticity of substitution is $\sigma = 1/(1 - \rho)$, a positive number; or, for $\sigma = 1$ (Cobb-Douglas case),

$$Q = L_0^\alpha K_0^{1-\alpha} = L_1^\alpha K_1^{1-\alpha} \qquad (1b)$$

where α is labour's share. In either case, L is the labour employed with newly installed capital, I (investment); and $_0$ and $_1$ refer to the position along isoquant Q before and after the factor price shift.

(2) If the marginal conditions for cost minimization hold, then the first derivatives of (1) can be used to derive:

$$\frac{r_0}{r_1} = \left(\frac{I_1}{I_0}\right)^{1/\sigma}; \quad \frac{w_0}{r_0} = \frac{\delta}{1-\delta}\left(\frac{I_0}{L_0}\right)^{1/\sigma}; \text{ and } \frac{w_1}{r_1} = \frac{\delta}{1-\delta}\left(\frac{I_1}{L_1}\right)^{1/\sigma} \qquad (2a)$$

for the CES case; and

$$\frac{r_0}{r_1} = \left(\frac{L_0}{I_0} \cdot \frac{I_1}{L_0}\right)^\alpha \qquad (2b)$$

for the Cobb-Douglas case; w and r are the wage and rental rates, respectively.

(3) Value added must be equal at both points along the isoquant, or
$$Q = w_0 L_0 + r_0 L_0 = w_1 L_1 + r_1 I_1 \qquad (3)$$

(4) The change in relative factor prices can be defined as
$$w^1 = (w_1/r_1 - w_0/r_0)/(w_0/r_0) \qquad (4)$$

(5) And the elasticity of substitution can then be given by
$$\sigma = - \frac{(L_1/I_1 - L_0/I_0)}{L_0/I_0} \cdot \frac{1}{w'} \qquad (5)$$

For the CES case, the first four sets of equations can be used to derive:

$$\frac{g_1}{g_0} = \left(\frac{1 + \left(\dfrac{\delta}{1-\delta}\right)\left(\dfrac{w_0}{r_0}\right)^{1-\sigma}}{1 + \left(\dfrac{\delta}{1-\delta}\right)\left(\dfrac{w_0}{r_0}(1+w')\right)^{1-\sigma}} \right)^{\frac{\sigma}{1-\sigma}}$$ (6a)

For the Cobb-Douglas case, all five equation sets are used to derive,

$$g_1/g_0 = 1/(1-w')^\alpha \; [16]$$ (6b)

As investment takes place at the new capital-labour ratio, k_1, total employment will vary as follows:

$$L(t) = (1/k_0)K_0(t) + (1/k_1)\int_0^t R(v)dv + (1/k_1)\int_0^t I(v)dv$$ (7)

where $L(t)$ is employment at time t; k_0 is the old capital-labour ratio; $K_0(t)$ is the amount of the initial capital stock, K_0, remaining after t years; $R(v)$ is replacement investment; and $I(v)$ is investment in new capacity. If the initial capital stock decays at the exponential rate β per year and replacement investment is just sufficient to keep output at the previous level,[17] then

$$K_0(t) = K_0 e^{-\beta t} \text{ and } R(v) = \lambda \beta K_0 e^{-\beta v}, 0 < \beta < 1$$ (8)

λ is the ratio of the new investment-output ratio $(I/Q)_1$ to the old $(I/Q)_0$.[18] During the first year after the change in relative factor prices, capital stock will grow at the reduced rate, g_1; thereafter it will grow at g_0, the rate of output. Hence

$$I(1) = g_1 K_0 \text{ and } I(v) = I(1)e^{g_0 v} = g_1 K_0 e^{g_0 v}, v > 1$$ (9)

Substituting (8) and (9) into (7); integrating; using the approximation, $e^{g_0} = 1 + g_0$ (which is very close for $g_0 < \cdot 10$); and using

$$k_0/k_1 = (L_1/I_1)/(L_0/I_0) = 1 - \sigma w'$$ (10)

which comes from (5); we get

$$L(t) = \frac{K_0}{k_0}\left[e^{-\beta t} + (1 - \sigma w')\left[\lambda(1 - e^{-\beta t}) + \frac{g_1}{g_0}(e^{g_0 t} - 1) \right] \right]$$ (11)

To get some idea of the magnitudes involved, take plausible estimates for a small industrial sector in a developing economy: $w' = -\cdot 25$, the roughly 25 per cent fall in the wage-rental ratio observed in Ghana from 1966 to 1970; $g_0 = 6$ per cent a year; $\beta = 10$ per cent a year, implying a half-life for capital stock of 7 years; δ, the distributive parameter for labour, or α, labour's share under the Cobb-Douglas function, at $0 \cdot 5$; alternative values for the elasticity of substitution, σ, of $0 \cdot 5$, $1 \cdot 0$ and $1 \cdot 5$; and corresponding values of g_1 and λ from footnotes 10 and 12, respectively. Table 3 compares values of $L(t)$ for permutations of parameters, taking $L(0) = K_0/k_0 = 100$.[19]

TABLE 3
GROWTH OF EMPLOYMENT
(VALUES FROM EQUATION 11 WITH $L(o) = K_0/k_0 = 100$ and $w' = -·25$)

Year after change	Case 1: $\sigma = ·5$ $\beta = ·1$ $\delta = ·5$	Case 2: $\sigma = 1$ $\beta = ·1$ $\alpha = ·5$	Case 3: $\sigma = 1$ $\beta = ·15$ $\alpha = ·5$	Case 4: $\sigma = 1$ $\beta = ·1$ $\alpha = ·67$	Case 5: $\sigma = 1$ $\beta = ·1$ $\alpha = ·4$	Case 6: $\sigma = 1·5$ $\beta = ·1$ $\delta = ·5$	No change
1	107	108	109	107	108	109	106
3	121	125	127	123	126	127	120
5	137	144	146	141	145	146	135
10	187	199	201	193	202	203	182
Annual growth rate to year 5 (%)	6·5	7·6	7·8	7·1	7·7	7·8	6·2[a]
Additional job creation to year 5 (%)[b]	6	25	31	16	29	31	—

[a] Differs from 6·0 per cent because compound interest tables were used to calculate five-year growth rates, but the table values are based on exponential rates.
[b] The increase in job creation in each case expressed as a percentage of job creation in the no-change case.

The model shows that for plausible parameter values, a 25 per cent decrease in the wage-rental ratio, acting only through future investment, would, over a five-year period, increase employment growth from an equilibrium rate of 6·2 per cent a year to a rate between 6·5 and 7·9 per cent. If the elasticity of substitution is only 0·5, only 6 per cent more jobs would be created over five years, but if the elasticity is 1·0 or higher and labour's share is not over 50 per cent, 25 to 31 per cent more jobs would be created. That is a significant response, indicating considerable scope for employment creation from adjusting factor prices. Allowing for substitution through changing output mix, elasticities of one or more for new investment in manufacturing seem reasonable.

INCOME DISTRIBUTION

Income equality and greater employment conflict only if the elasticity of substitution is less than one. If it is one or higher, lower relative wages induce enough labour-capital substitution so that labour's share of value added is maintained or increased. Although it seems likely that the elasticity is close to or greater than one for future investment, a pro-employment wage policy must reduce wages for all workers, including those employed by existing facilities for which elasticities are probably well below one in the short to medium term (say, up to ten years). For manufacturing as a whole, the relevant elasticity may be well below one and labour's share is likely to fall. How, then, can governments minimize or eliminate the medium-term conflict between employment and income distribution policies?

A good deal of reconciliation can be accomplished through a judicious selection of policy instruments. To avoid adverse investor income effects, some of the burden for wage-rental shifts must be borne by decreased real wages. However, the increased cost of capital services need not redound entirely to the benefit of capitalists and can be used to compensate wage earners. Taxes on profits (especially on devaluation-induced profits of exporters and import substituters) and tariffs on imported capital equipment can be spent by government on public goods consumed mainly by wage earners or simply transferred to them. In effect, government can tax capitalists to subsidize wages, which imparts precisely the desired employment incentive.

However, the income distribution problem is not fundamentally a matter of functional shares within the industrial sector. Rather, it centres on the distribution between the modern and traditional sectors. By and large, both manufacturing capitalists and workers are in the 'modern' sector, while the bulk of the population consists of low-income traditional farmers and underemployed workers in services. A neoclassical employment policy in manufacturing can contribute to narrowing the modern-traditional income gap only if government uses taxes on capital as its instrument to lower wage-rental ratios and spends the proceeds to benefit those in traditional occupations.

SUMMARY AND CONCLUSIONS

As guides to employment policy, econometric measurements of the CES production function measure the wrong concept of elasticity and may contain serious biases, mostly upward. More fundamentally, the CES function cannot incorporate (1) the greater ability of capital, rather than labour, to substitute for raw materials and (2) the possibility that more sophisticated management is required to produce efficiently with labour—intensive methods. These shortcomings suggest that there is less scope for intra-industry substitution than economists have been measuring. However, when changes in the output mix are considered, there is promise of enough labour-capital substitution in the aggregate to make a neoclassical factor price policy worthwhile.

Experience in Ghana during the past few years indicates that it is feasible to reduce wage-rental ratios substantially. However, part of the change in relative factor prices must be borne by lower real wages or investment will be discouraged enough to cancel much or all of the employment impact of factor substitution. And to ensure that investors' expectations undergo a similar adjustment, the new factor prices must be seen as a deliberate and permanent shift by a secure government. The last condition may be the most difficult to realize in practice, and eventually proved to be un-realizable in Ghana. If these conditions can be met, a 25 per cent fall in the wage-rental ratio is capable of creating up to 30 per cent more jobs in manufacturing over a five-year period than would otherwise have been the case.

The most powerful policy instrument for altering relative factor prices is exchange rate devaluation. Not only does it change the wage-rental ratio dramatically, but it also induces greater product substitution by altering the relative prices of outputs. If the country has comparative advantage in labour—intensive production, the observed aggregate elasticity of substitution will be higher for devaluation than for other relative price changes. Duties on capital equipment have an equally powerful effect on relative factor prices, but not on final product prices. Domestic interest rates must rise substantially to have much effect, especially because much of the investment in industry comes from overseas. Incomes policies which slow the rise in money wages can be combined with moderate increases in the cost of capital services to have a substantial impact on relative factor prices.

Because the aggregate elasticity of substitution for new and existing capital stock is probably below unity in the medium term, a neoclassical employment policy will cause income to be distributed less equally within manufacturing unless taxes on capital are transferred to wage earners. However, the real income distribution problem is between the modern and traditional sectors and not within the manufacturing sector.

These policy prescriptions implicitly condemn the investment incentives which have become part of most developing countries' industrial strategy. The commonly used incentives—low-interest loans, free infrastructure, profit tax holidays, accelerated depreciation and duty-free entry of capital equipment—all work to lower the rental rate on capital services and encourage substitution of capital for labour. Wage subsidies, seldom used, would be a superior incentive to any of these. Export subsidies (in lieu of devaluation) would also be effective, not only because these countries typically have comparative advantage in labour—intensive goods, but also because subsidies will encourage firms to use excess capacity to produce for the export market.

NOTES

1. I am indebted to the Central Bureau of Statistics of Ghana, especially to the government Statistician, Mr J. E. Tandoh, and Mr S. W. K. Sosuh and his staff, who made data available for this study; to the Harvard Institute for International Development (formerly Development Advisory Service) for financial and logistical support; to Mrs Belinda Dapice for computer programming; and to Mr Joost Miedema for statistical calculations.

2. Pooled data were used by Williamson [1971], who found elasticities of substitution well in excess of one for all manufacturing, for six sub-sectors, and for the four two-digit ISIC group studies.

3. Although in principle a wage expectations function with distributed lags could be introduced, this is not done here for three reasons: (1) the coefficients of the resulting equation cannot be separately identified; (2) the resulting model predicts an autocorrelated disturbance term; and, in any case, (3) the term in $\text{Log } q_{t-2}$ which is introduced by a distributed lag turns out to have statistically insignificant coefficients.

4. Before the completion of Akosombo Dam in 1966, power was both generated and distributed by small local companies; afterwards they stopped generating. Since this implies a different production function, only data from 1962 to 1965 were included in the regressions.

5. For a summary of the voluminous literature on the shortcomings of econometric estimates of CES parameters, see Nadiri [1970].

6. Mukerji [1963] has proposed a generalized neoclassical function in which one factor can have different elasticities of substitution with respect to various other factors. However, it is not then a homogeneous function and elasticities of substitution are variable (although ratios between any two are constant).

7. However, Winston [1971] has emphasized that the neoclassical models may

underestimate substitutability considerably, especially when the conventional elasticity is well below one, by not dealing explicitly with multiple shifts.

8. For instance, UNIDO [*1967*] uses engineering estimates to show, *inter alia*, that there is considerable scope for labour-capital substitution in cotton spinning and weaving. As one example, at a daily average wage below $4·00, simple, modern weaving machines which use 17 labourers per 1,000 yards of cloth per hour produce at a lower unit cost than more complex machines which use only 11 workers; at wages below $1·00 per day, second-hand machines using 30 workers per 1,000 yards per hour produce as cheaply as the simple modern units using 17 labourers.

9. A recent input-output study of 77 Indian manufacturing industries [*Hazari and Krishnamurty, 1970*] shows a very wide range of employment-output ratios: from over 1,000 employees per unit output for the top 9 sectors, all in food processing; to less than 100 for the bottom 29 sectors. The latter include many of the favourite import-substituters: chemicals, plastics, drugs, cotton yarn, cigarettes, fertilizer, etc.

10. For a particularly good diagnosis of the import-substitution syndrome, see Bruton [*1970*].

11. Table 2 summarizes an earlier paper by the author [*Roemer, 1972*]; the original paper contains further details of the calculations.

12. The coup was not entirely unrelated to some of the relative factor price changes discussed in this paper, although its root causes appear to lie elsewhere. As noted below, government stability is a pre-requisite for a successful neoclassical employment policy.

13. In early 1973, chaotic world currency markets and record prices for cocoa induced the military government to revalue the cedi by 10 per cent against the devalued dollar. With offsetting changes in the cedi-sterling and cedi-mark rates, this would, by itself, cause a further rise of the (non-tax) wage-rental index of only 2 percentage points.

14. In Ghana, the 23 per cent drop in the wage-rental index from 1966 to 1970 was accomplished by a 7 per cent fall in real wages and a 22 per cent increase in real rentals. This probably caused some negative income effect and reduced employment potential.

15. Bruton [*1972*] has shown that with Hicks—neutral technological change at a rate g_T, employment will grow at

$$g_L = g_Q - g_T + \sigma(g_T - g_W)$$

where g_Q is output growth, g_W is wage rate growth and σ is the elasticity of substitution. For our purposes, technological change can be ignored if either $g_T = 0$ or $\sigma = 1$.

16. For $w' = -0·25$ and $w_0/r_0 = 1$, g_1/g_0 is

σ	0·5	1·0	1·0	1·0	1·5
δ or α	0·5	0·4	0·5	0·67	0·5
g_1/g_0	0·93	0·91	0·89	0·86	0·80

17. This ignores the possibility that a lower wage-rental ratio might reduce the rate of replacement by making it cheaper to produce with existing capital.

18. $R(v) < \beta K_0(t)$ because, at the new capital-labour ratio, less capital is required per unit output. The ratio of new to old investment requirement is

$$\lambda = (I/Q)_1/(I/Q)_0 = (\delta/k_0{}^\rho + 1 - \delta)^{1/\rho}/(\delta/k_1 + 1 - \delta)^{1/\rho}$$

for the CES case and

$$\lambda = (k_1/k_0)^\alpha = 1/(1 - w')^\alpha$$

for the Cobb-Douglas case. For $w' = -0·25$, λ is given by the following table:

σ	0·5	1·0	1·0	1·0	1·5
δ or α	0·5	0·4	0·5	0·67	0·5
λ	0·90	0·91	0·90	0·86	0·87

19. Table 3 also reports calculations at $\sigma = 1·0$ for $\beta = 15$ per cent and $\alpha = 0·67$, and $\alpha = 0·4$, each taken separately. These show that more rapid depreciation can speed up employment creation slightly, while a higher labour share has a depressing effect because it lowers the initial growth rate, g_1. However, a higher labour share also means that more of the burden for a reduced wage-rental ratio can be borne by capital without a negative income effect on investors.

REFERENCES

Bruton, H. J., 1970, 'The Import Substitution Strategy of Economic Development: A Survey', *Pakistan Development Review*, 10: 2.

Bruton, H. J., 1972, 'Employment, Productivity and Import Substitution', Research Memorandum No. 44, Center for Development Economics, Williams College.

Hazari, B. R., and J. H. Krishnamurty, 1970, 'Employment Implications of India's Industrialization: Analysis in an Input-Output Framework', *Review of Economics and Statistics*, 52: 2.

Mukerji, V., 1963, 'A Generalized SMAC Function with Constant Ratios of Elasticity of Substitution', *Review of Economic Studies*, 30: 3.

Nadiri, M. I., 1970, 'Some Approaches to the Theory and Measurement of Total Factor Productivity', *Journal of Economic Literature*, 8: 4.

Roemer, M., 1972, 'Relative Factor Prices in Ghanaian Manufacturing, 1960–1970', *The Economic Bulletin of Ghana*, 1: 4.

UNIDO (V. Saxl), 1967, *Technological and Economic Aspects of Establishing Textile Industries in Developing Countries*, Vienna.

Williamson, J. G., 1971, 'Relative Price Changes, Adjustment Dynamics, and Productivity Growth: The Case of Philippines Manufacturing', *Economic Development and Cultural Change*, 19: 4.

Winston, G., 1971, 'Capital Utilization and Employment: A Neoclassical Model of Optimal Shift Work', (mimeo).

The Employment Effects of Wage Changes in Poor Countries

By *Frances Stewart** and *John Weeks***

It is commonly argued that a rise in 'modern' sector wage rates in poor countries will reduce employment as a result of factor substitution. However, it is shown that this need not apply, even assuming the existence of high elasticities of substitution, if there are segregated labour markets, as is common in poor countries. When all labour markets are considered, a rise in 'modern' sector wage rates may increase total employment opportunities through the shift in demand towards the more labour intensive low-wage sector. The effects of a rise in 'modern' sector wage rates must, therefore, be analysed in terms of its effect on the distribution of employment opportunities and income throughout the whole economy and not just in one sector.

A familiar conclusion of marginal analysis is that a rise in the wage rate will, *ceteris paribus*, lead to a fall in total employment; and conversely, a fall in the wage rate will increase the level of employment. The Keynesian revolution, and subsequent developments in the theory of distribution, have destroyed this proposition for policy purposes for developed countries.[1] Yet it remains a central proposition of policy in poor countries.[2] It is our contention that this central proposition—viz., that a rise in wage rates will reduce employment and a decrease will raise employment—is not valid for poor countries either; a rise in the wage rate may increase total employment in some plausible circumstances.

Before going into our argument, it is worth recounting briefly why the Keynesian analysis of the relationship between wage rates and employment is not generally accepted as relevant to poor countries. Broadly, two reasons have received emphasis. First, the type of unemployment to which Keynesian demand remedies apply is that associated with spare capacity in machinery—across the board—as well as spare capacity in the form of under-utilised labour. Although spare capacity in machinery does, notoriously, exist in poor countries [*Little, Scitovsky and Scott, 1970, Ch. 3; Brecher and Abbas, 1972, pp. 126–8, 131–8; ILO, 1972, Ch. 8*], it does not exist in a form which can be remedied by expansion of aggregate demand. It usually does not occur in a balanced form. Expansion of output

---

* Senior Research Officer at the Institute of Commonwealth Studies, Oxford and **Lecturer at Birkbeck College, London. The authors wish particularly to thank Charles Cooper, Science Policy Research Unit, University of Sussex, and Ajit Bhalla, International Labour Organisation, for their comments and collaboration in an earlier draft from which this paper emerged. Thanks also go to John Muellbauer, Richard Portes, and Paul Streeten for their valuable comments.

in excess-capacity industries is limited by simultaneous supply constraints elsewhere in the economy, such as basic power industries. Frequently, the spare capacity may be the result of the restriction on the importation of intermediates, which is a consequence of structural and chronic balance-of-payments disequilibrium. Thus the consequences of an increase in aggregate demand are bottlenecks in domestic capacity in key sectors, intensification of balance-of-payments pressures, and domestic price inflation. At most, Keynesian unemployment—i.e., the unemployment of labour that could be absorbed by fuller utilisation of existing machines resulting from an increase in aggregate demand—forms only a very small proportion of total labour under-utilisation [*Rao, 1952; Eckaus, 1955*].

Keynes, in contrast to many of his followers, did accept at least in part a marginal productivity theory of wages. He believed an expansion of employment would be accompanied by falling marginal productivity of labour and a falling real wage rate. However, he believed that the decline in the real wage would be a consequence of the expansion in employment, not a cause. It would not be a cause because the state had no control over the level of real wages; at best it could affect the level of money wages. What happened to real wages depended on the relationship between money wages and the price level. In an economy in which all sectors were affected by a change in money wages, the most likely consequence of a money wage change (upwards or downwards) was a similar change in prices, with no effect on the real wage rate. For this reason Keynes believed that manipulating wages would not be effective in determining employment since the policy makers could influence only the money wage, whereas the real wage was the key variable.

In developing economies, however, changes in money wages in the relatively small 'modern' sector may also constitute changes in real wages. The workers affected only spend a proportion of their incomes on the products they produce, and their consumption of these products accounts for only a relatively small proportion of total sales. Their wages, in general, are only a small proportion of the costs of the products they produce as compared with rich countries. Hence the price level of the products they produce is unlikely to be proportionately affected by a change in money wage rates, so that the ratio of money wages to product prices [3] is likely to be changed by a change in the money wage. The important point is that *prima facie* there is more reason to suppose that changes in money wages will cause changes in real wages, where the controlled sector forms only a small proportion of total activity, and this is the reason why the Keynesian attack on the idea of determining employment via control over money wages appears less effective in the context of developing countries; it is the dualistic nature of developing economies that reduces the effectiveness of the Keynesian critique. It is precisely this dualistic aspect of developing economies on which our main argument is based.

We assume:

(1) that there exist two markets, [4] or sectors, for non-agricultural labour, the controlled sector where the level of money wages is determined by trade union and employer bargaining and government intervention, and the

uncontrolled sector where incomes are determined by competitive forces. [5] In the controlled sector wages are above their competitive level in the sense that there is excess supply of labour at the ruling wage rate, and the rate would drop in the absence of trade unions, and government. The supply of labour to the controlled sector comes from the rest of the economy, including the uncontrolled sector. Wages in the controlled sector are above those of the uncontrolled sector. [6] The supply of labour for the uncontrolled sector comes from the agricultural sector, the unemployed and the under-employed (i.e., those working short hours in any part of the economy.) According to the Todaro model [*Todaro, 1959*], workers take into account incomes in the high-wage sector, and their estimates of the likelihood of getting a job, in deciding to migrate from the rural sector and deciding whether to look for a job in the urban sector. But his is a two sector model, and assumes that anyone without a high-wage job in the urban sector is unemployed. When we introduce a three-sector model—urban high-wage, urban low-wage and rural—the picture is substantially altered. Workers deciding to migrate to the urban sector must now take into account the near certainty of getting some sort of (low-wage) job in the urban sector as well as the possibility of acquiring a high-wage job, assuming, which seems reasonable, that employment in the low-wage urban sector does not rule out the possibility of acquiring employment in the high-wage sector. Thus supply of labour to the low-wage urban sector is increased by those who join the sector as a stepping stone to the high-wage sector. The greater the wage-differential between the high-wage sector and the rural sector, the greater the supply of labour to the low-wage urban sector for any wage. Whether or not there is surplus labour in this sector is partly a matter of definition and partly of fact. If we define surplus labour as excess of labour supply (in hours) at the ruling wage rate, so an expansion (diminution) of employment does not affect the wage rate, there is surplus labour in so far as marginal disutility of work is constant over the relevant range. In terms of labour hours, if not of labourers [*Sen, 1966*], this may be a reasonable assumption. In any case it seems likely that, if not infinite, the elasticity of supply of labour hours to changes in wages in the uncontrolled sector is very high.

(2) Each sector produces goods and services which are close substitutes with goods and services produced by the other sector. The two sectors compete in terms of final output (sold to consumers) and intermediate commodities (sold as inputs to each sector).

(3) We assume (initially) a closed economy. Both sectors sell only to final consumers or to each other—i.e., the net output (i.e., value added generated in the sector) of each sector is equal to

$$o_1 = c_1 + o_{12}$$
$$o_2 = c_2 + o_{21}$$

where o_1, o_2 = net output of each sector;

c_1, c_2 = net output sold to consumers;

o_{12} is net output of sector 1 sold as input to sector 2;

o_{21} is net output of sector 2 sold as input to sector 1.

(4) The sectors do not face identical technical/economic opportunities.

If they did, the low wage sector would be at an absolute advantage as compared with the high wage sector and would take the whole market. The two sectors differ in other respects besides the wage rate:

(i) they have differing access to capital funds, with the low-wage sector having much more limited access, and having to pay a much higher price for the funds it does raise;

(ii) they differ in scale; the large scale high-wage sector can use machines which, because of indivisibilities, are not possible for the low-wage sector because of the latter's more limited access to credit, foreign exchange, and foreign technology; and

(iii) their products and services are not perfect substitutes; the high-wage sector tends to produce a more modern and standardised product which allows it to charge a higher price and serve a different market than the low-wage sector.

We may thus view the two sectors as facing different production possibilities, and different factor prices, from each other.

Given these differences between the sectors (the three above and the wage differential), an equilibrium situation may arise in which the sectors produce competing goods and services. 'Equilibrium' here means that there is no endogenous tendency for one sector to drive the other from the market, at any point in time.[7]

The nature of the equilibrium, the levels of output and employment in the two sectors, and the response of the system to changes in wage rates depend on the assumptions we make about the production function each sector experiences, and the method of decision making. We start by exploring the implications of adopting neoclassical assumptions—viz., diminishing returns to additional employment and profit maximising. Sub-

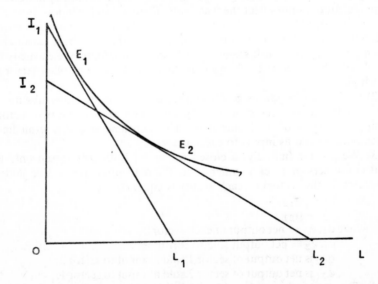

FIGURE 1

sequently we consider how our conclusions may need modification with more realistic assumptions.

Assuming diminishing marginal productivity of labour in each sector and profit maximisation, each sector will employ additional workers until the real wage is equal to the marginal product of labour. This is illustrated in Diagram 1 which shows the profit maximising equilibrium, E_1 and E_2 for the two sectors, assuming each is producing the same product—in quantity and quality—and they face different factor prices, represented by $I_1 L_1$ and $I_2 L_2$ in Figure 1. Under these assumptions, the low-wage sector will use more labour and less investible resources than the high-wage sector. The low-wage sector will be more labour intensive than the high-wage sector in terms of labour requirements per unit of output, and in terms of investment per man as compared with the high-wage sector. For stable equilibrium the marginal costs of each sector should be approximately the same. In this case, this requires that the extra cost of labour in sector 1, as compared with sector 2, is offset by lower cost of investment. In other words for production in both sectors along the same isoquant, the isoquant curve must also represent an isocost curve, given the differences in factor prices between the sectors. While this might seem to be a rather stringent requirement that makes it unlikely that both sectors would operate simultaneously and in equilibrium, there are other differences between the 2 sectors which make it more likely. In the first place there are *scale* differences. The high-wage sector generally only operates on a much larger scale than the low-wage sector. The large scale of the high-wage sector stems from the advanced country technology with which it operates, and the managerial requirements which are indivisible and make it worthwhile only to operate at a large scale. In contrast, the low-wage sector's limited access to capital and advanced country technology means that its scale of operations is much smaller. It is not necessary for our equilibrium that $MC_1 = MC_2$, only that they are not too divergent. The small firm, if family owned and run, may be content to operate at a lower unit profit. It is only necessary that the firm with the lower marginal costs does not sell at a price which is below the normal profit price level of the other firm. In addition, the very fact of getting larger leads to a rise in wages,[8] and hence a shift from low- to high-wage operations, as the firm becomes subject to union organisation, and government regulations. Thus the two sectors are not operating at the same scale as shown in Figure 1, but at different scales, as shown in Figure 2 below. Consequently, economies associated with scale may offset the extra costs generated by the higher wages sector 1 has to pay. It remains true that sector 1 is less labour intensive than sector 2 in terms of labour requirements per unit of output, and investment per man. Whether it is more or less capital using (i.e., has more or less investment per unit of output), depends on how far investment costs fall as scale rises. Further, the quality of the product produced tends to differ between the sectors. The high-wage sector product is more standardised, more advertised, and packaged, and often with more or higher quality attributes than the product of the low-wage sector. It can therefore sell for a higher price. Nonetheless, it is a close, if not perfect, substitute for the low-wage product

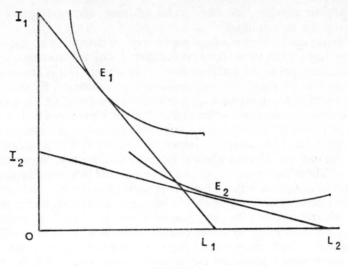

FIGURE 2

fulfilling many of the same needs. If w_1 is the wage in the high wage sector and w_2 the wage in the low wage sector, then

$$\frac{w_1}{w_2} = \frac{MPL_1}{MPL_2} \tag{1}$$

and by hypothesis $w_1 > w_2$. Since, therefore, $MPL_1 > MPL_2$, it follows that any switch in output from sector 1 to sector 2 will increase employment. Hence analysis of the employment effects of changing wage rates must take into account the effects of intersectoral allocation of tasks as well as the effects on the level of employment in relation to any given output level in each sector.

An increase in the money wage-rate. Δw_1, in the controlled sector may be expected to have the following effects:

The increase on the wage rate in the sector will tend to reduce the level of employment associated with any given level of output of the sector. It is also likely to curtail the level of output of the controlled sector in one, or both, of the following ways. If prices are determined competitively entrepreneurs will not be able to pass on the extra wages in prices, and will therefore curtail output, which will have the indirect effect of raising prices of the controlled sector. In so far as prices are determined oligopolistically the increased wage rate may be passed straight on to consumers in the form of raised prices.

The rise in price (and curtailment of output) of the controlled sector will lead to an increased incentive to use the output of the uncontrolled sector, where there are close substitutes, both for intermediate products and for final consumption. Increased output of the uncontrolled sector will lead to an increase in employment in that sector.

Thus the negative effects on employment of an increase in wages in the controlled sector—resulting from reduction of output in that sector, and substitution for labour [*Harris and Todaro, 1969*][9]—will be offset (in part, whole or even exceeded) by positive effects on employment in the uncontrolled sector.[10] We may summarise the effects algebraically, as

$$\Delta L = -\Delta L_1 + \Delta L_2$$

$$\text{where} \quad -\Delta L_1 = -\left[\Delta w_1 \times \frac{\Delta L_1}{\Delta w_1} + \frac{\Delta O_1}{\Delta w_1} \times \frac{OL_1}{\Delta O_1} \right]$$

$$\text{and} \quad \Delta L_2 = \left[\frac{\Delta O_2}{\Delta w_1} \times \frac{\Delta L_2}{\Delta O_2} - \Delta w_2 \times \frac{\Delta L_2}{\Delta w_2} \right]$$

$$\text{or} \quad \Delta L = -\left[\Delta w_1 \times \frac{\Delta L_1}{\Delta w_1} + \frac{\Delta O_1}{\Delta w_1} \times \frac{OL_1}{\Delta O_1} \right] +$$

$$\left[\frac{\Delta O_2}{Ow_1} \times \frac{\Delta L_2}{\Delta O_2} \quad \frac{\Delta w_2 \times \Delta L_2}{\Delta w_2} \right]$$

Most analyses look only at effects on employment *in the controlled sector*, and thus capture *only the negative effects* of a wage rise.

What, if anything, can we say about the magnitude of the changes, and therefore the net effect of the wage rise? First, we know that, because $w_1 > w_2$ and $MPL_1 > MPL_2$, then $\dfrac{L_1}{O_1} > \dfrac{L_2}{O_2}$. Thus, if we can assume that the total level of output is unaffected by the change, $\Delta O_1 = \Delta O_2$, then $\dfrac{\Delta O_1}{\Delta w_1} \times \dfrac{\Delta L_1}{\Delta O_1} = < \dfrac{\Delta O_2}{\Delta w_1} \times \dfrac{\Delta L_2}{\Delta O_2}$ so that the magnitude of the third term (positive effect) exceeds that of the second term (negative effect). The question, then, is whether the excess, $\left[\dfrac{\Delta O_2}{\Delta w_1} \times \dfrac{\Delta L_2}{\Delta O_2} - \dfrac{\Delta O_1}{\Delta w_1} \times \dfrac{\Delta L_1}{\Delta O_1} \right]$

is greater than the sum of the remaining terms, which are both negative. The first term is the elasticity of substitution for labour in sector 1 in response to a wage rise. Many would argue that this is likely to be low, particularly in the short run when capacity (and the technique) is fixed. However, further discussion of this must await relaxation of the basic neoclassical assumptions below. The fourth term has not been discussed so far. It represents the elasticity of substitution for labour in the uncontrolled sector, and will only appear if wages in that sector rise too, i.e., if $\Delta w_2 > 0$. Whether wages do rise in that sector depends on the labour supply in that sector. If there is surplus labour—i.e., excess supplies of labour at the ruling wage—as suggested earlier—then $\Delta w_2 = 0$. In the absence of surplus labour, the wage in that sector will tend to rise with an increase in employment in the sector, but given the labour supply situation the rise in wage is likely to be extremely small.

A key assumption is that the overall output level is unaffected—i.e., $\Delta O_1 = \Delta O_2$: what happens to the level of output, in response to a wage rise, is a complex matter depending on the propensity to consume of different classes, the effects of any price rises on the level of demand, and the response of the government to the changes in question. In a closed economy, no change in the level of output seems a reasonable assumption as the rise in purchasing power among workers enjoying a wage rise may offset any effect of a price rise—though of course this depends on what happens to the total wage bill, in both sectors combined. In an open economy the level of output also depends on foreign demand. In many developing countries, the overall level of output is set by foreign exchange availability in relation to propensity to import, as output expands. What happens to this balance, in this case, depends on price changes, subsequent exchange rate changes and flows of international capital, and the propensities to import of the two sectors. This is clearly a complex matter with which we cannot fully deal here. One can be fairly confident of two (offsetting) directions of change: on the one hand the wage rise and price rise, unless fully offset by exchange rate changes, may diminish the net trade balance and reduce the inflow of capital. On the other hand the propensity to import is likely to be higher in the high-wage than in the low-wage sector.

The discussion has been concerned with output and employment consequences of a wage change, where the 2 sectors are assumed to be producing substitute goods. Some of the output of the high-wage sector may be complementary, rather than competitive, with output of the low-wage sector. Some activities may be simultaneously substitutes and complements, in the sense that the activity as a whole—e.g., housing or repairs —is positively related to the level of output of the high-wage sector, while both sectors compete with one another in performing the activity. It might seem that where goods are complements rather than substitutes a reduction of output in the controlled sector will actually reduce output and employment in the low-wage sector. However, this only follows if the relation of complementarity holds between the output of the controlled sector and output of the uncontrolled sector, but *not* between output of the uncontrolled sector, and itself. In general, the opposite situation is likely. The uncontrolled sector is more likely to be complementary with itself (produce its own inputs and provide for its own consumption) than to be complementary with the high-wage sector. For example, repairs, transport and construction activities for the low-wage sector are likely to be performed by other enterprises in the sector, because members of the sector have close contacts with each other, and cannot afford the prices of the high-wage sector, whereas only a proportion of repairs, etc., needed for the high-wage sector are likely to be performed by the low-wage sector. Similarly, workers in the low-wage sector are more likely to live in houses produced in the uncontrolled sector, than workers in the controlled sector. This tendency for each sector to use more of its own inputs and consumption goods, relatively, than those of the other sector, means that any initial switch of output between the sectors will tend to be reinforced, or multiplied, by a subsequent switch as source of inputs and consumption goods are also switched.

Two of the assumptions made above seem unrealistic: the nature of the production function facing firms in the two sectors, and the assumption that workers are employed so long as their contribution exceeds their wage. This last assumption is probably a reasonable assumption to make for the controlled sector. However, the uncontrolled sector is largely composed of family enterprises, some of whom may have an obligation to provide for family members irrespective of their contribution to the enterprise. In such a situation, the extra cost of employment may be close to zero. This means that the ratio of the labour intensity of the sectors may be greater than an assessment of the ratio of their wage levels would suggest. It is also likely to lead to a situation where many of the employees are underemployed (i.e., working few hours, or very unintensively.) In this situation while the method of production employed for an extra output will tend to be labour intensive, relative to the controlled sector, increased production may reduce underemployment of existing employees, rather than adding to the total *numbers* employed. An assessment of the effect on employment of a wage change (as in the expression above) should be calculated in terms of *labour-hours:* the effect on *labourers* depends on the extent and response of underemployment among existing workers.

It was assumed above that there was diminishing marginal product of labour in both sectors, and no distinction was made between the short run and the long run, nor was there any discussion of the investment implications of a change in the share of output of the 2 sectors.

The assumption that the wage is equated with workers' marginal product requires the existence of continuous variability between factors (men and machines) *and* that marginal product of labour diminishes as employment increases, both in the short run and the long. Fixed coefficients may prevail in some processes, particularly in the short run. Moreover, the amount of equipment available in each sector is fixed in the short run. If this capacity is underutilised, output is likely to increase more than proportionately with employment—i.e., the marginal productivity of labour is greater than the average product, and thus the real wage must be less than the marginal product of labour. As full capacity is reached, the marginal product drops sharply until it approaches zero. In the modern high-wage sector a form of J-shaped cost curve may often be the best approximation to reality.[11]

Consequently, the assumption made above of steadily diminishing marginal product of labour as employment increases, equated with the real wage, is unreal. So long as there is spare capacity, average product of labour is rising and the marginal product exceeds the wage. When full capacity is reached marginal product of labour is indeterminate or falls sharply below the wage rate. In contrast, the neoclassical model in which capital equipment may be gradually spread more and more widely, and used more and more intensively, with an increase in employment, may be nearer to an approximation of reality in the low-wage sector. The obvious example is land, which may be used more and more intensively. But other forms of complementary assets—tools and equipment—may also be used more or less intensively. However, even in this sector there are areas where there is spare capacity of capital equipment and where output may increase more than proportionately with employment.

Once we drop the assumption that the wage is equated to the marginal product of labour in each sector, we can no longer assume that the ratio of the wages in the two sectors shows the inverse of the relative labour requirements for producing additional output. With spare capacity in each sector, we may assume that the wage sets the lower limit to the marginal product of labour in each sector. If there is spare capacity in each sector and,

$$
\left. \begin{array}{l}
MP_1 = \dfrac{\Delta O_1}{\Delta L_1} \geqslant w_1 \\[4mm]
MP_2 = \dfrac{\Delta O_2}{\Delta L_2} \geqslant w_2
\end{array} \right\} \tag{2}
$$

For given change in output, $\Delta O_1 = \Delta O_2$

$$
\frac{\Delta L_2}{\Delta L_1} = \frac{(\geqslant w_2)}{(\geqslant w_1)}
$$

then we may assume that the ratio of the wages gives some guide to the labour requirements.

Alternatively, we may assume that, while there is spare capacity in the controlled sector, the uncontrolled sector displays neoclassical diminishing returns and the wage is equated to the marginal product of labour. i.e.

$$
\left. \begin{array}{l}
MP_1 = \dfrac{\Delta O_1}{\Delta L_1} \geqslant w_1 \\[4mm]
MP_2 = \dfrac{\Delta O_2}{\Delta L_2} = w_2
\end{array} \right\} \tag{3}
$$

Therefore, for given increase in output, $\Delta O_1 = \Delta O_2$

$$
\frac{\Delta L_2}{\Delta L_1} = \frac{(\geqslant w_1)}{w_2}
$$

Or, as discussed above, we may assume that family obligations to provide employment mean that the wage sets the *upper* limit to the marginal product of labour, i.e.,

$$
\left.
\begin{aligned}
MP_1 &= \frac{\Delta O_1}{\Delta O_2} \geqslant w_1 \\[2em]
MP_2 &= \frac{\Delta O_2}{\Delta L_2} \leqslant w_2
\end{aligned}
\right\} \tag{4}
$$

and for given increase in output, $\Delta O_1 = \Delta O_2$

$$
\frac{\Delta L_2}{\Delta L_1} = \frac{(\geqslant w_1)}{(\leqslant w_2)}
$$

These alternative assumptions have different implications for the change in employment consequent upon a wage increase in the controlled sector. (2) above, as argued, may have similar implications, to that assumed initially, of $w_1 = MP_2$ in each sector. (3) above means that for any change in output, employment changes in the controlled sector are *less*, while those in the uncontrolled sector are the same, as under neoclassical assumptions. Hence the net employment effect is more likely to be positive (or likely to be smaller in a negative direction) than under neoclassical assumptions. Finally, the fourth set of assumptions (4) are likely to give the greatest positive, or the smallest negative, employment effect.

Thus a more realistic approach to the nature of available equipment capacity suggests modifications to the above analysis. The general proposition—that a switch in output from the high-wage to the low-wage sector is likely to increase labour use—remains true, but the wage rates in the 2 sectors cannot be taken as indicators of the changing employment requirements.

In the longer run a change in sectoral allocation of output will have implications for investment requirements. In so far as the investment costs per unit of output are lower in the low-wage sector, investment requirements, for a given output growth, will also be lower. But we argued above that this was not necessarily always the case. The impact on savings must also be considered. The normal assumption that more labour intensive employment reduces savings does not apply here, because it supposes a uniform wage rate between techniques, whereas here the wage rate is assumed to differ between the sectors. The impact on savings available for reinvestment depends on the wage bill as a share of output in each sector, and the propensities to save of entrepreneurs and workers in the 2 sectors. The evidence on these propensities is scanty and unreliable. The frequent predominance of foreign investment in the high-wage sectors (and its complete absence in the low-wage sector) also influences, via remitted profits, the availability of savings for local investment.

There are also consumption effects of the wage increase, which in the long run might have an important impact on the sectoral distribution of output, independent of relative price changes. This is difficult to analyse *a priori*, because we cannot predict with confidence the impact of an increase in the controlled sector wage on the wage bills in the two sectors. Let us take the case where a higher wage and less employment in the controlled sector results in a higher wage bill (the demand for labour is inelastic). Higher wages may make this larger wage bill more import and sector 1 intensive, if such goods are characterised by high income elasticities. In such a case, there could be a secular shift in demand away from the low-wage sector by high-wage workers.

However, if the rise in the controlled sector wage results in an increase in the sector 2 wage bill which is greater than the increase in the sector 1 wage bill, one would have to know the consumption patterns of low-wage workers in order to reach an overall conclusion. As argued above, workers in the low-wage sector, because of their lower incomes and their close relationship with the sector, would tend to spend a higher proportion of their income on products from sector 2 than would be the case for high-wage workers.

It is, perhaps, illuminating to compare the relationship between high- and low-wage sectors *within* a poor country, to that of the relationship between a developed (high-wage) country and a poor (low-wage) country. Given fixed exchange rates—which of course are implicit in the relationship between sectors within a country (a single monetary area)—and in the absence of tax/subsidy arrangements, a rise in wage rates in the high-wage country will reduce its competitiveness *vis-a-vis* the low-wage country, and, to the extent that output between the 2 countries is competitive, will increase the share of output produced by the poor country. Given the greater labour input per unit of output in the poor country, and the availability of surplus labour in that country, world employment will be increased as a result. The switch in output towards the poor country is likely to lead to a greater use of inputs and consumption goods from the poor country, reinforcing the original change, on the assumption that there is spare capacity in the poor country. As with our two sector model, the net effect on output and employment will depend on the effect on the total level of world output, as a result of the change. The analogy between the two situations breaks down here, however. In the first place, given restrictions on migration of labour, the high-wage country does not have access to surplus labour from the low-wage country, as the high-wage sector does from the low-wage sector. In the second place, the rich countries can be assumed to give priority to full employment of *their* labour force, in their policies, and pay no attention to employment in the poor country. In the third place, and most important, the rich country has control over its monetary, exchange rate and budgetary policy, and may therefore react in a way that will offset the initial change, which may not be possible for the high-wage sector in the poor country.

DISTRIBUTION OF INCOME WITH DIFFERING HIGH-WAGE SECTOR WAGE RATES

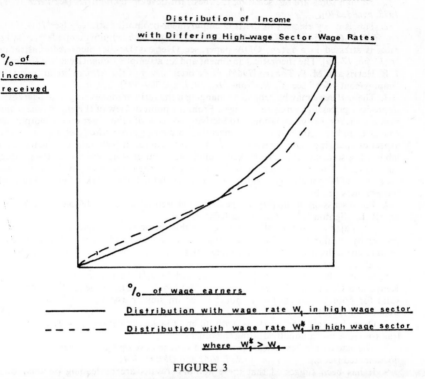

FIGURE 3

We have not been concerned here to discuss the welfare implications of the possible strategies. A lower wage rate in the controlled sector may involve greater employment opportunities there, and less in the low-wage sector. A higher wage rate, while diminishing employment opportunities in that sector may expand them more than proportionately in the low-wage sector. Which is better, from a welfare point of view, is a complex matter depending on how one values the relative welfare of different groups of workers and different income categories. This is a situation where Lorenz curves cross, as indicated in the diagram below. To draw welfare implications in such situations is notoriously difficult.

In conclusion, we stress that our model may not be sufficiently realistic. In particular, we have dealt for the most part only with a closed economy. We have not examined, in detail, possible supply constraints in the low-wage sector. Nor have we examined the implications of the differing incidence of technical progress over time. However, we feel that analysing the employment effects of changes in wage rates in a two sector framework is an improvement on the one sector analysis, and the 2 sector approach must be pursued if intelligent wages and employment policies are to be formulated.

NOTES

1. Though some are resuscitating the thesis for developed countries [see *Peter Wiles*, *1973, pp. 83, 330*].

2. This is a key element in the ILO employment-promoting strategy [see *ILO, 1961, pp. 56 ff; ILO, 1964, pp. 141 ff; ILO, 1970, pp. 185 ff*]. The 'employment effect' of wage rates is stressed in a recent ODA paper, see Overseas Development Administration [*1972, pp. 17–20*]. The theoretical argument and an attempt to quantify it are found in J. R. Harris and M. P. Todaro [*1968*]. For a brief survey of the African literature on the 'employment effect' see [*C. R. Frank, Jr., 1971, pp. 799–801*].

3. The *real wage* may be defined as changing if the ratio of money wages, in aggregate, to product prices, in aggregate, changes. From the point of view of the entrepreneur this means that, for any given labour productivity, the cost of labour per unit of output has changed, and therefore there is an incentive to change production methods. It is this aspect of changing real wages which is relevant to choice of technique and demand for labour. It also means that the workers' command of purchasing power over the product has changed. This is the relevant aspect determining the standard of living of workers, the supply of labour and aggregate demand (in real terms) from workers' expenditure for the products produced.

4. For discussion of 'duality' in the industrial sector, see R. R. Nelson, T. P. Schultz and R. L. Slighton [*1966, Ch. 4*] and Kilby [*1969*].

5. A major proportion of employment in this sector is self-employment. However, for brevity, we normally refer to the sector as 'low-wage sector' because this emphasises its fundamentally distinguishing characteristics, access to low cost labour, in contrast to the high-wage sector.

6. See P. Kilby [*1967*], ILO [*1972, Ch. 13 and 1970*], for documentation for Nigeria, Kenya and Colombia. The existence of a dual labour market is generally accepted as valid for poor countries. For a model based on similar assumptions to ours, see D. Mazumdar [*1973*].

7. Over time technical progress, with differing incidence between the 2 sectors, may lead to one sector gradually ousting the other.

8. The association between wage rates and scale in developing countries has been well documented [see e.g., *Dhar and Lydall, 1961* and *Okita, 1964*].

9. It has been suggested that these authors' results are misleading on their own grounds, see C. R. Frank, Jr. [*1971*].

10. Todaro [*1969*] has also argued that an increase in the wage-rate may increase employment, but on quite different grounds. He argues that firms will suffer a reduction in income as a result of the wage increases. Given a rigid capital constraint this loss in income will mean that they cannot afford to buy (indivisible) machinery, and will therefore use more labour intensive methods of production than before. The effect on employment will thus be positive, assuming that the income effect out-weighs the substitution effect of the wage rise—i.e., assuming that labour is a Giffen good.

11. See J. S. Bain [*1968*], *Industrial Organisation*, for empirical evidence of J (on its side) and U-shaped cost curves in the US.

REFERENCES

Bain, J. S., 1968, *Industrial Organisation*, (2nd Edition), Wiley.

Brecher, I. and S. A. Abbas, 1972, *Foreign Aid and Industrial Development in Pakistan*, London: Cambridge University Press.

Dhar, E. N. and H. F. Lydall, 1961, *The Role of Small Enterprises in Indian Economic Growth*, Asia Publishing House.

Eckaus, R. S., 1955, 'The Factor Proportions' Problem in Underdeveloped Areas', *American Economic Review*, 45, September.

Frank, C. R., Jr., 1971, 'The Problem of Urban Unemployment in Africa', in R. G. Ridker and H. Lubell, (eds.), *Employment and Unemployment Problems of the Near East and South Asia*, Delhi: Vikas, Vol. II.

Harris, J. R. and M. P. Todaro, 1968, 'Urban Unemployment in East Africa: An Economic Analysis of Policy Alternatives', *East African Economic Review*, 4; 2, December.

Harris, J. R. and Todaro, M. P., 1969, 'Wages, Industrial Employment and Labour Productivity in a Developing Economy', *Eastern African Economic Review*, 5: 1, June.

ILO, 1961, *Employment Objectives in Economic Development*, Geneva.

ILO, 1964, *Employment and Economic Growth*, Geneva.

ILO, 1970, *Towards Full Employment: A Programme for Columbia*, Geneva.

ILO, 1972, *Employment, Income and Equity*, Geneva.

Kilby, P., 1967, 'Industrial Relations and Wage Determination: Failure of the Anglo-Saxon Model', *Journal of Developing Areas*, I: 1, July.

Kilby, P., 1969, *Industrialisation in an Open Economy: Nigeria 1946–1966*, London: Cambridge University Press.

Little, I., T. Scitovsky, and M. Scott, 1970, *Industry and Trade in Some Developing Countries*, London: Oxford University Press.

Mazumdar, D., 1973, 'The Theory of Urban Under-Employment in Less Developed Countries', Washington: IBRD ms.

Nelson, R. R., T. P. Schultz, and R. L. Slighton, 1971, *Stuctural Change in a Developing Economy*, Princeton: Princeton University Press.

Okita, S., 1964, 'Choice of Techniques: Japan's Experience and its Implication', in K. Berrill (ed.), *Economic Development with Special Reference to East Asia*, Macmillan.

Overseas Development Administration, 1972, *Underemployment in Underdeveloped Countries*, paper prepared for Institute of Development Studies—Overseas Development Administration Seminar on Aid Policy.

Rao, V. K. R. V., 1952, 'Investment Income and the Multiplier in an Underdeveloped Economy', *Indian Economic Review*, February.

Sen, A. K., 1966, 'Peasants and Dualism with or without Surplus Labour', *Journal of Political Economy*, October.

Todaro, M. P., 1959, 'A Model of Labour Migration and Urban Unemployment in Less Developed Countries', *American Economic Review*, 59: 1, March.

Todaro, M. P., 1969, 'A Theoretical Note on Labour as an 'Inferior' Factor in Less Developed Countries', *Journal of Development Studies*, 5: 4, July.

Wiles, P., 1973, 'Cost Inflation and the State of Economic Theory', *Economic Journal*, June.

Skill Acquisition in the Imformal Sector of an African Economy: The Kenya Case

By Kenneth J. King*

This article explores the acquisition of a wide variety of skills by low income Kenya Africans, outside the scope of government and voluntary agency programmes. Many thousands of such (mostly young) Africans arrange types of unofficial fee-paying apprenticeships for themselves at the feet of older, often illiterate craftsmen. The process represents an indigenisation in Kenya of important elements of East African Indian craft training—not least in the product types and the innovative re-use of scrap materials. It appears to have important implications for the success of the government's official formal sector apprenticeship schemes, but indicates considerable difficulties for any attempt to identify this informal world as an autonomous sector of Kenya's larger economy.

Following the widespread recognition that formal enumerated employment was not expanding with anything like the speed necessary to absorb the products of the national and private school systems, there has been a recent switch of interest amongst economists and educationists to the untapped potential of informal employment and informal schooling. Unfortunately, so far the informality has been taken to refer to two rather different types of activity in these two spheres. Thus, for instance in Kenya, the informal sector of the economy can be described as that lying between subsistence or small scale cash crop agriculture on the one hand and the arena of government and private company employment on the other. Under this title one can usefully subsume the tens of thousands of people who work providing services and consumer goods to the lower income Africans across the country. Their informality derives from their being unrecognised in government employment statistics, and operating in the main out of makeshift shelters on urban wasteland, roadsides and forest fringes. As the ILO report on Kenya has recently stressed, there are important historical reasons why this whole sphere, like that of squatter housing, should receive little government attention—apart from the occasional attempt to sweep some of its urban members out of sight [*ILO, 1972, Ch. 13*]. By contrast, informal or non-formal education has been taken to mean the whole range of vocational training available to young people and adults outside the monolithic formal educational system. It usually means educational opportunities outside the Ministry of Education, but invariably these turn out to be the initiatives of other ministries or of private church or aid bodies—such as village polytechnics, farm schools,

---

* Lecturer in African education in the Centre of African Studies, Edinburgh University.

national youth services, 4K clubs, functional literacy or vocational training centres. Unlike the other informal sector, this educational one turns out to be one that is recognised, sponsored and on which data is relatively easily obtained [*Sheffield, 1971*].

The purpose of this present paper is rather to explore the informal educational system which *does* prepare Kenyans for operating in the informal sector that has been described above. It will be seen shortly that there is in fact a significant training function attached to the informal sector, and which shares with it a lack of recognition by the relevant Ministries of Labour and Education. Partly, this lack of recognition may be attributed to ignorance or apathy, but principally it derives from government concentrating its attention upon its own vocational training programmes, and particularly over these last two years with integrated schemes for producing skilled tradesmen in larger numbers. Briefly, the ingredients of the government's programme are (1) a Canadian-aided technical teacher training project based on the Kenya Polytechnic; (2) an ILO-aided expansion of the National Industrial Vocational Training Centre, and (3) introduction of an Industrial Training Act (on the lines of the one presently being abandoned by Britain); (4) formulating policy to incorporate Harambee Technological Colleges, once these begin to come to fruition. [1] With such a vast build up of government and popular interest in formal technical training and apprenticeship at the intermediate and higher levels, it is understandable that the non-institutional skill training of the informal sector has been overlooked. It should however be stressed that there are probably greater numbers moving through this level than there are in the whole of the government's technical school and training projects. [2] And it may therefore be of some advantage to those aiding and implementing the latter to appreciate something of the scale and dynamism of skill acquisition in the 'twilight' sector.

It is the intention to deal here primarily with the productive crafts in this sphere rather than the multiplicity of service industries; and this means rather neglecting Nairobi's whole network of informal transport, costermongering, brewing and renting—apart from stressing that almost all the hardware on the service side is produced in the craft sector. It is unfortunately not possible, either, to give space to the production of the few traditional craft items—gourds, clay pots, ornaments and others, which continue to be made for a gradually decreasing market. Rather, the focus will be on carpentry, tinsmithing, sheet metal work, automobile mechanic crafts and panel beating. Within this restricted field it should be possible to gauge some of the dimensions of this sector—its internal structure, diffusion potential, some attitudes of its participants, and its links with the more formal Indian and Western production enterprises. For the moment, much that is suggested here must remain tentative, since the research to support it has only been carried on with some 50 roadside operators in the Nairobi-Thika-Kiambu triangle of Central Kenya, but enough of a pattern emerges to make a preliminary report worthwhile. [3]

First of all, it is possible to examine the sector as one that has developed out of a primary school education that from the time of independence stopped having any vocational component. Upper primary during the late colonial period (the old intermediate schools) had insisted on trade courses (principally carpentry) being combined with work for the junior secondary entrance. The abandonment of the colonial syllabus was perhaps inevitable in the face of primary expansion and its now almost total pre-occupation with entrance to academic secondary schools. But by the mid-sixties it had become obvious to most observers that, with government secondaries only able to take a fraction of the primary leavers, there would be left many thousands in any one year who could not push their academic careers much further. For those with richer parents the struggle to rejoin the educational mainstream could be continued for a few more years in the self-help (harambee) schools; others would retake the primary leaving (or more appropriately secondary entrance) examination for a further two or three years. But the group with which we are concerned began, in this situation, to pay money to the lowest level of African artisans in exchange for their instruction. In fact at the very time that the National Christian Council of Kenya was initiating its apparently novel concept of Village Polytechnic—to offer the primary dropout or leaver some simple trade skill to live off, many thousands of young people had already set about acquiring such skills on their own [*Anderson, 1970*]. Indeed, the presence of a large scale indigenous training programme must be seen as one reason for the continued failure of the village polytechnics to gain substantial support at the grassroots. By a strange paradox, those students who do use the polytechnics seem determined to manipulate their structure into being institutions for entry to formal employment, while down in the autonomous informal sector there are large numbers of learners with precisely the polytechnic ideals of small scale, skilled rural or urban *self*-employment [*Court, 1972*].

The critical factor in the informal training industry is that the trainees are prepared to pay for their skill. Most of them have been paying primary school fees of between £3 and £4 per annum over the previous ten years, and they now make arrangements with experienced African artisans (fundis) to pay them sums that will fall somewhere in the range from £5 to £50 for a complete training. In fact like the apprenticeship principle in Britain until the early years of this century, trainees pay their masters to accept them, and expect only some form of maintenance or subsistence in return. Of course, this has the effect of placing these many thousands of trainees and their masters quite outside the present law of the land, recently formalised in the relevant sections of the Industrial Training Act. It may therefore be useful to sketch briefly the disposition of apprentice-ship in the formal sector, particularly if some way is to be found to recognise what presently is unacknowledged.

The government system recruits its apprentices primarily from the eight secondary vocational schools, where they will have been exposed to some basic craft practice in one or other of the City and Guilds courses. Follow-ing the escalation of schooling credentials widespread in the formal sector, this group which used to be apprenticed at Standard VIII, then at forms II and III, will from now be almost entirely form IV leavers. They will proceed to some of the public corporations and to the larger, mostly British owned, companies in the field of construction, engineering and automobile maintenance. The number formally registered in any one year has not recently been much above a hundred, although it is hoped that the levy/grant system will substantially raise the figure.[4] Parallel with current British practice, this little group have formal contracts of apprenticeship drawn up and lodged with the Ministry of Labour, wages are laid down industry by industry, and the employers' obligations to instruct and provide training facilities and release are insisted upon. There is in practice some gap between the best paid apprentice who with, say, Construction Equipment will be getting £42 a month in his fourth year and others who will start at about the rate of the minimum wage of £7 to £8. All however, are paid, and can protest to their ministry if the training component appears inadequate. All expect to rise rather swiftly in the years immediately following the completion of their time.[5]

By contrast, with this increasingly formalised structure, there is the main body of apprentices in Kenya who illegally pay for their training after primary school, but in the process provide an essential input to their very undercapitalised masters. It is not being suggested that for most of the roadside sector the training fees are necessary to understanding the economics of informal small scale industries. There is such a range of fees and of organisation that no generalisation of this sort is really feasible. In some of the larger concerns the importance of the fee has meant that production and training can be very profitably combined. Peter Training School in Machakos, for instance, accepts apprentice fees from 20 young people every second year, and gives instruction on the job in tinsmithing [K.I.E., n.d., pp. 90–91]. The precise fees levied by this production unit are not known, but in general tinsmithing trainees pay between £3 and £20 depending on diversity of operations learnt. Even so, the value of fee capital from the trainees could be considerable, especially when it is necessary to obtain a large consignment of scrap metal from Nairobi at any time. However, in the more expensive trades like automobile mechanic, the temptation of the fees (which range from £15 to £50 depending on the size and location of the industry) can lead to the exploitation of the training function displacing the productive element in importance. For example, one roadside panelbeater who has been operating out of a vacant lot in Nairobi for several years, discussed his plans to expand dramatically his training function from his present 8 apprentices to batches of 40 who would move through his hands in six month courses.

The stage beyond this is when the entrepreneur actually crosses into the formal sector, describes his premises with garage attached as a technical college, and levies on his trainee students up to £80 a year if they are boarding. In terms of value for money, what students receive from some of these institutions is clearly inferior to straight apprenticeship in the informal sector. They do however point to a demand even in the remoter areas of Kenya to get access to a marketable skill. Indeed, the majority of the trainees in such colleges are migrants from up country Kenya or neighbouring Tanzania where the roadside fabricating apprenticeship has not yet penetrated. Lacking government technical facilities in their home areas, or relatives with whom they can board in Nairobi, they respond to the advertising of the private technical academies:

> We are among the First Kenya Schools to introduce this system of Education which presently provides technical training opportunities to students in Secondary Schools. What is one's hope nowadays in the Continent of Africa without a technical qualification? (*University Central Academy, 1972*)

As soon as there is this transition into the formal sector, the fees become much higher, and are related to specific terms and years of study; the courses too make much of being geared towards the government trade tests. With the smaller fabricator and his group of trainees, by contrast, the fee is for the length of time it takes the individual student to master the skill, the bright student being expected to serve his time in a few months and the slower student up to a year or more. In addition, the fee is not fixed; a relationship through kin or friendship can reduce it substantially or dispense with it altogether; and there are a number of differences depending on whether the trainee decides to ask for shelter or not. In exchange for this sum, the trainee usually receives morning tea and lunch, and in Nairobi is often given a shilling for transport, if he is not actually sleeping on the site. As will be seen shortly, the system is rather different in the rural areas proper, which has important implications for the spread of this phenomenon more widely.

This informal apprenticeship is, then, in complete contradiction to the spirit of the government system. Moreover, it suffers from some of the same occasional harassment that other informal operations in Kenya encounter [*ILO, 1972, pp. 226–7*]. Labour officers can make a lot of trouble or expense for masters who are thought to be receiving fee-money and paying no wages to those who are learning to work. Paradoxically, this government concern that people be either formally employed or formally apprenticed has led some roadside operators to prefer school children (like Britain's old 'half-timers') who can then produce evidence that they are not really unpaid labour but just off school for a day or two. But the situation where the conflict between the two modes of training has become most clear cut is with the Indian skilled class. No longer impeded by the restrictions of the caste-like colonial society, many of this community's craftsmen have moved out of employment into running their own engineering companies, automotive workshops and other precision industries. They have become in the process much less possessive of some of the skills that they once deliberately guarded from their African employees or fellow workers. At the very point, however, when large numbers of African parents, aware of this, are trying to arrange for their sons to be taken on at a fee in such Indian concerns, the regulations about what constitutes apprenticeship have made it very unlikely that there will be an Indian-African skill transfer through the same medium as has been described above. Admittedly, a number of the operators who were interviewed had been trained by Indians in the same fee-paying system, but without any food, shelter or transport. And it was not uncommon during the 1960s for Africans who agreed to such an arrangement to sign a lawyer's letter to the effect that they were receiving wages of so many pounds (even though they were getting nothing). This proved, however, to be not a very effective protection against some of the labour inspectors and trade union officials, and once a few Indian firms had been prosecuted and forced to pay several thousand shillings of back pay to their one-time apprentices, there was a general reluctance to become involved further in this fee-paying training. In fact, in a brief survey of the small Indian workshops in one area of Nairobi, only two or three were found who were prepared to risk becoming skill models in the way that the Africans had developed into an accepted pattern, on the waste lots nearby.

It might seem inappropriate to berate government harassment of this indigenous system, particularly when the Ministry of Labour is trying through its new levy/grant system to promote British style apprentice arrangements amongst certain Indian companies.[6] There are, however, perhaps two justifications for criticism: the first, that the transplant is being attempted without any very clear understanding of how people are used to acquiring new skills in the Indian and African sectors; secondly, there seems no evidence that those who undertake fee-paying apprenticeships are prepared to be used as cheap labour. Indeed, there is rather less likelihood of this in the informal sector than there is with the formal time-bound apprentice contract of the government. As there is no codification in the informal world, but only the axiom that apprentices should go at their own pace, there is no possibility of maintaining for a long period a workshop with a very high ratio of trainees to journeymen. This, incidentally, seems to mark off Kenya's style of informal apprenticeship from that described by Callaway in 1964 for Nigeria, where it appeared that the contractual element was very much more significant [*Callaway, 1964, pp. 62–79*].

The most obvious feature of the system is the determination of those under training to move as rapidly as possible to establishing their own little workshop or industry. Very often the brightest trainees are absorbed within a month or two into a co-operative arrangement with their former masters. They may begin to do a little work on a contract basis, but as soon as they see how much their master gets from a single job in, say, panel-beating, they will either ask to become one of the qualified helpers in the company and share its profits, or will, after accumulating sufficient capital from piece-work or contracts, set up on their own. Within a few months, therefore, in exceptional cases, the former trainee has his own apprentices. In addition, many of the older masters seem very aware of the number of people who have gone through their hands, and are able to identify with some pride precisely where their former pupils are now operating their own businesses. At the moment the system seems so open to the enterprising that there is probably little objection felt amongst participants to the premium payments. (The few masters who were asked about this pointed out that Kenyatta himself had said after detention that free things got finished a long time ago!)

It may be useful at this point to sketch in some of the characteristics of the apprenticeship group of young people, especially as this may help to clarify some of the issues about the origins of the self-employed, and the profitability of the enterprises in which they get engaged. It should however be mentioned that because of the very uncertain status of both masters and their trainees in government eyes, it is not possible to administer anything resembling a structured series of questions. Nevertheless, such has been the concern amongst (predominantly Western) social scientists during the 1960s about un- and underemployment of school leavers that this particular example of small scale dynamic self-employment should be looked at closely. Admittedly, by the 1970s, research interest had begun to abandon the primary school leaver in favour of the allegedly more political form IV students; the younger leavers, it was assumed, were ready to accept any sort of job at all, now that all hope of 'modern' sector employment had passed them by. It was discovered that this vast group of young people were peacefully adjusting their aspirations to the realities of low income and poverty; they were not even determined to migrate and remain in the towns to the extent that it was once feared was inevitable.[7]

There is clearly some truth in this conventional picture of the cooling out of the standard seven leaver, as he competes to grasp in the 1970s the sort of openings that his preceding cohorts despised in the late '50s: shoe shiner, *shamba*-boy, spanner-boy, day-labourer on the building sites, tea and coffee picker. It does not however adequately cover the self-employed producers—many of whom see themselves training for a situation where they will easily outstrip the remuneration of a government clerk. In a number of cases, contrary to expectation, the trainees or their master had come to the informal sector of the economy not because they could not obtain a position in the enumerated sector, but because the jobs they had in the modern sector had insufficient pay and prospects. Often such a distinction is drawn between the wage-and-salary sector and the unenumerated that it is assumed that any job in the former is worth retaining for its security and steady income. The reality is that there is a great deal of restless movement in the bottom reaches of the 'modern' sector as people search out an income above £8 a month. Several claim that once they had set up on their own, they found they could make more in a day that they had previously made in the month, while avoiding most of the former expenses and overheads. Whatever the reality of their earnings may be, most artisans or their trainees have a fierce determination not to be employed again.

Many however clearly do measure up to the model of a cooling out of their earlier aspirations. They will have spent some time approaching the few relations or contacts they have in the city centres, and are then faced with one of several possibilities. Money may finally be extracted for one final course in, say, accountancy or book-keeping in one of the myriad of private urban schools or colleges. Others will take a temporary job to enable them to search further for what they feel appropriate, and gradually the temporary job may become permanent. It is always possible also to take labouring jobs on a daily basis, particularly on construction sites, or working for some of the rapidly growing small African contractors. Many undertake such *kibarua* work (as it is called) in rather the same way that their great grandfathers first worked for the whites—on a target basis. They may work for a week at the daily rate of 5/- to 6/- in the towns, or 3/- to 4/50 in the rural areas, and then have enough to travel home to their family, or to buy a particular item of dress. In such work, they are increasingly being joined, in Nairobi at least, by form II and form IV leavers, the latter scrupulously not disclosing their educational qualifications, and working as far away as possible from the area in which they have their room and friends. [8]

It seems hard, however, to generalise on the rather motley group that finally approach some of the older skilled men, and ask to be shown how to do bicycle repair, carpentry, automobile maintenance, amongst many others. Some may be the first of their family to go into these modern trades, others appear to be continuing the older tradition (amongst certain tribes) of families concentrating on one particular skill. Indeed, what was in the precolonial period a rather restricted category of blacksmith families and woodworkers may well become more common over the next few decades. Already there is some evidence that all the male children in certain roadside operator families are following the same skill as their father. This is in some way an insurance against the future—just as primary school children have begun on their own to combine schoolwork with, say, tinsmithing and the clothes trade, where light fingers are at a premium.

It would appear that the marriage of the traditional to the modern skill, which is a feature of the Yoruba apprentice system, is really rather a rarity in East Africa. However, there are one or two quite notable examples of where a traditional craft skill has taken new shape in the informal sector. Thus in one of the families interviewed, the grandfather had been of the Kikuyu *muturi* clan of blacksmiths; the father had a substantial workshop in Kiambu District with some 38 hand-operated machines, making fence-post nails, bolts and ladles, and designing his own machines. One of the sons was operating in the open on one of Nairobi's wastelands, producing the cheapest bicycle carriers and bicycle foreguards (front wheel strengtheners) in the country. He too had a whole range of hand-operated machines for metal pressing and cutting which he had designed himself, and like his father had a mixture of trainees and qualified helpers. Amongst these were standard VII workers, and also a form IV Kamba and a form IV Maasai boy. Unlike the restricted market of his grandfather, he was producing within the informal sector large orders of goods for different parts of the country. His team could make 20 dozen foreguards per day, and up to 10 dozen of the metal carriers. Far from the conventional picture of informal sector stagnation and petty trade, this team of smiths and metal workers had just returned from a promotion trip to Kisumu, 200 miles away, and had come back with orders for 35 dozen carriers and 25 dozen bicycle stands.

The more common pattern however is to approach a friend, or an acquaintance of the family who has been following a trade for some time, who is usually a man of the same tribe, but by no means always so in Nairobi. In many cases the result is that, in order to gain their skill, the younger and more schooled are actually going to craftsmen who are frequently illiterate. In turn, these older men tend to be those who gained their skill from the Indians during the 1940s and '50s. Strictly speaking, this first generation of older *fundis* who became the source thereafter of informal sector skills did not so much learn from the Indians as extract the craft secrets for themselves. They describe a situation where at that time they were employed as sweepers or simple cutters of metal, but gradually they found out the secrets of soldering and welding which were often carried on by the Indians in another room. This was in fact merely the Indian strategy for survival at that time, analogous to the white farmers' ban on African coffee and pyrethrum production. Once the skill had been thus acquired, there seems to have been little objection with the new cohort of African masters to making training open to all who might apply (and pay). The Indian tradition of father to son transfer has certainly not yet become the predominant pattern.

Taken as a group, the trainees and their models are largely drawn from the poorer strata of society (though not the poorest), and they are primarily the Mount Kenya peoples—Embu, Meru and particularly Kikuyu. The diffusion of specific skills amongst African craftsmen is still of sufficiently recent origin that it is possible to trace, say, the making of wick lamps (from soldered tins) to an identifiable group of Embu who gained the secret from Indians in the 1940s. The Kikuyu themselves may attempt to explain their own pre-eminence in these roadside areas by stereotyping most other tribes as not wanting to dirty their hands (frequently alleged of the Luo). It is more adequately explained however by a cluster of historical factors— still allowing for the place of a trading tradition amongst many Kikuyu. First, many Kikuyu were forced into various sorts of informal sector activity during the Emergency, when many of the government and company jobs were suddenly closed to them for security reasons. Secondly, as Nairobi is very much the county town of the Kikuyu, they can operate with a head-start the network of trade-offs and connections that some informal sector activity requires. It is not in fact easy to set up as a solitary independent producer in this arena any more than it is in the modern sector, since scrap wood and metal have to be obtained through the various link men in the garages and factories from where they are principally derived. This necessitates cordial relations with suppliers who legally and illegally sell the scrap to the hand-cart operators and other delivery men, and also with the transporters and retailers up country. Finally, as Nairobi is the only really large, scrap-producing centre, its major group of inhabitants had an immediate advantage, if they chose to exploit it. However, as the informal sector is very much the satellite of the modern industrial area, some account does need to be taken of the personal and material linkages between the two sectors by any planners concerned to promote rural or urban industries in another context.

It is difficult to estimate to what extent this diverse group sees itself as set apart from the industrial mainstream. There is admittedly a tendency for operators within it to stress that only those prepared to work hard and long in dirty conditions need think of entering apprenticeship. A number of the owners actually share with their European and Indian counterparts in the 'modern' sector precisely their contempt for the secondary school boy as someone who will be unable to accommodate himself to the work. It is assumed by all three that his education will have unfitted him for hard labour in exacting conditions, even though, increasingly, poor secondary school leavers are turning to this type of training. Amongst the majority of secondary school boys, however, it is still regarded as something of a joke to find one of their classmates translated into a self-employed carpenter ('doing what he shouldn't be doing' in popular parlance). However, despite the disadvantages of working without access to piped water, electricity or shelter from rain and mud, it seems difficult to conceive of the informal artisans as a race hammered apart, in the same way as the hard core squatters have been made to feel. For one thing, while it remains true that the informal sector aims its products principally at the low income African market, some of its wares cannot be distinguished from 'modern' sector artifacts. Cars that have been spray-painted or been panel beaten in a vacant lot only differ substantially from Indian garage work-manship in price—the informal operators nearly always having initially learnt their skill from the Indians. Similarly the wardrobes and kitchen furniture that are made under makeshift shelters of polythene duplicate the products of some formal operators. In fact, there are very few items that can be considered informal sector products exclusively, since scrap materials are widely used by artisans who have moved into premises and to that extent have become formalised. Furthermore, the majority of the roadside operators aspire to get formal workshop premises (at the moment in very short supply in Nairobi), and probably do not see themselves as different in kind from those, more successful, who have managed to rent or buy accommodation already. Whether looked at from the angle of materials, product, premises or apprenticeship, the attempt to separate very rigorously formal from informal appears as rather an academic exercise.

To many planners, however, a critical question must be how widely these simple industrial techniques seem likely to spread within Kenya—whether a mode of production that can apparently thrive without shelter or official interest can be duplicated elsewhere. It has been shown that large numbers of trainees are being turned into quite adequate artisans. Can these be expected to use their skills in the rural areas? Here there are two facets of diffusion to be discussed, the first being the readiness of people to buy the products of the informal sector, and the second being the readiness of the producers to transfer to the smaller townships and villages.

As far as product and services diffusion are concerned, it is not easy to generalise when there is such a range of cheap and expensive goods made in the informal sector. It is interesting to observe that some of those goods for which there is an almost insatiable demand from the rural areas and from neighbouring countries are originally Indian artifacts such as char-coal burning braziers made from scrap iron, wick lamps, and *kerais* (shallow metal cooking bowls). Whole strings of the wick lamps are for instance exported to as far afield as Zambia from the Nairobi centre;

similarly it is very common to see the tops of country buses festooned with braziers and other informal sector products. It does however say something about the complexities of promoting intermediate technology as a policy, that of all the centres where Indians have been concentrated in East and Central Africa, only Nairobi seems to have adopted products once made for Indian domestic consumption, on a large scale. There is the additional difficulty, on the promotion side, that although informal sector products are now receiving the attention of economists for their employment poten- tial (through their labour intensity), it should be realised that the informal sphere is very much a satellite of the large scale firms or of some of the products they import at first hand; appropriate technology in the informal sector may be derived from inappropriate technology and import patterns in the 'modern' sector.

Let us take an example. Kenya's policy on the importation of cars is frequently criticised now as being to *laissez-faire*, it being considered in- appropriate that so much foreign exchange should go on the purchase of cars for the still rather small local and foreign elite. On the other hand, the informal metal working industry is directly dependent on the detritus from the modern car industry for much of its own dynamism. The vast numbers of motor oil cans collected daily from Nairobi petrol stations provide the informal sector with the most satisfactory supply of cans for the making of soldered wick lamps. Bought at approximately 5/- or less per hundred from the petrol stations, they are converted often the same day into lamps that retail at 40cts in the towns and 50cts up country. Additionally, oil and petrol drums and much of the car body is central to the fabrication of the charcoal braziers which retail at 4/- to 5/-. Even the bedmaking industry— which is one of the fastest growing on the carpentry side—is dependent for all its springing on the availability of second hand tyres, from which the long criss cross strips can be cut. The car therefore makes a rather impor- tant contribution to the informal sector products, quite apart from the numbers of mechanics and panel beaters who keep cars, buses and lorries on the road long after they would have been scrapped in the West. Any decision such as that of Tanzania recently, to restrict radically the import of new cars could well alter patterns of production amongst the various informal ancillary industries. A similar point could be made about the industries which operate largely with the wood derived from packing cases and crates.

There are a series of problems when it comes to considering the spread of the actual craftsmen into the rural areas. Some of these can only be touched upon, but they do highlight the difficulty of surmounting urban- rural imbalance even in the informal sector. Initially, of course, it has to be admitted that the market for informal sector goods, though vast and largely untapped, is determined to a considerable extent by the state of agricultural incomes, and can therefore be sluggish in taking up even cheap innovations quite close to Nairobi. The craftsmen who do however decide to practice in their home area (after acquiring the skill usually in Nairobi) are naturally attracted by the idea of being one of the few or often the only such in the village or small town. It became clear however, from conversation with some who had taken this step, or who had taken it and then returned to practising in Nairobi, that there really are quite substantial difficulties in operating outside the metropolis. First there is the task of obtaining scrap materials from Nairobi. The road system is now very adequate to the majority of small trade centres in Central Province at least, but even this is a mixed blessing for the young entrepreneur; the very multiplicity of country buses, and the tendency for most rural families to have two households, one of these in Nairobi, means that it is very often easier to buy beds, chests, braziers from amongst the much greater variety of Nairobi and send them up on the bus. Quality also is still very much better in Nairobi than in the smaller market centres.

Secondly, the would-be rural entrepreneur cannot take advantage of the apprentice system to the same extent as his urban counterpart. He often, especially at the village level, does not have sufficient work to justify keeping an apprentice, and as it is not customary to sack or send off apprentices for lack of work, they would have to be maintained during periods of slack.By contrast, daily paid labour can be taken on and dropped as the occasion arises. In fact at the very lowest level of the village carpenter or tinsmith, apprenticeship is often not a feasible proposition. Many of the craftsmen combine their craft with agriculture, and only make one-off goods to order. At the level of the larger district towns like Murang'a and Thika and Kiambu, apprenticing is much more common, but the fees tend to be higher than Nairobi. Trainee metal workers can be charged up to £15 in Murang'a compared with £5 to £7 in Nairobi. Mechanics, too, in Thika can be charged up to £40 or £50—very much more than their Nairobi counterparts. The result is that many intending apprentices who have Nairobi contacts will prefer to acquire their training there. For one thing, they will learn a much wider range of skills through urban apprenticeship than by attending a master who is restricted by limited rural demand and lack of materials.

Thirdly, a number of artisans gave the definite impression that they are much more troubled over licensing in the rural areas than if they were set up on one of the large vacant lots in Nairobi. There the City Council do not attempt to enforce licensing upon sections of the carpenters and scrap metal workers; but it is impossible to avoid it in many rural townships. Why this should be so is not clear, but is one of the many anomalies of the licensing regulations which could be reconsidered in the post colonial situation.

Nevertheless, despite the attractions of Nairobi for migrant apprentices, the informal fabrication sector is very much on the increase in townships like Nyeri, Thika and Murang'a. Quite rapidly they have become self-sufficient in certain informal sector goods and may in turn begin to supplant Nairobi in supplying the smaller villages around them.

It is also apparent that there is a very definite innovative strain in much of the production in the informal sector, contrary to the usual picture of its doing second-hand things in a second-rate way. Any single item such as the wick lamp can be shown to have had several variations and improvements made in it in the period since it was wholly taken over from the

Indian *fundi*. It is, for example, less of a fire risk and more easily adjusted than it was before. Similarly, with the bent wood garden furniture industry that started in the Nairobi suburb of Banana Hill in 1956, there has been spatial spread through the ten ex-apprentices and also a diversity of styles and techniques. The inventiveness and skills of the blacksmith family, already mentioned, are perhaps of a different order. Their ability to design hand operated machines (and sell some of them) places them in a category of their own, between the remaining Indian precision metal-working shops and the vast crowd of informal operators using hand tools only. The particularity of their position does however focus on the issue of how the considerable skill reserve of the Indian workshop can be transferred to the more successful of the informal artisans, who have begun to move into premises. Having long since abandoned to the African some of the products that have been described, it still remains to be seen whether any Africanisation policy can be sensitively enough designed to encourage training in precision skills.

The whole engineering industry (Indian and European) will shortly have a levy/grant principle applied to it, in the hope of extracting more rigorous training and an increased number of apprentices. But these will be apprentices of the official form IV type, who will have to be paid for their learning period at rates far beyond those current for learners in the smaller workshops. The result will probably be that many small Indian firms choose to regard the levy as a tax and simply pay it, rather than take on a type of trainee worker that is paid and trained according to a series of rigorous specifications. And the illicit paid training in the informal sector will continue as before to expand.

From a policy point of view, the priorities would seem to be the recognition that these clusters of small industries do fulfil a valuable function, scattered as they are through 10 or 11 semi-permanent sites in Nairobi alone, and in many others in the district townships. It would be important to acknowledge that such industries will want to continue being located close to both the low income African markets and the town's major 'modern' sector, if any. In some such locations, many operators would clearly be interested in the provision of basic facilities through site and service arrangements, and would be prepared to build appropriate structures for their trade, where now the construction of anything resembling a more than makeshift shelter is thought likely—at least in Nairobi—to provoke the attention of the local authorities.

As far as the present fee-paying element of apprenticeship is concerned, there seems little ground for indignant attempts at eradication. It does of course mean that apprentices are not drawn from the most indigent households, just as the previous British system of apprentice premiums discriminated against the lowest income levels. Similarly, young people who lack extended family connections cannot afford not to be paid a wage. At the moment this appears to be much more true of the rural areas, where money is much tighter, than in the cities. But even so, the Kenya informal apprenticeship does not mean foregoing real wages for the five to seven year period that was the norm in Britain until relatively recently; it can be as little as two months in some skills and not much above a year in others.

Over the last ten years and more, a system has grown up almost entirely unnoticed by educationalists and government, which has quietly been producing hundreds of artisans yearly with basic craft skills. Most important, the bulk of the group in their anxiety to be self-employed have paid little attention to the system of government trade tests (Grade III to Grade I) which are the decisive factor in assessing salary for the government's technical departments and the larger firms. They share with the Indian artisans a healthy disregard for paper qualifications and schooling credentials; they are aware that grade tests in many cases can actually be 'purchased', but know for all this that grades are irrelevant in a situation where the hardest worker makes the most money. Like the Indians, they say of a skilled colleague: he's illiterate, unqualified, but equivalent to Grade I. Over against this ungraded sector with its very low training costs, there is a counter ideology (or myth) spreading throughout the country that there is still a vast reservoir of intermediate and higher level wage and salary technical positions waiting to be Africanised. Never until the last two years have there been so many applications for entry into some of the eight secondary vocational schools. And to provide institutions for the higher reaches of technical training (sub-university), communities have been competing to tax themselves on a scale unprecedented in the history of African self-help. Both these thrusts are directed to the hope of technical employment (rather than self-employment), and unfortunately not very much attention has been paid to the difficulties already encountered by many technical school graduates in finding a job today. Technical preparation for the formal sector employment is in fact rapidly becoming a high cost activity, and the tendency for its products will be, in Kenya as in Nigeria, to have technical 'qualifications' without industrial or workshop experience.

A case could however be made out that there is really a very limited demand, in the short term, for candidates with these higher technical aspirations. The problem is instead how to flood Kenya with people of a skill level immediately above that of the present informal sector operator. Two sources seem likely to provide this—those whose aspirations for higher technical positions become gradually adjusted downwards through unemployment, and those moving up from the present informal sector. In either case, they will require a relevant skill model and workshop experience. Thus the argument returns to the role of the Indians. Something more imaginative than the present style of government apprenticeship will have to be thought up if the Indian skill reservoir is not to be lost to Kenya completely—as recently occurred in Uganda. At the present moment, Indian co-operation in transferring some of their skills to Africans would probably require a corresponding agreement by government to allow the transfer of some Indian capital out of the country; any conventional tax relief as a quid *pro quo* for training would no longer provide adequate incentive. As to the trainees, in any such compromise, there are none more closely adjusted to the attitudes of the Indian skilled class than the informal sector Africans described in this paper. With them, some form of apprenticeship might well be then worked out which retained the dynamic character of the arrangements such Africans are now accustomed to.

NOTES

1. For example *Kenya* [*1972*]; for further discussion of these institutes, see Godfrey and Hassenkam [*1972*] and King [*1972*].

2. Preliminary discussion of the numbers engaged in informal sector activity is contained in ILO [*1972*], Technical Paper No. 3. By no means all such activity has a training function attached to it, but in the productive crafts, there are usually at least as many trainees as there are qualified men.

3. Research carried out by the writer during July-September 1972, through the assistance of a Hayter Travel Grant.

4. Approximately 115 new apprentice contracts had been registered by mid-1972.

5. In a survey of some 80 vocational school boys shortly to leave form IV, it was found that rather more than half expected to have reached the grade of foreman or assistant foreman, supervisor or assistant supervisor within 2 years.

6. For further detail on an aspect of the levy/grant operations, see King [*1973*].

7. For a useful overview of school leaver research, see Anderson [*1972*].

8. The writer has recently finished editing material on the city life of Kenya's educated school-leavers, which should be available in early 1974 under the title of *Jobless in Kenya: the Social Life of the Educated Unemployed.*

REFERENCES

Anderson, J. E., 1970, 'The Village Polytechnic Movement', Institute of Development Studies, Nairobi.

Anderson, J. E., 1972, 'The Rationality of the School leaver: Africa's Teenage Problem', in *Development Trends in Kenya*, Centre of African Studies, Edinburgh (hereafter *Developmental Trends*).

Callaway, A., 1964, 'Nigeria's Indigenous Education: the Apprentice System', *ODU*, 1:1, pp. 62–79.

Court, D., 1972, 'Dilemmas of Development: the Village Polytechnic Movement as a Shadow System of Education in Kenya', in *Developmental Trends*.

Godfrey, E. M. and Hassenkam, H., 1972, 'Technical and Vocational Education and Training in Kenya', Institute of Development Studies, Nairobi.

ILO, 1972, *Employment, Incomes and Equality*, Geneva.

Kenya: Ministry of Education, 1972, 'Analysis of Harambee Technical Institutes', mimeo.

K.I.E. (Kenya Industrial Estates Ltd.), n.d., 'Techno Economic Survey: Report of Selected Centres', Nairobi.

King, K. J., 1972, 'Some Notes on Technological Self-help in Kenya' in *Developmental Trends*.

King, K. J., 1973, 'Indian-African Skill Transfers', paper delivered to Institute of Commonwealth Studies Conference, 23rd March, London.

Sheffield, J. R. and Diejomaoh, V. P., 1971, *Non-Formal Education in African Development*.

Universal Central Academy prospectus, 1972, Thika, Kenya, mimeo.

The Relation between Tourism and Employment in Kenya and Tanzania

By Walter Elkan*

The unqualified enthusiasm of some for the development of tourism as a strategy for the development of low income countries is only matched by the equally unqualified scepticism of others. Few have felt neutral or considered the possibility that its effects might depend on the country concerned or the type of tourist development to be undertaken. This paper, based on a survey of employment in the hotel and tourist industries of Kenya and Tanzania, begins with an exposition of the general case for and against tourism as a way of promoting the development of low income countries, and then presents some of the findings of the East African survey. It pleads the case for less generalization and a more eclectic approach to an assessment of the costs and benefits of tourism and points out that, as is so often the case, the balance of advantage is greatly dependent upon the policies pursued with regard to the particular form of hotel and tourist development.

Supporters of tourist development have been particularly impressed by its potential to create employment. It has come to be accepted that the development of manufacturing industry of the type that uses much power driven machinery may contribute substantially to the growth of GDP or total output, but that it creates very little employment. Since income from employment is the principal means by which the benefits of industrialization are likely to be spread, the lack of much additional employment is now seen by many as a serious shortcoming of the kind of industrial policy that has been pursued by African countries in the last decade or two.

Tourist development has seemed much more promising. Not only does it earn foreign exchange but, above all, being a service industry it was regarded as intrinsically more labour intensive, to provide more employment and therefore to be more efficient in spreading the benefits of development around. There would be much employment in the hotels. In addition, the tourists' spending would create further income earning opportunities outside the hotels—they would want taxis, entertainment, hand-made curios, guides, restaurants, travel agencies and so forth. The building of the hotels would also provide much employment, since the

---

*Walter Elkan is Professor of Economics at the University of Durham and was Visiting Research Professor at the Institute for Development Studies, University of Nairobi in 1972–73. An earlier version of this paper was presented to a Seminar on Tourism at the Centre of African Studies, University of Edinburgh. He is grateful, especially to Henry Ord, for critical comments at that time.

construction industry is also labour intensive. Finally, tourism was expected to generate additional demand for food and as agriculture, too, tends to be labour intensive, this would further spread the benefits of tourism in ways that manufacturing did not [*Dag Hammerskjold Foundation, 1969; Popovic, 1972; World Council of Churches, 1970*].

There is evidence from Kenya and Tanzania, where I undertook a tourist employment survey last year, that all these things have indeed happened though in very varying degrees according to locality. In general, they have happened much more in Kenya than in Tanzania, and within Kenya there have been marked differences between Nairobi and the Coast or, looked at differently, between the type of hotel established. East Africa's experience points to some lessons for an optimal development strategy to which we shall return at the conclusion of this paper.

Before presenting a summary of the findings, something needs to be said about the case *against* tourist development as it is most commonly put. First, it is argued that the advocates of tourism point only to the foreign exchange which tourists bring to the country and forget to allow properly not only for the imported materials and furnishings that go into the new hotels, but also for the imported food, sun-tan lotions, film, food and liquor on which tourists spend part of what they bring into the country. Further, it is argued, that since much tourism is of the package variety, the operators and foreign airlines often skim off the greater part of the sum that tourists actually pay to come. Lastly, tourism is said to have adverse cultural and social effects; it is said to be distasteful to bring the very rich into countries that are very poor. The former's affluence makes the poverty of the latter the more galling, and to generate material ambitions that are totally out of their reach. A tactless dispensation of largesse is said to be corrupting, and corrosive of established society so that, for example, the one-time proud Masai now demean themselves to selling trinkets and begging for sweets. And of course it encourages prostitution.

Each of these 'adverse' effects is certainly to be found somewhere in the world, though it is improbable that there is a coincidence of all of them in any one place. For example, Bryden [*1973*] is probably right about the adverse balance of payments effects in the Caribbean but would be quite wrong, as Mitchell has shown, if he were to apply his findings to Kenya [*Mitchell, 1968, 1970*]. Whether having poor waiters serve rich tourists is to be deplored, is largely a matter of personal judgment.

Turning now to the survey, this was carried out by means of a postal questionnaire followed up by personal visits wherever possible if the questionnaires had not been returned by a certain date. Forms were sent to all known hotels and lodges and also to a small number of restaurants in Nairobi which were known to cater for tourists. A different form was sent to all tour operators, travel agents, car hire firms, safari outfitters and airline offices. The principal aim was to elicit information about the numbers employed in different occupations, to estimate the total wages bill, and to provide an idea of the numbers of non-Africans engaged in the industry. Since the object of the survey was also to assess the need for training, questions were included to this end and especially questions designed to help in estimating the probable expansion of employment in the different occupations.

The survey was in one sense very restricted. No attempt was made to measure the total impact of tourism on employment, let alone on other forms of income earning opportunities. Consequently, there is no estimate of employment in the Ministries of Tourism or the Game Departments, or in the construction industry. Nor are the incomes earned by taxis, guides or curio sellers estimated. Since there were already *guess*timates galore concerning tourism, it was thought more useful to concentrate on those activities about which it might be possible to get some 'hard data' without having to resort to guesswork.

The results were encouraging: in Kenya, the rate of response from hotels and lodges was such as to account for 90 per cent of all beds—only 3 out of 128 failed to respond, and 70 out of 86 tour operators etc. responded. In Tanzania, where tourism is on a much smaller scale except in the Game Parks which are contiguous with Kenya and generally visited by tourists who come initially to Kenya, 35 hotel establishments out of a total of 90 failed to respond, but 10 of these were described as guesthouses and at most 2 or 3 of the remainder would ever be visited by tourists. In the case of the tour operators, etc., we had only a 60 per cent rate. The 2 surveys will henceforth be, somewhat misleadingly, referred to as the 'hotel' and 'tourist' survey respectively.

TABLE 1

HOTEL: EMPLOYMENT BY TYPE AND LOCATION OF ESTABLISHMENT

| Type/Location | No. of Hotels | No. of Beds | Beds per Hotel | Employment | | | Employees per bed |
				Male	Female	Total	
Kenya							
Nairobi Hotels	31	3,556	114	3,021	181	3,202	0·9
Nairobi Clubs	3	274	91	260	15	275	1·0
Nairobi Restaurants	7	—	—	156	13	169	—
Wildlife and Scenic	25	1,517	60	1,528	63	1,591	1·0
Business Hotels	12	570	48	356	19	375	0·7
Coast Hotels	37	4,700	127	3,236	123	3,359	0·7
	115	10,617	92	8,557	414	8,911	0·84
Tanzania							
Dar-es-Salaam	22	2,363	107	1,877	115	1,992	0·8
Arusha-Moshi	12	716	60	422	62	484	0·7
Wildlife and Scenic	12	1,140	95	855	11	866	0·8
Rest of Country	10	272	27	187	9	196	0·7
	56	4,491	80	3,341	197	3,538	0·80

Table 1 presents the basic findings of the hotel survey and relates the figures of employment to the number of beds. It shows that in Kenya there were some 9,000 employees in 115 establishments, whilst in Tanzania much less than half that number were employed in 56 hotels. In both countries, the overwhelming majority were men. The ratio of ·8 employees per bed was the same in both countries, but with a rather higher variance in Kenya than in Tanzania.

The number shown by the 'tourist' survey to be employed by tour operators, etc., as shown in Table 2 is much smaller, especially in Tanzania, and even in Kenya, where this side is much more highly developed, it adds only 2,000, making a total there of some 11,000 directly employed by the hotel and tourist industry. When one remembers that total enumerated employment in Kenya is about 700,000 and in Tanzania at most 400,000, it becomes at once apparent that tourism is not quite so important in relation to total employment as might have been supposed, even if one doubled or trebled the numbers to take account of its indirect and multiplier effects.

TABLE 2

EMPLOYMENT IN THE TOURIST SERVICE TRADES

	No. of Firms	Male	Female	Total
Kenya				
Tour Operators	36	1,091	182	1,273
Travel Agents	8	52	19	71
Car Hire Firms	6	193	16	209
Airline Offices	11	128	44	172
Hunting Firms	9	279	26	305
Total	70	1,743	287	2,030
Tanzania				
Tour Operators	13	219	34	253
Travel Agents	8	39	5	44
Car Hire Firms	3	35	1	36
Airline Offices	10	46	12	58
Total	34	339	52	391

It is, however, perhaps more relevant to draw comparisons, not with total enumerated ('formal', 'modern sector') employment, but with employment in manufacturing industry. In Kenya, this was provisionally given as 72·9 thousand in 1972 (including repairs), and in Tanzania in 1969, and evidently using a broader definition, as 40·3 thousand [*Kenya, 1973, p.135; Tanzania, 1970–1, p.141*]. In relation to *these* totals, tourism is clearly a more important provider of jobs.

This comparison then naturally leads to the question of what it costs to provide jobs in tourism on one hand and in manufacturing on the other.

The response to questions which were included in the survey about the cost of construction and furnishing the hotels was too erratic and unreliable to be used. Instead, we obtained information from the Kenya Tourist Development Corporation concerning the initial capital outlay on 20 hotels and lodges recently established or under construction and are able to compare this with the figures quoted in the Little Report for Tanzania [*Little, 1973*]. The capital outlay figures have been translated into 'cost per bed' and then converted into 'cost per workplace' by using the previously arrived at average coefficient of ·8 employees per bed. The results are presented in Table 3.

TABLE 3

COST PER WORKPLACE: KENYA AND TANZANIA

	No. of Hotels	No. of Beds	Average No. of Beds per Hotel	Cost per bed	Cost per Workplace
Kenya				£	£
Nairobi	5	1,968	394	3,343	4,179
Game Lodges	9	831	92	2,111	2,638
Coast	6	1,064	177	1,761	2,201
All Hotels	20	3,863	193	2,642	3,304
Manufacturing and Repair					1,233
Tanzania					
City Hotels				3,800	4,750
Game Lodges				3,100	3,875
Beach Hotels (Medium)				2,500	3,125

SOURCE: Information provided by the Kenya Tourist Development Corporation; Kenya [*1972*] and Little [*1973*].

The Kenya and Tanzania figures are not really comparable as the former are 'actual' figures whilst those relating to Tanzania are estimates to be used for planning a programme of hotel expansion and may prove to be wrong.

But in both cases, the order of cost per bed is the same, lowest at the Coast and highest in the cities where, in general, more expensive building materials and methods of construction have to be used. But cost is also in part a function of the size of hotels and the higher cost in Nairobi is partly explained by the greater size of the hotels although, taking the two largest, the difference between the cost per bed exceeded 100 per cent.

Table 4 analyses the cost per bed of the 20 Kenyan hotels by the size of hotel and shows clearly that the larger the hotel, the greater the cost per bed which leads equally clearly to the policy implication that if one is trying to maximize hotel employment from given outlays of capital expenditure, it is better to go for small hotels.

TABLE 4

COST PER BED IN 20 KENYA HOTELS BY SIZE OF HOTEL

No. of beds	No. of hotels	Average cost per bed
		£
Less than 100	3	1,295
100–199	10	2,253
200–299	4	2,320
300 or more	3	3,389

SOURCES: As for Table 3
NOTE: The three largest hotels are all in Nairobi

It needs of course to be stressed that these 'costs per workplace' only relate to the employment directly created in the running of the hotels. They take no account of employment created in the building of hotels, or in the manifold ancillary activities which tourism creates. The more tourists there are, the more people will be employed in travel agencies or as taxi drivers, curio dealers and, still more indirectly, in agriculture, breweries and bottling plants.

For Kenya, we computed comparable figures of cost per workplace in that sector of the economy which the official statistics of GDP and employment describe as 'Manufacturing and Repair'. We did so very crudely by relating the increase in employment in that sector between 1970 and 1971 to that sector's gross capital formation in current prices in 1970, as shown in the *Economic Survey* of 1972.

If these figures are to be believed, then it would seem that the hotel industry is more capital intensive than is usually supposed. The average cost of establishing one workplace in a hotel is K£4,179, compared with an average of K£1,233 for the component of GDP described as Manufacturing and Repair. Too much should not be read into such comparisons. First, it is not at all certain that a one year lag is the right interval to choose and different intervals yield very different results.

Secondly, the ancillary activities created by the operation of hotels are probably greater than for 'manufacturing and repair'.

Thirdly, 'manufacturing' and 'repair' are really very different activities; and to have to lump them together for lack of a breakdown in the official statistics is probably greatly to understate the cost per workplace in manufacturing—the sector in which one is specifically interested. One has also to bear in mind that the cost of establishing a workplace in manufacturing contains a larger element of imports than the cost of a workplace in a hotel. Given Kenya's overvalued currency this will make the workplace in manufacturing appear relatively cheaper than would otherwise be the case.

Fourthly, it is, of course, quite wrong to assume, as has been done here, that a given increase in employment was directly attributable to capital formation in some earlier year. Employment can also increase simply because an increase in demand for goods and services calls for more workers to man the previously existing capital stock, and there is no knowing, simply by looking at such figures, how much of an increase in employment to attribute to each of these influences. Lastly, some forms of capital formation in industry have as their very object to replace labour by machines; in such a case, the effect of capital formation would in any case be to reduce employment, not to increase it.

Having entered all these reservations about the figures, it is nevertheless surprising—and quite contrary to common belief—that the cost of creating one hotel job should be apparently so much higher than in manufacturing. Only in the smallest hotels—mostly Game Lodges—are the costs at all alike.

To conclude, it needs to be stressed again that it would be wrong to draw strong inferences about the costs and benefits of tourism or even about the employment generated by tourism from so narrowly circum- scribed a survey as the one on which this paper is based. Everything, in a sense, depends upon the linkage or indirect effects created by tourism and these have been left out of account. But it is clearly possible to say *some- thing* about these indirect effects. For example, without question Kenya's tourists eat a great deal more domestically produced food than do Tanzania's. Tanzania's tourists not only eat a good deal of food that is imported, but some of these imports no longer even come from her East African Community partners but from China, whilst virtually none of the food eaten by Kenya's tourists is imported. Even Tanzania imports much less food than some of the tourist island resorts of the Caribbean so that in both Kenya and Tanzania there is less foreign exchange drain on this count than in the Caribbean. Tanzania could do a good deal more to produce 'tourist food' domestically, but the ambivalent attitude of the government to tourism is delaying the necessary measures to bring this about.

Bryden in his careful study of tourism in the Caribbean argues that public sector resources are diverted to tourism and implies that this is to the detriment of other, more socially advantageous forms of capital formation [*Bryden, 1973*]. The same argument is often heard in East Africa and especially in Tanzania. Tanzania has, however, almost gone out of her way in the development of her beach hotels to maximise the infra- structure cost of these hotels, by insisting that they be built at a safe distance from Dar-es-Salaam, where tourists would be less likely to exert an influence on the residents of the capital. Locations closer to Dar-es- Salaam would not only have economized the use of scarce resources, but would probably have made the hotels more attractive to tourists who might enjoy spending occasional evenings in Dar-es-Salaam which is a beautiful town.

This is instanced only to reinforce the general conclusion that the cost and benefits of tourism are by no means immutable, but depend on the policies chosen to promote it. The East African survey shows clearly that small hotels provide more employment for any given investment than large hotels. If it is thought that the employment effects of tourism development are its principal benefits, then it will clearly pay to pursue a strategy accordingly.

REFERENCES

Bryden, J. M., 1973, *Tourism and Development: A Case Study of the Commonwealth Carribean*, London: Cambridge University Press.

Dag Hammerskjold Foundation, Stockholm, 1969, Report of a Seminar, mimeo.

Kenya, Government of, 1972, 1973, *Ecomonic Survey*.

Little, A. D., Inc., 1973, *Tourism in Tanzania*, Consultants Report, Cambridge, Mass., 2 volumes.

Mitchell, F., 1968, *The Costs and Benefits of Tourism in Kenya*, Institute for Development Studies, University of Nairobi.

Mitchell, F., 1970, 'The Value of Tourism in East Africa', *Eastern African Economic Review*, 2: 1, June.

Popovic, V., 1972, *Tourism in Eastern Africa*, IFO Institut, Munich: Weltforum Verlag.

Tanzania, Government of, *Economic Survey and Annual Plan 1970–71*.

World Council of Churches, 1970, *Leisure Tourism: Threat and Promise*. Geneva: Report of a Conference.

Class, Caste and Community of South Indian Industrialists: An Examination of the Horatio Alger Model

By E. Wayne Nafziger*

'Unto every one which hath shall be given; and from him that hath not, even that he hath shall be taken away from him'. Luke 19: 26

Development economists have been preoccupied with the problem of increasing the size of the GNP pie to the relative neglect of the distribution of this pie. Despite the recent disenchantment with the viewpoint that all classes share in the benefits of industrial growth, empirical data on the distribution of income, business opportunity, and economic power are in short supply. This study, which focuses on the origins of manufacturing entrepreneurs in a newly industrializing city in coastal Andhra, India, offers one perspective on vertical socio-economic mobility, and the differences in economic opportunities between the privileged and underprivileged portions of the population. A highly disproportional number of the entrepreneurs (especially successful ones) are from twice-born castes and from families with a high economic status. Members of the dominant castes, leading classes, and large business houses can avert the threat of democratization, industrialization and modernization to the positions of their families by using the advantages of the past—property, influence, status and so forth—to obtain the concessions, experience, education, training, and industrial capital usually essential for successful industrial undertakings.

Much of the literature on entrepreneurship in underdeveloped countries, if not apologetics for ruthless capitalist exploitation as Baran suggests [*1957, pp. 254–257*], is a celebration of the virtues of the capitalist entrepreneur without a critical look at his class origins and monopoly advantage. To Schumpeter, entrepreneurs, whose class origins are rather varied, are heroic figures, with the dream and will to found a private kingdom, to conquer adversity, to achieve success for its own sake, and to

*Research Fellow, Technology and Development Institute (TDI), East-West Center, Honolulu, and Associate Professor of Economics, Kansas State University. Author's thanks to TDI, Andhra University, and the Fulbright Foundation; and B. Sarveswara Rao, M. Jagadeswara Rao, S. A. R. Sastri, Ben Finney, Alok Chakrabarti, and Kusum Nair.

experience the joy of creation [*1961, pp. 78–79, 93–94*]. McClelland's scheme, labelled a moral theory of entrepreneurship by one critic [*Bernstein, 1971, p.148*], preceives the efforts of the entrepreneur, in his exercise of control over production in both capitalist and socialist economies, as largely responsible for the global association between high *n* Achievement (a psychological measure of the urge to improve) and rapid economic growth. The entrepreneurial role is assumed to be characterized by moderate risk-taking as a function of skill not chance, energetic and/or novel instrumental activity, individual responsibility, inner satisfaction that arises from having done well, an interest in money primarily as a measure of achievement, and long-range planning and organizational abilities [*McClelland, 1961, pp.36–239*]. For Papanek, Pakistan's 'success' in achieving rapid industrialization can be attributed in large part to the private entrepeneur, who is frugal, hard-working, far-sighted, remarkably able, and willing to take political risks [*1967, pp. 2, 25–36, 199*].

Recent empirical studies of the socio-economic mobility of the entrepreneur have reinforced a heroic notion of the entrepreneur. Collins, Moore, and Unwalla found that most of the entrepreneurs in medium manufacturing firms in Michigan 'clearly moved a long way from the somewhat impoverished economic level of their childhoods' [*1964, p.238*]. Both Nigerian and Greek industrialists were considered highly upwardly mobile in status by two other investigators [*Harris, 1971, pp.336–337* and *Alexander, 1964, pp.80–95*]. I shall call these views of upward mobility to success in business the 'Horatio Alger model', although obviously these empirical works are far more systematic and less simplistic than the heroic fictional biographies by the nineteenth century US author. This model is consistent with the paradigm of neoclassical economics, which in its analysis of entrepreneurship tends either to abstract from considerations of conflict and political power [see *Higgins, 1968, p.227*] or to assume relatively open competition in a polity characterized by the balancing of independent interests. Below I show that the appearance of substantial upward socio-economic mobility in these three empirical studies results from the peculiar way in which the question is posed, and that the data can be interpreted as corroborating the low degree of vertical class mobility I find in the South Indian case.

A period of rapid industrial growth and economic modernization, as in India's independence era, does not remove the advantages of ascribed status, even in entrepreneurial activity in manufacturing. The traditional Indian upper classes—local rulers and administrators, landlords, and Brahmins—whose strength is a legacy of the feudal and colonial periods, have allied, and in some cases overlapped, with the capitalist, political and bureaucratic elites, most of whom originated from high-income families, to control much of the access to key business positions. Families and communities with wealth and position use the monopoly advantage resulting from ready access to capital, greater information and mobility, superior education and training, privileged access to licenses and concessions from government, and a low discount of future income, to become industrial entrepreneurs in disproportional numbers.

CONCEPTS, METHODS AND PROCEDURES

A sample of 54 manufacturing entrepreneurs in the southeastern port city of Visakhapatnam (Vizag), Andhra Pradesh was interviewed.[1] The rapidly-growing municipality of 335,045 people (1971), which has experienced an industrial boom in the post-Independence period, is located about halfway between Calcutta and Madras by rail.

Although several empirical studies have investigated the socio-economic origins of entrepreneurs in parts of India, these studies lack the data essential for comparing the origins of entrepreneurs with that of the population as a whole, and for relating socio-economic characteristics of the entrepreneurs to their success. (Nafziger [1971, pp.287–316] surveys studies of Indian entrepreneurs.) In this paper, data on the distribution of entrepreneurs by caste, and class (parental economic and occupational status) are compared with information on the population at large, and are related to the educational attainment, occupational background, entrepreneurial and managerial experience, initial capital, access to governmental assistance, and business success of the entrepreneurs. The value added of the firm and the income class of the entrepreneur are the major indicators used for business success.

To cope with the problem of identifying quantities of entrepreneurship, it is assumed that there is one unit—the entrepreneur—in each firm. He is identified as the person with the largest capital share in the enterprise [see Knight, 1961, pp.296–298]. Even though there are a large number of family enterprises in Vizag, one can readily distinguish the principal of the firm, usually the father or elder brother.

CASTE, FAMILY AND SOCIAL COMMUNITY

Entrepreneurs are classified according to caste, i.e., the ancient four-rank varna system for Hindus—Brahmin (priest), Kshatriya (warrior), Vaishya (trader), and Sudra (artisan), in addition to the 'untouchables' (or Harijans); and religion in the case of the non-Hindu population. More specific than the varna is the jati, which is still the basic kinship and social particle in a system of hierarchically arranged, locally integrated, occupationally and ritually specialized, endogamous social strata. Yet the concept of varna, recognized by the courts during the colonial period and supported by the leading castes to legitimize their status, has helped to shape social reality and is accepted by ordinary Indians as a conceptual device to understand the caste system [Gould, 1963, pp.427–438; Srinivas, 1962, pp.63, 69; Rudolph, 1967, p.119].

Caste is not an immutable system where the position of each jati is clearly fixed for all time. In the middle regions of the varna hierarchy, caste standing is at times vague and flexible. In fact, the Sudra categories range from powerful and rich jatis with a relatively high ritual status to those whose assimilation into Hinduism is only marginal. Some of the former Sudra jatis have been able to rise to a higher position in the varna hierarchy in a generation or two through Sanskritization (the adoption of the rituals of twice-born castes, Brahmins, Kshatriyas and Vaishyas) [Srinivas, 1962, pp.7–8, 42, 65].

The *Varna* model is used in most of the article, even though Sudras designate themselves by *jati*. By and large, the sample is too small to make generalizations about *jatis*. In addition, the ritual status of a caste aids in defining and identifying a person socially. Although *varna* may include a number of *jatis*, it is highly correlated with family socio-economic status and class in Vizag [*Ramana, 1970, pp.132–134, 139–140*], as well as India in general, and can with other indicators of these rankings, help in analysing social mobility. Despite the diversity of the Sudras, in the aggregate they correspond to the middle socio-economic group between twice-born castes and Harijans.

Data on the caste composition of the sample and city indicate that high Hindu castes, and Muslims were over represented among the entrepreneurs. Fifty-two per cent of the entrepreneurs (in contrast to only 11 per cent of blue-collar workers) were from twice-born Hindu castes which comprise only 26 per cent of the population of Vizag city. None of the entrepreneurs, but a disproportional share of blue-collar workers, were from low-caste background (i.e., Harijans and Protestant or Roman Catholic Christians).

TABLE 1 [2]

CASTE ORIGIN OF SAMPLE ENTREPRENEURS COMPARED TO THE POPULATION OF VIZAG

Caste	Number of entrepreneurs (Total)	Percentage of entrepreneurs (Total)	Percentage of of blue-collar workers in Vizag[a]	Percentage of population of Vizag[b]
Brahmin	11	20·36	2·22	21·45
Kshatriya	5	9·26	8·89	2·35
Vaishya	12	22·22	0·00	2·15
Sudra	15	27·78	57·78	56·86
Harijan	0	0·00	15·56	11·25
Muslim	7	12·96	6·67	1·30
Christian (Prot. & Cath.)	0	0·00	8·89	4·55
Christian (Syrian)	1	1·85	0·00	0·00[c]
Sikh	2	3·70	0·00	0·00[c]
Parsi	1	1·85	0·00	0·00[c]
Unknown	0	0·00	0·00	0·10
Total	54	99·98[d]	100·01[d]	100·00

[a]Ramana [*1970, p.137*]

[b]Ramana, [*1970, p.29*]

[c]None of the three groups are represented in the Ramana sample. Sikhs comprise 0·09 per cent and Parsis 0·01 per cent of the population of Vizag City, according to the 1961 census. Syrian Christians are not separated from Protestant and Catholic Christians in the census, but Ramana suggests that less than 1 per cent of the Christians (i.e., less than 0·05 per cent of the total population) are Syrian.

[d]May not add to 100·00 because of rounding.

If the Hindu population in Vizag is divided into high castes (twice-born castes), middle castes (Sudras) and low castes (Harijans), there is a significant positive relationship between caste ranking, on the one hand, and education, income, occupational status, and perceived class and status, on the other [Ramana, 1970, pp.130—131]. Thus, as expected, the paternal economic status of entrepreneurs from twice-born castes was significantly higher than those of Sudras[3] (see table 2). Largely as a result of this high economic status, the median initial equity capital of the firms of high-caste entrepreneurs was Rs. 60,000 (or about $8,000 at the official exchange rate), and 14 out of the 28 received the bulk of their initial capital from their families (ancestors, siblings, spouses and descendants). The median initial capital of the Sudras, on the other hand, was only Rs. 37,500, and only 5 out of the 15 acquired initial funds from their families. The median and model educational class for entrepreneurs from twice-born castes was a bachelor's degree, compared to a secondary certificate for Sudras. High caste families, with a disproportionate number of enterprises and connections with business friends, could more readily arrange management experience for their sons. Thus the median prior management experience of twice-born entrepreneurs was higher than for Sudras. Prior to the involvement in their present firms, the major previous occupation of 20 of the 28 high-caste businessmen and only 5 of the 15 Sudras involved entrepreneurial or managerial responsibility. The lesser socio-economic status, access to capital, educational achievement, entrepreneurial and management experience, and access to government [Nafziger, 1972, p.66] of Sudra businessmen was associated with a lower level of median income and a smaller median gross value-added of the firm (Table 2).

Despite the lack of low-caste entrepreneurs, there were 3 Protestants, 1 Catholic and 1 Harijan who were the top day-to-day managers of enterprises (usually on the technical rather than the sales and personnel side). This is consistent with a pattern of a relatively high predisposition by members of low-caste communities in Vizag for salaried positions with a secure tenure and a low propensity for self-employment. Ths risk of business activity is not attractive to Harijan castes, whose designation as 'backward' castes entitles them to a portion of the quota of university seats and civil service positions (even though usually at the lower echelons). In addition, Harijans and Christians are low in family income, access to capital, business experience, training, and education [Ramana, 1970, pp. 131—141, 198, 200] (despite scheduled caste legislation in recent years). Furthermore, they lack connections in high government positions, a network of relationships within the business community, and (analogous to the black supervisor of white American workers) a secure psycho-cultural acceptance of their positions of authority.

Among the Sudra jatis, only the Kammas and Naidus, each with 2·27 per cent of the population and 5·56 per cent of the entrepreneurs (i.e., 3) were as highly represented in the sample as in the population as a whole. The Kammas, a sizeable and prosperous farming caste primarily in the coastal districts of Andhra, are together with the Reddis among the

TABLE 2

SELECTED DATA ON FIRMS AND ENTREPRENEURS BY CASTE ORIGIN AND BIRTHPLACE OF THE ENTREPRENEUR

Caste/ Birth-place	Number of Entrepreneurs	Median Value added[a] of the firms	Median Income Class of the Entrepreneurs[b]	Median Employment of the Firms[c]	Economic Status of the Entrepreneurs' Father			Major Occupation of the Father of the Entrepreneur[f]		Median Initial Capital of the Entrepreneurs	Median Education of the Entrepreneurs[e]	Median Years Prior Management Experience of the Entrepreneurs[d]
					High	Med-ium	Low	Business	Non-business			
Brahmin												
A.P.	9	62,300	2,501-5,000	12	3	5	0	2	6	35,000	Bachelor's	6
Other	2	30,000	2,501-5,000	23·5	0	2	0	2	0	12,500	Bach. Mast.	7
Total	11	41,000	2,501-5,000	12	3	7	0	4	6	30,000	Bachelor's	6
Kshatriya												
A.P. (Total)	5	37,500	0- 2,500	15	1	3	0	1	3	80,000	Secondary	16
Vaishya												
A.P.	4	37,500	5,001-10,000	11	0	4	0	2	2	35,000	Secondary	3
Other	8	325,000	50,001 & above	20·5	7	1	0	8	0	425,000	Bachelor's	18·5
Total	12	105,000	50,001 & above	12	7	5	0	10	2	125,000	Some U. Bach.	13
Sudra												
A.P.	14	21,000	5,001-10,000	9	2	7	4	7	7	30,000	Secondary	3
Other	1	230,000	10,001-25,000	16	0	1	0	0	1	70,000	Some Sec.	0
Total	15	28,000	5,001-10,000	10	2	8	4	7	8	37,500	Secondary	2

Muslim										
A.P.	8,350	5,001-10,000	5	1	2	0	2	1	Secondary	2·5
Other	21,000	5,001-10,000	10	2	1	0	1	2	Secondary	7
Total	19,000	5,001-10,000	7	3	3	0	3	3	Secondary	5
Other (Sikh, Syrian Christian, Parsi) Outside A.P.										
(Total)	94,000	10,001-50,000	40	1	3	0	2	2	Bachelor's	10
Entire Sample										
A.P.	37,500	5,001-10,000	12	7	21	4	14	19	Sec. Some U	5·5
Other	122,500	25,001-50,000	18	10	8	0	13	5	Bachelor's	10
Total	40,500	5,001-10,000	12	17	29	4	27	24	Some Univ.	6·5
Total Twice-Born										
A.P.	41,000	2,501-5,000	12	4	12	0	5	11	Sec. Some U.	6
Other	160,000	50,001 & above	20·5	7	3	0	10	0	Bachelor's	13
Total	50,000	10,001-25,000	13	11	15	0	15	11	Bachelor's	9

a Refers to gross value-added, which equals the value of output of a firm minus purchases from other firms.
b Measured in rupees per annum (in fiscal year 1969-70).
c Measured in terms of average number of full-time wage-earners in the firm in fiscal year 1969-70.
d Refers to the median experience in entrepreneurial and/or management positions (outside agriculture and the professions) prior to the establishment of the firm.
e The total of responses may be less than the number of entrepreneurs because of cases where there is a lack of response or where the answer is unknown.
f Business as a major occupation refers to the management and/or ownership of any business unless it is agricultural or professional.

politically dominant castes in the state. Members of this caste have used their economic advantage, political access and hard work to facilitate movement from farming and rural trade to business and the professions in the urban areas[4] [see *Epstein, 1962, pp. 243–254, 276-278, 293*]. There was no separate Naidu *jati* before the twentieth century. Some of the Harijans and (as in the cases of the families of the three entrepreneurs) lower Sudras in Andhra who were upwardly mobile tried to escape discrimination by identifying as Naidu, considered a Sudra caste of some standing.

Among twice-born castes, the Vaishya (mercantile) community, with about 22 per cent of the entrepreneurs in comparison to about 2 per cent of the population of Vizag, was especially well represented. Most of the Vaishyas were born out-of-state. The fathers of out-of-state Vaishyas have the highest economic status and the highest percentage (100 per cent) engaged in management and/or ownership of non-agricultural business. This family background, in part, has enabled the Vaishyas from the outside to rank the highest in median education, median prior management experience, median initial capital, and the percentage who have received the major share of their initial capital from other family members. Not surprisingly, if entrepreneurs were classified according to birthplace (whether in-state or out-of-state) and caste, out-of-state Vaishyas had the highest median value added of the firm and medium income (see Table 2).

Each of these eight Vaishya entrepreneurs, together with other members of their families, had at least 5 or 10 business units scattered throughout India, while four of the families had more than 20 firms. Three entrepreneurs were Khatri, Sindhi, and Bhatia, major trading and financial communities beginning in the eighteenth century. Five in the sample were Marwaris, primarily originating from rural trading *jatis* in agriculture-poor Rajasthan. Although they did not enter major urban manufacturing until about 1920, several decades after the earliest indigenous industrial venture, today the Marwaris are the leading Indian business community. Under the umbrella of British military power during the colonial period, all four of these communities conducted entrepreneurial activity in alien linguistic or religious communities (e.g., Khatri and Sindhi Hindus in Islamic northwestern *undivided* India).

Outsiders from specialized business communities were not expected to participate in the network of traditional obligations or to become local community members. Prior to Independence, these communities, including the 8 business families, entered sectors of trade and finance (and in a few cases after World War I even manufacturing) that, by and large, did not compete with British industrial interests. In these endeavours, they amassed capital and business experience which were used to make substantial moves into manufacturing (in some cases buying existing enterprises from the British) after Independence in 1947, with the protection of industry, the accompanying decline of trade, and the more favourable government policy toward indigenous enterprise. For example, A. R. Balchandani (a pseudonym), a radio importer in the 1940s and 1950s, switched to the manufacture of electronic components and other radio parts in Madras and Vizag in the 1960s after increased forms of protection restricted the supply of imported radios. Although the Indian political elite was less favourably inclined toward private capitalism than the British, and at the state level, less accessible to outsiders, the economic power of the major business communities and families was sufficiently well-established and the economic resources sufficiently abundant, so that they could pull the political levers essential to insure the security and expansion of their business interests.

Gradually they moved beyond major industrial cities such as Calcutta and Bombay to establish manufacturing firms in many of the other cities in India, including Visakhapatnam in the 1960s. These leading families continued control of the far-flung industrial empire despite the abolition of the managing agency system (where two or more legally separate companies are controlled by a single managing firm) in 1970, and the legislation designed to restrict the expansion of large business houses. The country-wide network of firms maintained a 'community of interest' through the ties between the family members with management and ownership interest in the various enterprises. In fact, frequently the companies were controlled by one or two principals in the family who for tax purposes dispersed the ownership of enterprises in the names of other family members. Large business families, because of their accumulation of resources, knowledge, organizational skill and influences, were most likely to receive licenses for the establishment of a new enterprise or the acquisition of materials, and were in a better position to take advantage of government schemes to encourage small industry and geographical diversification. Frequently, large industrial houses owned a series of 'small-scale' industrial enterprises, which under other institutional arrangements would be described as branches of a large-scale enterprise based in a large manufacturing city. In two instances in the sample, a large industrial house prevented from establishing new enterprises without an explicit industrial license was able to purchase an establishment that had already been granted a license.

The large business families, because of their wealth and financial security, have the latitude to provide the training, education, travel and business experience of their sons, and the spending on plant and equipment that is most appropriate for the entrepreneurial development of their sons. As youngsters, the sons learn the nature of the enterprises and are exposed to a business milieu. During school vacations and after graduation each son is moved from job to job within the family's firms, gradually having his responsibility increased so that in his early 20s he may be in charge of day-to-day responsibility at one of the plants, and a few years later he may be entrusted to make major decisions in a plant in a minor industrial city (such as Vizag) away from the family's headquarters. Marriage may be arranged in part to further an economic alliance with another large business family.

Manufacturing units in Visakhapatnam had only a peripheral role in determining the overall business success of these families. Despite the fact that 7 of the 8 entrepreneurs had a 1969–70 annual personal income exceeding Rs. 50,000, 4 of the 8 entrepreneurs were incurring business losses from their manufacturing units in Vizag. Although the size of the firms were substantial compared to others in the sample, the firms were small when compared to other enterprises of the entrepreneur in other parts of India. Among the firms where information was available and which had existed for over five years, the rates of growth in employment and production for out-of-state Vaishya firms were substantially less than the rest of the sample. Three out of 4 of these firms declined in output and employment in the 5 years previous to 1969-70, while one had an increase in both categories. In contrast, among other firms, 14 grew in output, 2 remained the same, and 3 declined; in employment, 11 increased, 6 stayed constant, and two declined.

In India, the licensing of capacity and materials to specific firms is done by the state government. The evidence concerning growth, profits and capacity utilization is consistent with the contention that most large business houses acquired licenses to establish factories in Vizag (one of the cities in less industrialized states favoured by government policy) not so much for purposes of expansion, but to obtain licensed imports and materials, undertake transfers of these to sister firms, and foreclose the growth of licensed capacity by other competitors in the industry [*Nafziger, 1972, pp.13, 83, 85*].[5]

Komatis (the local name for Vaishyas) comprise over one-half of the traders in Vizag city [*Rao, 1971, pp.30–31*]. However, unlike Vaishyas in many other parts of India, Komatis have virtually no experience in manufacturing. Coastal Andhra, because of its comparative advantage in agriculture, its deficiency in power resources and basic raw materials, its lack of a number of social overhead services, and the relative neglect of its economic development when part of Madras State until 1953, has long been backward industrially, and thus has never developed an indigenous industrial community. Although Vaishyas are disproportionately represented among in-state entrepreneurs, their income class and firm value added were not even above the median of entrepreneurs born in Andhra, partly as a result of a relatively low family economic status, associated with low educational attainment and business experience (see Table 2).

For the Brahmins, merchant and industrial entrepreneurship is far removed from the traditional caste occupations of priesthood, teaching, the professions, and government service. Relatively few of the fathers of Brahmin entrepreneurs were involved in business and none were engaged in the same business as the son (see Table 2.) Yet is it not surprising that the major previous occupation of 5 out of 11 was trade and sales, or that 50 per cent of the businessmen with an entrepreneurial background in commerce were Brahmins.[6] For prospective industrialists with a lack of personal or familial expertness and capital, investment and experience in petty trade is a natural stepping stone to a larger, more fixed and more complex manufacturing enterprise. Nor is it surprising that a disproportionate number of these entrepreneurs acquired their initial capital from their own resources (7 out of 11 compared to only 20 out of 43 in the rest of the sample) and that their median initial capital was below the sample median. Since none could obtain their start in a relative's business, they obtained prior experience and (in some cases) capital as merchants, engineers, technicians, or sales managers in the same industries they established, or as professionals. Nevertheless, the median value added of their firms is as large as that of the sample. This may be attributed in part to their high level of education, with 72·7 per cent having at least a bachelor's degree, compared to 46·3 per cent of the sample as a whole.

The fact that Brahmin participation in industrial entrepreneurial activity in Vizag is about as high as their percentage in the population results from several 'push' and 'pull' factors. A major 'push' factor has been the administrative orders which limit the number of Brahmins in government departments. The wealth and influence available to facilitate investment in training and new enterprises are 'pull' factors.

The proportional representation of Muslims in entrepreneurial activity in Vizag is almost as high as for the Vaishyas. Muslim participation can be explained partly because of limited alternatives in the civil service, and the absence of traditional barriers to occupations that are polluting to Hindus. For M. C. Ahmed, who was an administrative head and whose father was police superintendent in former princely states, past wealth and influence stemmed a decline in options in government service in the 1950s and 1960s by facilitating 2 industrial ventures in Vizag.However, none of the other 6 Muslim entrepreneurs, 4 of whom were born within the state, had ties with the old Muslim ruling class of the princely states. Local Muslim entrepreneurs, like Muslims in general, did not enjoy a high parental economic status or high educational status [Ramana, 1970, pp.120, 134]. This socio-economic background was partially responsible for the low level of initial capital, value added, and income associated with Muslim business endeavours.

In general, the entrepreneurs, by virtue of being engaged in the 'modern' sector, manufacturing, rarely pursued the traditional caste-assigned occupations. The superior efficiency and market power of modern capitalistic firms undercut the viability of caste-assigned craft enterprises, and impelled most self-employed persons to seek another occupation in the capitalist sector.

BIRTHPLACE

The birthplaces of entrepreneurs were divided equally between Vizag District, the state of Andhra Pradesh outside Vizag District, and South Asia outside Andhra Pradesh. The percentage born outside the state was over five times their share of the population of Vizag city by place of birth, and others born outside Vizag District were also disproportionately represented. This is not surprising, as there is less regional segmentation in the market for high-level manpower, such as entrepreneurs, than for ordinary labour.

Those born outside of Andhra Pradesh were most successful and those born within Vizag District generally least successful as entrepreneurs [Nafziger, 1972, p.53]. The four entrepreneurs born outside India's present borders—3 who were refugees from West Pakistan in 1947, and 1 who left Burma as a result of business nationalization in 1965—were among 13 entrepreneurs in the top 2 income classes and their firms were all among the top 10 in value added.

Why were entrepreneurs from outside the state more successful than entrepreneurs from within the state? Due to the financial, psychological, and linguistic barriers to interstate migration, entrepreneurs were not likely to immigrate without some wealth and education, and the prospect for substantial economic advantage. Thus, outside entrepreneurs who migrated to Vizag, a city which lacked local industrial skills and experience, originated from a select portion of the population, as the sample totals in Table 2 show. In addition, the challenge of a new environment to immigrants may have had beneficial educational and psychological effect in breaking tradition and enhancing innovation and success. A related factor was that the geographical dispersion of friends, relatives and neighbours of the migrants may have allowed the rejection of local values, obligations and sanctions, such as notions of caste propriety, which impeded rational business practices.

PATERNAL ECONOMIC STATUS

The median personal income of entrepreneurs was Rs. 5,001-10,000 per annum in fiscal year 1969-70, which divided by the median number of persons dependent upon the entrepreneur's income, 5, gives a median per capita income of Rs. 1,000-2,000, substantially above the 1969-70 all-India average per capita net national product of Rs. 589·3 (itself higher than the median figure) [India, 1971, p.78]. Responses by entrepreneurs indicated that the economic status of the fathers was high in the aggregate (see Table 2).[7] This view is reinforced by the fact that only 20 per cent of the fathers were in cultivation and 2 per cent in agricultural labour compared to 45 per cent and 25 per cent respectively in India's working population in 1931 [Dewett, Singh, and Varna, 1970, p.45]. In addition, the major occupation of 27 of 51 of the fathers was some form of non-agricultural business (see Table 2).

The economic status of the father was closely related to the entrepreneurial success of the son.[8] A high economic status of the father assists the prospective entrepreneur in acquiring resources for investment in education,[9] training, and plant and equipment (see below p.143). The median education of the entrepreneurs, who were all male, was some university, which is extremely high when compared to the male population of Vizag District urban areas, 63 per cent of which had not completed primary school. Among entrepreneurs, there was a positive relationship between educational attainment and business success.[10] In addition, businessmen with a greater paternal economic status, because of more education and erudition, a more extensive network of influential acquaintances, and more resources available to acquire information, were more likely to be successful in receiving government assistance.[11]

ENTREPRENEURIAL AND MANAGEMENT EXPERIENCE

For the entrepreneur, the lack of technical, managerial and marketing experience and training in business is perhaps one of the major barriers to success. The small-scale entrepreneur usually needs to have a minimum level of skills in production, engineering, marketing, financing, purchasing, organisation, labour relations, and relationships with government, as the unit cost of acquiring high-level personnel for such a size firm may be prohibitive. Most entrepreneurs who did not belong to the large out-of-state business families did not have the network of relationships with business-oriented friends and relatives to obtain access to trustworthy management personnel or even to acquire a reliable evaluation of the ability and integrity of prospective managers. In addition, those with greater experience in business had more time to acquire retained earnings to increase the capital available for their initial venture in manufacturing.[12] Thus, there was a significant positive relationship between the experience of the respondent in entrepreneurial and managerial positions (outside agriculture) and the success of the entrepreneur.[13]

SOURCES OF INITIAL CAPITAL

Entrepreneurs in single small-scale enterprises have not usually had access to funds from organized financial institutions, at least prior to bank nationalization. In addition, in Indian society a prospective lender or partner usually did not feel that the social sanctions and networks of relationships were available to feel secure in advancing funds to a person who was not a close relative, of the same caste, or linked together in a customary patron-client relationship. Thus, raising the initial capital of the firm was a major barrier to entry. Even the smallest industrial enterprise may require Rs. 5,000-10,000, equivalent to a few years earnings for prospective entrepreneurs with a median income.

The extended family, because of its age composition and size, may be able to mobilize funds that the prospective entrepreneur, whose median age of entry into the sample firms was 35, would not have available. Sixty-one per cent (33 out of 54) of the entrepreneurs indicated that a part of the initial capital for the firm was raised from other members of the family. Forty-four per cent received most or all of their initial capital from the family. The figure for at least partial assistance from the family is greater (74 per cent), if you consider capital raised for the entrepreneur's initial business venture (i.e., not necessarily the sample firm).[14]

The family economic status of the entrepreneur is a crucial factor affecting the availability of capital for new industrial enterprises, and thus the supply and success of industrial entrepreneurs. Extrepreneurs with high paternal economic status had a median initial capital of Rs. 167,000, compared to Rs. 35,000 for those with a low and medium economic status. It is reasonable to assume that this relationship between parental economic status and initial capital is the tip of the iceberg whose surface depicts a positive relationship between parental economic status and entry into industrial entrepreneurship.

Those with high parental economic status are more likely to be able to receive their initial financial support from their family. Ten of 17 with a high father's economic status received most of their funds from their family, while 4 additional ones received some support from this source. In contrast, only 14 of 33 with low or medium economic status received most of their initial financial support from their family, with 8 more receiving some support from it. Those who received most of their initial financial support from their families had a higher median capital, Rs. 70,000, than those who provided their own support, Rs. 45,000. Finally, major industrial families used their control of banks, prior to bank nationalization in July 1969, to fund the enterprises of their own families and business communities.

COMPARATIVE DATA

A number of studies of Indian industrialists point to a concentration of entrepreneurial activity among the sons of the members of the large business houses, who represent a small fraction of the population (see the survey in Nafziger [1971,pp.291–306]). Although Berna remarks on the extremely varied backgrounds of sample industrialists in the state of Tamil Nadu, 41 of the 46 Hindu entrepreneurs with some caste designation (excluding the three designated by social community, not always indicative of caste) are from twice-born castes, and the rest are Sudras [1960, pp.43, 83]. A highly disproportionate number of the fathers of manufacturing entrepreneurs in Pakistan, which had a common history with India before 1947, were from traditional business communities while a low percentage of fathers were in wage employment or agriculture. This pattern would suggest, contrary to Papanek's interpretation, that the socio-economic class status of entrepreneurs was high when compared to the population [1962, pp.50-58]. Indigenous managers of large public, foreign and private enterprises in India also originate from a highly select portion of the population, as none of the fathers were labourers, only 10 per cent were farmers (all of whom were small farm operators or large farm owners), and the rest were white-collar workers, government officials, business executives, professional men, and business owners [Prasad and Negandhi, 1968, p.27]. Adding a perspective to the social origin of businessmen is a study of factory labourers in Poona indicating no significant difference between caste and social community of the workers and the city population [Lambert, 1963, pp.33–34, 36–38].

Contrary to a widely-held viewpoint, this low degree of socio-economic class mobility is found not only in India but also in most of the rest of the non-socialist world, at least if evidence is based upon empirical studies of entrepreneurs. (Views about the peculiarity of a rigid social structure in underdeveloped countries such as India [e.g., Hoselitz, 1960, pp.154–156] are criticized by Berreman [1960, pp.120–127]). The proportion of fathers of Filipino manufacturing entrepreneurs from an upper socio-economic position was 36 times that of the population [Carroll, 1965, pp.100, 126]. Despite the conclusions of the authors cited above concerning upward mobility, data from their studies of Nigerian, Greek and Michigan entrepreneurs reinforce my findings concerning the high socio-economic class origins of industrialists. The select nature of their sample firms (with the usual elimination of newly established firms, which biases the sample in favour of units profitable in the long run, and the exclusion of smaller firms), results in an overestimation of the upward mobility of entrepreneurs. Also, none of these authors adjusted the comparative status of father and son for the inter-generational advance in economic well-being and skill composition of the labour force which accompanies economic growth. Nevertheless the knowledge that industrialists enjoy a higher occupational status and material level of living than their fathers, like analogous information about New York bankers and their fathers, is not trivial. But an exclusive focus on this concept of socio-economic mobility distracts from the highly contrasting socio-economic class background between entrepreneurs and the general population, information available but not discussed by the authors. We can surmise, from the fact that the major occupation of 56 per cent of the fathers of industrial entrepreneurs in the Harris sample was in a non-agricultural sector compared to 21 per cent of the Nigerian male population, and that 54 per cent of the fathers of industrialists studied by Alexander were big merchants, industrialists, professional men or business executives compared to 2 per cent of the working population in Greece, that the socio-economic class of the entrepreneurs was far above that of the population at large [*Harris, 1971, p.335; Nigeria, 1963, p.21; Alexander, 1964, pp.45, 87*].

Those for whom today's 'modernized' societies present an image of the future of 'traditional societies' envision a movement in history from a 'rigid' social structure and underdeveloped economy to a fluid social structure and developed economy, whose archetype is the US and Western Europe [*Smelser and Lipset, 1966, pp.9, 44; Alexander, 1964, p.80; Harris, 1971, p.337*]. But if studies of businessmen are any indication, the fluidity of the prototypical modern country, the US, does not vary much from that of India. Doubtless the two-thirds of the Michigan sample entrepreneurs who described their early family life as poor or underprivileged (rather than 'affluent' or 'well off', the other two choices) were sincere [*Collins, Moore and Unwalla, 1964. p.238*], even though perhaps evaluating parental family income in terms of contemporary standards (the 1960s) and in comparison with their own high level of economic well-being. But the vast under-representation of Michigan sample fathers in unskilled, semi-skilled, clerical, sales and kindred work (24 per cent from the sample and 61 per cent from the general labour force), and the disproportional representation of fathers in business, executive, managerial, and official, farm ownership and managerial, and professional work (57 compared to 26 per cent), points to median incomes substantially above the corresponding population of their period [*US, 1943, p.87; Nafziger, 1972, p.73*].[15] It is not surprising that despite the readily available data, US business scholars and development economists, who tend to assume a harmony of interests between the goals of the businessmen and the community at large, do not generally consider it important to raise questions about the economic class origin of entrepreneurs.

These data contradict the Horatio Alger myth of Western business and economic thought, and suggest that the socio-economic class status of businessmen is substantially higher than the general population not only in India, but probably also in a large part of the rest of the non-socialist world.[16]

NOTES

1. The universe consisted of the entrepreneurs of the 55 private industrial establishments, with at least 50 per cent indigenous ownership, registered with the Industries Department of Vizag District from 1958 through 1970, listed as having 5 or more employees, and operating at the time of interview (January-April 1971). The interview schedule and a detailed discussion of methods are available in Nafziger [*1972, pp.1–3, 75–85*].

2. Statistics of Vizag are based on the universe of 2,000 households from eight representative areas within the city as indicated in Ramana [*1970, pp. 21–9*] a source consistent with the 1961 census data on the distribution of the population of Vizag city by religion.

The caste standing of the Syrian Christian, represented in the sample, closely approximates that of the Kshatriya [*Atiya, 1968, p.377*].

3. Entrepreneurs were asked: 'Was your father's economic status high, medium or low?'

4. Interestingly enough, all 3 Kammas received financial assistance from government agencies, although only 7 of the other entrepreneurs received this assistance. In addition, the median Kamma entrepreneur had more education, management experience and initial capital, and greater success than the median entrepreneur in the sample, despite the fact that all 3 had established their businesses since 1966. Because of the small number of sample Kammas, these findings can only be suggestive.

5. In order to arrive at the entrepreneur's perception of capacity utilization, I asked the following question. 'Assume that the price of your products remains the same, and that you use the same plant and equipment. How much more could you have produced (in rupee value) in 1969-70 if you could have sold all that you produced?' In 4 of the 8 instances, capacity utilization for one shift was perceived by the entrepreneurs to be less than 50 per cent.

6. I found no evidence that Brahmins who are entrepeneurs in Vizag are any less inclined than other entrepreneurs to do dirty manual work when that is required in their unit. This is in contrast to the Brahmins of Howrah, West Bengal as viewed by Owens [*1973*].

7. This is despite the fact that respondents judged the status of unskilled factory workers as low, even though it is at least medium when one considers that 70 per cent of India's working population is in the low-income agricultural sector.

8. Where Y is net income class (1 for less than 0, 2 for 0–2,500, 3 for 2,501–5,000, 4 for 5,001–10,000, 5 for 10,001–25,000, 6 for 25,001–50,000, 7 for 50,001 or more), X_1 is father's economic status (1 for low, 2 for medium, and 3 for high) and X_2 is the entrepreneur's age (in years), $Y = 1 \cdot 1353 + 1 \cdot 389X_1 + 0 \cdot 0071X_2$, $t_1 = 2 \cdot 3082$, and the multiple regression coefficient on X_1 is significant at the 5 per cent level.

9. E.g., there is a positive correlation between the economic status of the fathers and the education of the entrepreneurs. Where Y is educational achievement (0 for none, 1 for some primary, 2 for primary, 3 for some secondary, 4 secondary, 5 for some university, 6 for a bachelor's degree, 7 for a master's degree, 8 for above a master's degree) and X is the economic status of the father (see previous note), $Y = 3 \cdot 13083 + 0 \cdot 72100X$, $t = 2 \cdot 15510$, and the regression coefficient is significant at the 5 per cent level.

10. I explain these relationships in more detail [*1970, pp.349–360*].

Where Y is 1969-70 gross value-added and X is the entrepreneur's educational achievement (as indicated in note 9), $Y = -219{,}070 + 84{,}840X$, $t = 2 \cdot 0518$, and the regression coefficient on X is significant at the 5 per cent level. Where Y is net income class (as indicated in note 8) and X is educational attainment, $Y = 2 \cdot 0208 + 0 \cdot 45451X$, $t = 2 \cdot 5986$, and the regression coefficient on X is significant at the 2 per cent level.

11. Those who receive government assistance, especially financial help, have a higher degree of success than others (although causation may run in two directions) [*Nafziger, 1972, pp.41, 67, 70*].

12. There is a significant positive relationship between initial share capital (Y) and the number of years of management and entrepreneurial experience prior to the establishment of the business (X). $Y = 35,661 \cdot 62500 + 12,089 \cdot 4765X$, $t = 2 \cdot 82741$, and the regression coefficient is significant at the 1 per cent level.

13. Where Y is net income class and X is the number of years of experience of the major entrepreneur, $Y = 2 \cdot 88302 + 0 \cdot 089694X$, $t = 2 \cdot 48273$, and the regression coefficient is significant at the 2 per cent level. Where Y is 1969-70 gross value added and X is the number of years of experience of the major entrepreneur, $Y = -53670 \cdot 37500 + 15114 \cdot 0078X$, $t = 2 \cdot 14681$, and the regression coefficient is significant at the 5 per cent level.

14. Even though Vizag entrepreneurs are very dependent upon the family for initial funds, they are slightly less dependent on the family than a sample of Nigerian entrepreneurs (from the same size of firms) [*Nafziger, 1969, p.29*].

15. Executives in large joint-stock companies in the US are likely to originate from an economically more select portion of the population than medium-scale industrial entrepreneurs. In terms of socio-religious communities, there is a rough parallel between the position in the business establishment of white Protestants of northern and western European origin in the US to that of the Hindu twice-born castes in India, and of black Americans to Indian untouchables [*Newcomer, 1955, pp.48, 55; Warner and Abegglen, 1955, pp. 41–42, 239–249; Collins, Moore and Unwalla, 1964, p.239; Domhoff, 1967, pp.29–30*].

16. The hypothesis might be broadened to include most of the socialist world as well. For example, the representation of sons of white-collar employees, professionals, or business owners in industrial executive positions in the Soviet Union in 1936, the latest data for reliable information on parental occupational origins, was 6 times as high as that of the sons of manual workers and farmers. This occurred despite the revolution of 1917 which overturned the existing class structure [*Granick, 1961, pp.39–40*].

REFERENCES

Alexander, A. P., 1964, *Greek Industrialists*, Athens: Centre of Planning and Economic Research.

Atiya, A. S., 1968, *The History of Eastern Christianity*, London: Methuen and Co.

Baran, P. A., 1957, *The Political Economy of Growth*, New York: Modern Readers Paperbacks.

Berna, J. J., 1960, *Industrial Entrepreneurship in Madras State*, New York: Asia Publishing House.

Bernstein, H., 1971, 'Modernization Theory and the Sociological Study of Development', *Journal of Development Studies*, 7: 2, January.

Berreman, G. D., 1960, 'Caste in India and the United States', *American Journal of Sociology*, 66.

Carroll, J. J., 1965, *The Filipino Manufacturing Entrepreneur*, Ithaca: Cornell University Press.

Collins, O. F., D. G. Moore, and D. B. Unwall, 1964, *The Enterprising Man*, East Lansing: MSU Business Studies.

Dewett, K. K., G. C. Singh, and J. D. Varna, 1970, *Indian Economics*, Delhi: S. Chand and Co.

Domhoff, G. W., 1967, *Who Rules America?*, Englewood Cliffs: Prentice-Hall, Inc.

Epstein, T. S., 1962, *Economic Development and Social Change in South India*, Manchester: Manchester University Press.

Gould, H. A., 1963, 'The Adaptive Functions of Caste in Contemporary Indian Society', *Asian Survey*, 3, September.

Granick, D., 1961, *The Red Executive: A Study of the Organisation Man in Russian Industry*, New York: Anchor Books.

Harris, J. R., 1971, 'Nigerian Entrepreneurship in Industry', in Kilby [*1971*].

Higgins, B., 1968, *Economic Development: Problems, Principles and Policies*, New York: W. W. Norton.

Hoselitz, B. F., 1960, *Sociological Aspect of Economic Growth*, New York: Free Press.

India, Government of, 1971, *Economic Survey 1970–71*, Delhi

Kilby, P., (ed.), 1971, *Entrepreneurship and Economic Development*, New York: Free Press.

Knight, F., 1961, *Risk, Uncertainty and Profit*, Boston: Houghton Mifflin Co.

Lambert, R. D., 1963, *Workers, Factories, and Social Change in India*, Princeton: Princeton University Press.

McClelland, D. C., 1961, *The Achieving Society*, Princeton: D. Van Nostrand Co.

Nafziger, E. W., 1969, 'The Effect of the Nigerian Extended Family on Entrepreneurial Activity', *Economic Development and Cultural Change*, 18; 1, Part I, October.

Nafziger, E. W., 1970, 'The Relationship Between Education and Entrepreneurship in Nigeria', *Journal of Developing Areas*, 4, April.

Nafziger, E. W., 1971, 'Indian Entrepreneurship: A Survey', in Kilby [*1971*].

Nafziger, E. W., 1972, 'South Indian Industrialists: A Profile of Entrepreneurs in Coastal Andhra', Technology and Development Institute, East-West Centre, Working Paper No. 34.

Newcomer, M., 1955, *The Big Business Executive: The Factors That Made Him, 1900–1950*, New York: Columbia University Press.

Nigeria, Federal Republic of, 1963, *Annual Abstract of Statistics 1963*, Lagos: Office of Statistics.

Owens, R., 1973, 'Peasant Entrepreneurs in an Industrial City', in Milton Singer, (ed.), *Entrepreneurship and Modernization of Occupational Cultures in South Asia*, Durham: Duke University Press.

Papanek, G. F., 1962, 'The Development of Entrepreneurship', *American Economic Review*, May.

Papanek, G. F., 1967, *Pakistan's Development: Social Goals and Private Incentives*, Cambridge, Mass.: Harvard University Press.

Prasad, S. B. and A. R. Negandhi, 1968, *Managerialism for Economic Development: Essays on India*, The Hague: Martinus Nijhoff.

Ramana, K. V., 1970, 'Caste and Society in an Andhra Town', Ph.D. diss., University of Illinois.

Rao, N. A., 1971, 'The Commercial Entrepreneurs in Visakhapatnam City: A Survey', Department of Cooperation and Applied Economics, Andhra University, Waltair.

Rudolph, L. I. and S. H. Rudolph, 1967, *The Modernity of Tradition: Political Development in India*, Chicago: University of Chicago Press.

Schumpeter, J. A., 1961, trans. Redvers Opie, *The Theory of Economic Development: An Inquiry into Profits, Capital, Credit, Interest, and the Business Cycle*, New York: Oxford University Press.

Smelser, N. J., and S. M. Lipset, (eds.), 1966, *Social Structure and Mobility in Economic Development*, Chicago: Aldine Publishing Co.

Srimivas, M. N., 1962, *Caste in Modern India and Other Essays*, New York: Asia Publishing House.

US, Bureau of the Census, 1943, *Sixteenth Census of the United States: 1940, Vol. III, The Labour Force: Occupation, Industry, Employment and Income; Part I, U.S. Summary*, Washington, G.P.O.

Warner, W. L., and J. C. Abegglen, 1955, *Occupational Mobility in American Business and Industry*, Minneapolis: University of Minnesota Press.

Education, Individual Earnings and Earnings Distribution

By Keith Hinchliffe*

This paper attempts to explore the relationships between educational development, earnings differentials and earnings distribution. Initially it is argued that for such analyses, lifetime earnings are a superior measure to average earnings and this is followed by a discussion of the data sources used here—age-education-earnings streams from rate of return to education studies in ten countries—and their limitations. Earnings streams are then discounted and presented in ratio form as the basis for comparison. The pattern of these ratios which widen as we move from high to low income countries is then discussed. In the final section an illustrative example is developed from data for three countries of a 'potential' earnings distribution for the whole labour force differentiated by educational level.

INTRODUCTION

The expansion of educational provision in the poor, newly independent countries has been one of the most pervasive social phenomena experienced in the last decade or so. The rationale for such expansion was based initially on social criteria adopted from the liberal democracies of the former colonial powers. Soon however these criteria were supplemented by new and powerful voices—the economists of education who, by employing techniques from capital theory, came forward with analyses which gave a 'scientific' credibility to those who had for a long time perceived the economic value of education. From both a social and economic standpoint, the rapid expansion of education was seen as a 'good thing' for the poor underdeveloped countries. The provision of education was seen as conferring endless social and economic advantages with little thought being given to the problems which might be created first in the actual provision and secondly in the consequences of such provision.

The last few years of the 1960s saw the emergence of two concrete problems related to educational expansion, first the existence of a large body of unemployed school leavers for whom it was impossible to provide jobs on a level with their aspirations and secondly the crippling effect of educational finance on government budgets. Both these problems have

*Lecturer in Development Studies, School of Development Studies, University of East Anglia, Norwich. Much of the original work for this page was undertaken whilst the author was a Research Officer at the Higher Education Research Unit at the London School of Economics participating in a project with Dr G. Psacharopoulos, concerned with an international comparison of rates of return to investment in education. He would like to thank Dr G. Psacharopoulos, Professor R. S. Bhambri, Mr G. Williams, Mr J. B. Knight and Dr S. Merrett for comments and suggestions on earlier versions of this paper.

now been realised and efforts are being made in many countries (albeit often unsuccessfully) to control them. Another by-product of education, however, has often escaped serious consideration, yet it could be a source of great potential stress on the social and economic fabric of such societies. This is the wide distribution of earnings potential between those who have consumed varying amounts of education consequent on the necessarily large degree of selection at each level of the educational system. It is towards an analysis of this question that this paper is directed.

The procedure to be followed in this investigation of the relationship between education and earnings is in two parts. First we use data from 10 countries at widely differing levels of economic development to measure and compare earnings differentials and secondly, an illustrative example is developed of how to translate these measures of earnings, which refer to the average graduate of each educational level, to derive an earnings distribution based on educational distribution, for the labour force as a whole.

METHODOLOGY AND DATA

All previous studies of international comparisons of earnings differentials by skill or educational level have used average earnings [*Taira, 1966; Gunter, 1964; OECD, 1965; Chiswick, 1971; Papola and Bharadwaj, 1970; Lydall, 1968*]. However, for any study which bears at all on comparative earnings across countries, the use of average earnings is unsatisfactory for 2 major reasons. First the level of average earnings partly depends on the population structure and countries with relatively young populations will have low average earnings relative to countries with more balanced age structures since earnings generally increase with age. Thus use of average earnings may tell us more about population structures than about patterns of relative earnings. Secondly if we are considering the impact of education or skill acquisition on earnings, it is more relevant to consider the whole length of lifetime earnings rather than average earnings at one point in time.

The first major difference of this study compared with previous analyses of (mainly skill or occupational) wage differentials is that expected or potential lifetime earnings are used. In this case the focus is not on the average wage paid to all workers at one point in time, rather the emphasis is on the whole of the working life for persons educated to 3 different levels of education and those with no education at all. The data for this exercise are taken from studies conducted over the last decade of the rate of return to investment in education. Although such studies, in one form or another, have covered at least 30 countries, not all these have presented sufficient data on age-education-earnings profiles for detailed analyses of lifetime earnings. Earnings data for 10 countries—United States, Canada, Israel, Mexico, Colombia, Philippines, Ghana, Kenya, Nigeria and India—are used here.

The first practical problem posed by these lifetime earnings data for purposes of international comparison is to decide upon the equivalent schooling groups which are to be used. Two possibilities exist, either years of schooling or level of schooling completed, and there are advantages and disadvantages to both. The advantage of using years of schooling is that absolute equivalence could be arrived at, but unfortunately the data for all our countries are not so comprehensive. As to levels, the advantage is that earnings do not increase smoothly by years of schooling, rather they are usually geared to the completion of a particular level. The disadvantage of this procedure is the non-equivalence of levels across countries; for instance the length of primary school varies from 5 to 8 years in our sample of countries.

In fact it was decided to use a mixture of the 2 methods. At the primary schooling level the most satisfactory procedure for equalising the levels of education is to use 8 years of schooling. From the individual country studies we have earnings associated with 8 years of education for 8 of the countries, while for both Kenya and the Philippines the first division occurs after 7 years. The second division is a little more complicated but generally comes about 4 years after the first division. For some countries this corresponds to the end of the secondary cycle and immediately before university. For the others, chiefly those educational systems based on British influence, the break is pre-sixth form. In all countries the division corresponds to 11 or 12 years of schooling except for Ghana where it is after 13 years. The final category, higher education, corresponds to university or sixth form plus university and in most cases is 5 years in length. It should be noted that the years per course explained above are in many cases the minimum number and particularly in the underdeveloped countries, the actual time taken to complete each course may be much longer.

Before we leave this discussion of the data sources it is necessary to discuss their limitations. Rate of return studies up to the present have usually been far from explicit in stating whether they are supposed to reflect ex-post, ex-ante or some other type of lifetime earnings. Ex-post earnings by educational level should ideally be derived by following a given cohort through time, and ex-ante earnings by accurately forecasting the paths of future earnings. In fact, because of the problems of such estimation, rates of return have been calculated on the basis of today's cross-sectional earnings by age and educational level and then extrapolated either backwards or forwards in time and used as ex-post or ex-ante at the whim of the author. Only to the extent then that cross-sectional observations accurately reflect the path of expected or potential lifetime earnings will the data used here accurately reflect lifetime earnings differences by educational level. It is our opinion, however, that despite the limitations, use of cross-sectional lifetime earnings data is an improvement on the single point data normally used in studies of earnings differentials and earnings distribution.

Whatever type of data we use to represent lifetime earnings the fact remains that it is covering a forty or fifty-year time span and therefore the problems associated with discounting arise. Lydall, in a discussion advocating the use of lifetime earnings for analyses of earnings distribution states the position well,

. . . and presumably something should be done to bring incomes of different years into a single reckoning. Theoretically, this involves discounting; but what rate of discount is appropriate? And in which direction should the discounting be done? . . . Should one rate of discount be used for all? Or should it vary between persons? (*Lydall, 1968, p. 47*).

Generally personal income is discounted on the basis that for various psychological reasons individuals exhibit a natural preference for present over future income—what Pigou labelled our 'defective telescopic faculty' [*1924, p.25*] and also because of the diminishing marginal utility of income as income rises. Following Fisher's conclusion that time preference rates are chiefly determined by the character of a man's income 'as to its size, time shape and probability' [*1930, p.80*], we could conclude that the appropriate rate to discount personal earnings streams varies between individuals both within and between countries according to the size and pattern of earnings. Ideally then, we should not only discount the earnings of the uneducated, the primary, secondary and higher education graduate in one country by different rates but we should also use a different set of rates for each of the ten countries to be analysed.

The problem however in reaching this ideal is that even if it is accepted that inter-personal comparisons of marginal utilities may be made (and if it is not then there is no reason why rates of discount will vary between individuals at all) we cannot say for sure whether these rates will increase or decrease as we move up the educational hierarchy. Diminishing marginal utility of income would lead us to believe that not only should we apply higher discount rates overall to those in low income countries but also that the rates should be *higher* for the primary than for the secondary school graduate and so on. On the other hand we know from our age-education-earnings profiles that earnings increase most rapidly for the higher education groups. And this leads us to suppose that because of these earnings expectations, the discount rate will be *lower* for the primary than for the secondary graduate. To what extent the pattern of discount rates based on differences in present earnings is affected by differences in expected earnings is unknown. Not only therefore do we not know the actual appropriate discount rates to use in each case, it is not even possible to state whether these will increase or decrease by educational level. In the following analyses then we have not applied 4 different discount rates for each of the 10 countries; rather we have simply used 2 rates of 5 and 10 per cent, arbitrarily chosen, and have applied each of these to each educational level and country. The purpose of using 2 rather than 1 discount rate is first to see whether variation of the rate in fact does lead to much difference in the results and secondly to test the strength of 2 separate determinants of the shape of the earnings profiles.

INDIVIDUAL LIFETIME EARNINGS

As previously stated all lifetime earnings profiles, taken from rate of return studies, were discounted at rates of both 5 and 10 per cent. Since the absolute results are not comparable for all countries due to currency differences, absolute earnings were converted into ratios for each set of educational level comparisons. The results of this exercise are presented in Table 1 with countries grouped into three descending income groups: Group A, United States and Canada; Group B, Israel, Mexico and Colombia; Group C, Philippines, Ghana, Kenya, Nigeria and India.

TABLE 1

RATIO OF GROSS DISCOUNTED LIFETIME EARNINGS BY EDUCATIONAL LEVEL COMPARISONS

Country and rate of discount (1)	Educational Level Comparisons				
	Primary None (2)	Secondary Primary (3)	Higher Secondary (4)	Higher Primary (5)	Higher None (6)
United States					
5	—	1·53	1·56	2·38	—
10	—	1·68	1·65	2·76	—
Canada					
5	—	1·57	1·76	2·76	—
10	—	1·59	1·81	2·89	—
Israel					
5	1·59	1·56	1·42	2·20	3·52
10	1·56	1·83	1·42	2·61	4·07
Mexico					
5	2·94	1·46	2·39	3·49	10·26
10	3·08	1·39	2·71	3·78	11·65
Colombia					
5	3·29	2·74	1·77	4·86	16·00
10	3·45	2·46	2·12	5·21	17·99
Philippines					
5	2·34	1·54	1·45	2·23	5·21
10	2·56	1·71	1·52	2·60	6·64
Ghana					
5	2·25	1·92	4·77	9·19	20·66
10	2·53	2·03	4·48	9·08	22·97
Kenya					
5	1·70	2·32	2·63	6·12	10·43
10	1·72	2·48	3·04	7·55	12·97
Nigeria					
5	2·72	2·21	4·25	9·40	25·58
10	2·32	2·30	4·45	10·25	23·77
India					
5	2·77	1·48	3•56	5·26	14·57
10	3·38	1·60	3·54	5·65	19.11

SOURCES: United States: Hanoch [1967, p.316, 317]; Canada: Podoluk [1965, p.43]; Israel: Klinov-Malul [1966, p.29, 100, 101]; Mexico: Carnoy [1967, p.362]; Colombia: Selowsky [1968, p.90]; Philippines: Williamson and Devoretz [1967, p.24]; Ghana: Hinchliffe [1969, Appendix]; Kenya: Thias and Carnoy [1969, p.82, 92]; Nigeria: Bowles [1965, p.139]; India: Blaug et al. [1969, p.171].

Before we compare the results across countries it is interesting to see the effects of using 2 different discount rates in the overall pattern of earnings ratios. The first point is that variation of the discount rate while making large differences to the absolute level of discounted earnings has little effect on ratios comparing earnings for 2 different education levels. Even so, it is the case that the majority of earnings ratios, and therefore the measures of inequality, do increase as the discount rate rises. Out of the 28 relevant ratios (columns 2, 3, 4) a higher discount rate increases the ratio in 21 cases and the remaining cases where the ratios decrease do not present any systematic pattern when split into either education level comparisons or income groups. Why is it the case that higher discount rates produce wider relative earnings variations?

In the discounting process, a high rate of discount acts more strongly on later earnings relative to initial earnings than does a low discount rate. This produces two opposing tendencies on the relative earnings of, say, higher and secondary educated graduates. First, since peak earnings occur later in life the higher the educational level, a high discount rate tends to depress the higher/secondary education earnings ratio. On the other hand, if we are discounting back to the first year of working life, the secondary educated earnings stream is longer than that of the higher educated. Thus a higher discount rate will depress the earnings of the secondary educated relative to the higher educated so that the higher/secondary earnings ratio increases. Since Table 1 shows that the majority of earnings do in fact increase as the discount rate is increased from 5 per cent to 10 per cent, the effect of the longer working life of the secondary school graduate overrules the fact that peak earnings occur earlier in life relative to the higher education graduate. This argument also extends to the earnings of the secondary as related to the primary graduate, and to the primary graduate compared to the person with no schooling at all.

Turning back to comparisons of lifetime earnings ratios across countries it is obvious that overall, the ratios increase as we move from high to low income countries. This is especially apparent from columns 5 and 6 which reflect lifetime earnings differences corresponding in the first place to post primary education and secondly to the educational cycle as a whole. For instance, in West Africa the average university graduate can expect discounted lifetime earnings over 20 times the amount received by the individual with no education and 9 times the primary school graduate whereas in the United States the average university graduate can expect only two and a half times the earnings of a member of the least educated group. From columns 1, 2 and 3 although the secondary/primary education earnings ratio is generally greater for the low than the high income countries, it is obvious that the main reason for the widening ratios for the educational cycle as a whole is the differential between university and secondary educated individuals. This particular earnings ratio moves from (at 5 per cent rate of discount) 1.56 for the United States to 4.77 for Ghana.

Average lifetime earnings differentials associated with different levels of education are far greater in developing countries than in high income countries as exemplified by the United States and Canada, according to our data from a sample of 10 countries. This result corresponds to the results of those studies which have been made using average earnings based on skill level, but in this analysis we have been able to disaggregate the labour force more than is usually done and we have been able to consider earnings differentials over a lifetime. Attention is now turned to speculation of the causes of the wider earnings differentials in low income countries, abstracting from any historical or institutional circumstances and laying emphasis solely on economic factors.

a. Physical Capital per Man

If complementarity of factors of production is the key to productivity and if relative productivities determine relative earnings then the results from Table 1 imply that the ratio of physical capital used per higher education graduate to physical capital used per secondary graduate is greater in low than in high income countries (and the same would be true of the secondary/primary capital ratio). This could be the case if in low income countries, production is both highly capital intensive utilising a few highly trained workers and the rest of the production techniques are highly labour intensive using little physical capital and many units of labour, including secondary school graduates. Compared to the situation in high income countries where almost all production techniques are capital intensive this could lead to wider ratios of capital used per man for university and secondary educated workers in low income countries, thus leading to greater earnings ratios between the two categories of workers.

b. Scarcity Factor

A second possible explanation of the earnings ratio may be found in the often-invoked scarcity argument. For this to be used to explain our relative earnings pattern it has to be the case that, for instance, the ratio of university graduates to secondary school graduates is lower in low income countries than in high income countries and hence that university graduates are in relatively more scarce supply. This argument of course deals only with the supply side and says nothing about the different demand conditions operating within and between countries.

c. On-the-Job-Training

Finally it may be that the groups delineated in the analysis are in fact badly defined, depending as they do solely on years of formal education. If we allow that earnings potential is due not only to formal education but also to other types of less formal education usually referred to as on-the-job training, then a third explanation of the earnings pattern may be invoked, this being the relative amounts of post-formal education training. For explanation of our pattern of earnings ratios this would require that, for instance, the amount of training given to university graduates relative to secondary graduates is greater in low than in high income countries. Casual observation leads one to believe this is in fact the case.

The 3 sub-sections above provide possible explanations of the lifetime earnings ratio patterns shown in Table 1. The true explanation may be one, all or none of these but as a first step in this type of analysis they may be useful suggestions and all 3 could conceivably be tested. In fact the second. hypothesis has already been tested using earnings and labour force data for 18 countries and it was found that 35 per cent of the difference in the secondary/primary average earnings ratios and 50 per cent of the difference in the higher/secondary ratios across countries could be explained by relative stocks of educated manpower. [*Psacharopoulos and Hinchliffe, 1972*]. Even if the hypotheses above could be tested and if they 'explained' the relatively wide earnings ratios in low income countries this does not mean that such patterns have to be encouraged or even tolerated. The example of Israel in our sample of countries shows that institutional and political forces can counteract economic forces to some extent. Up to this point emphasis has been placed solely on the 'average' graduate of each educational level. This is important and interesting for several reasons including analysis of wage structures but greater interest potentially lies in the analysis of how these differences in individual earnings aggregate up to the level of the total distribution of earnings for the labour force as a whole.

EDUCATION AND EARNINGS DISTRIBUTION

Unfortunately, the lack of data for all countries in our sample except the United States, concerning the level of education by age of the labour force precludes a conventional analysis of the actual distribution of earnings by level of education. There is however, an alternative, and for some purposes, superior approach which can be used although again at present there are data limitations. This approach rests on the availability in several countries of estimates of gross discounted present values of lifetime earnings used in the previous section together with distributions of the labour force by educational level. From these 2 sets of data, it is possible to derive what we term a 'potential earnings distribution' which refers, not to the division of total earned income in one particular year, but to the total earnings past, present and future of the current members of the labour force. This type of distribution analysis helps to identify the impact of educational distribution on earnings distribution in a much fuller and more relevant way than a simple distribution relating to one moment in time. In other words the earnings distribution is here placed in a dynamic rather than a static framework, even though it relates to a single educational distribution at one time period and will alter as the latter changes.

The calculation procedure of a 'potential earnings distribution' by educational level is shown by way of a hypothetical example in Tables 2 and 3. Table 2 presents the absolute and percentage distribution of the total labour force by educational level (columns 2 and 3), the discounted lifetime earnings associated with each level (column 4) and finally the total 'potential' lifetime earnings in absolute and percentage terms corresponding to each educational group (columns 5 and 6). Table 2 therefore indicates that the 43 per cent of the labour force with no education earn only 16 per cent of the total potential earnings of the labour force, the 40 per cent with primary education receive 44 per cent of total

TABLE 2

DISTRIBUTION AND LIFETIME EARNINGS OF THE LABOUR FORCE BY LEVEL
OF EDUCATION

Level of Education	Distribution of Labour Force		Discounted Lifetime Earnings per man	Total Discounted Earnings by Educational level	
	No. (m)	%	£	(£m)	%
(1)	(2)	(3)	(4)	(5)	(6)
None	4·3	43	1,000	4,300	16
Primary	4·0	40	3,000	12,000	44
Secondary	1·5	15	6,000	9,000	33
Higher	0·2	2	30,000	2,000	7

TABLE 3

CUMULATIVE DISTRIBUTION OF THE LABOUR FORCE BY EARNINGS AND
LEVEL OF EDUCATION

Level of Education	Cumulative Distribution of Labour Force by Level of Education (%)	Cumulative Distribution of Potential Earnings by Level of Education (%)
(1)	(2)	(3)
None	43	16
Primary	83	60
Secondary	98	93
Higher	100	100

FIGURE 1

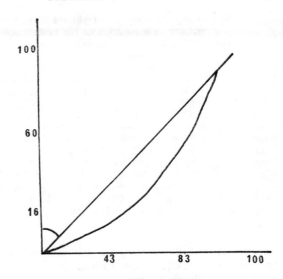

Total potential
lifetime earnings
of labour force
(%)

Labour force (%)

potential earnings and so on. So as to make these percentages easier to handle and capable of being described within the framework of the Lorenz earnings distribution curve, Table 3 converts columns 3 and 6 of Table 2 into cumulative distributions. Table 3 is then transformed into a Lorenz curve in Figure 1 above, the distance between the curve and the 45 degree line measuring the degree of potential earnings inequality. Since this section of the paper is largely illustrative, the above procedure was only followed for three countries, India, Ghana and the United States.

THE RESULTS

Before the results of the potential earnings distribution are presented it should be made clear that the educational divisions used are very broad and therefore much detail has been lost. For example, since the discounted lifetime earnings used here, and in the previous section, refer approximately to no education, 8 years, 12 years and 16 years of education there is no specific place for those educated to, say, 2 or 6 years. In this case, those members of the labour force have been relegated, rather unsatisfactorily, to the 'no education' category. This means that for India and Ghana this category encompasses very large sections of the labour force, and therefore little is known about the lower sections of the Lorenz curve. This however does not obscure the overall patterns but it does make them appear less dramatic than they probably are in reality. The detailed, underlying calculations of the cumulative percentages of the labour force by education and potential lifetime earnings, based on the OECD publication 'Statistics of the Occupational and Educational Structure of the Labour Force in 53 Countries' [OECD, 1969] and the individual rate of return studies respectively, are not presented here, but the final results are shown in Table 4. As an example of the information presented in Table 4,

TABLE 4

CUMULATIVE DISTRIBUTION OF THE LABOUR FORCE BY LEVEL OF
EDUCATION AND LIFETIME EARNINGS: INDIA, GHANA, UNITED STATES

Level of Education	India		Ghana		United States	
	Labour Force (%)	Lifetime Earnings (%)	Labour Force (%)	Lifetime Earnings (%)	Labour Force (%)	Lifetime Earnings (%)
(1)	(2)	(3)	(4)	(5)	(6)	(7)
None	90·0	65·4	84·4	64·3	—	—
Primary	97·3	83·3	98·3	91·1	41·7	27·5
Secondary	99·4	91·6	99·8	96·9	88·6	79·2
Higher	100·0	100·0	100·0	100·0	100·0	100·0

SOURCE: columns 2, 4 and 6: OECD [1969, pp.181, 161, 112]: column 3: Blaug et al. [1969, p.171]; column 5: Hinchliffe [1969, Appendix]; column 7: Hanoch [1967, pp.316, 317].

we can say that, considering the labour force with higher education, in India 0.6 per cent of the labour force receive 8.4 per cent of total potential earnings, in Ghana 0.2 per cent receive 3.1 per cent and in the United

States 13.4 per cent receive 20.8 per cent. In other words the total earnings of higher education graduates in India and Ghana are a much greater portion of overall total earnings in relation to their relative size than is the case for the similar educational group in the United States. Similar comparisons can be made for the other educational groups.

Transforming Table 4 into a Lorenz curve in Figure 2 below, a clear pattern emerges of the lifetime earnings distribution in India, Ghana and the United States, even allowing for the very aggregated divisions of the labour force by educational level. Inequality of potential lifetime

FIGURE 2

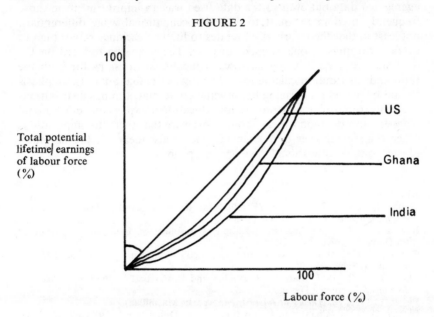

Labour force (%)

earnings between different educational groups of the labour force is much greater in low income countries such as India and Ghana than in high income countries such as the United States.

It may be objected here that the final result of the distribution analysis developed in this paper is no different from the results obtained by conventional distribution analysis since the labour force, however differentiated, has one single earnings distribution. There are two points however which differentiate this distribution analysis from other analyses. First the above distribution has been based on lifetime earnings and thus goes beyond previous efforts and secondly by using educational levels as a base, explanation has been incorporated into what is usually pure description. As has been pointed out previously this part of the paper is meant to be largely illustrative and the data used are of a rough order and highly aggregated. On the other hand, education-earning data are available in very raw form for several countries and it should be possible in the very near future to refine this data further.

CONCLUSION

It was intimated at the beginning of this paper that different patterns of educational provision have different consequences for the distribution of earnings and that this had not yet been fully realized, let alone analysed, particularly with the developing countries in mind. This paper has been an attempt to rectify this situation, albeit in a rudimentary way, by analyses which start with the individual graduate of each educational level and move on to earnings of educational groups as a whole. The latter investigation was somewhat stunted by the necessity of using highly aggregated data but even so the data used was an improvement on those frequently used in the past to analyse occupational wage differentials, not least in that the information relates to lifetime earnings rather than to average earnings at one moment in time. The next step forward on the data side must lie in using narrower educational divisions for both the ratio and distribution calculations. In terms of actual analysis, emphasis should be placed on deriving hypothetical potential earnings distributions resulting from different strategies of educational expansion. Educational planners and decision takers should be aware that there are implications other than manpower and financial ones consequent on the adoption of each specific educational development proposal.

REFERENCES

Blaug, M., Layard, P. R. G. and Woodhall, M., 1969, *The Causes of Graduate Unemployment in India*, London: Allen Lane.

Bowles, S., 1965, 'The Efficient Allocation of Resources in Education', unpublished Ph.D. thesis, University of Harvard.

Carnoy, M. 1967, 'Rates of Return to Schooling in Latin America', *Journal of Human Resources*, Summer.

Chiswick, B. R., 1971, 'Earnings Inequality and Economic Development', *Quarterly Journal of Economics*, February.

Fisher, I., 1930, *The Theory of Interest*, New York: Macmillan.

Gunter, H., 1964, 'Changes in Occupational Wage Differentials', *International Labour Review*, March.

Hanoch, G., 1967, 'An Economic Analysis of Earnings and Schooling', *Journal of Human Resources*, Summer.

Hinchliffe, K., 1969, 'Educational Planning Techniques for Developing Countries with Special Reference to Ghana and Nigeria', unpublished M. Phil. thesis, University of Leicester.

Klinov-Malul R., 1966, *The Profitability of Investment in Education*, Jerusalem: Maurice Falk Institute for Economic Research in Israel.

Lydall, H. B., 1968, *The Structure of Earnings*, Oxford: Clarendon Press.

OECD, 1965, *Wages and Labour Mobility*, Paris.

OECD, 1969, *Statistics of the Occupational and Educational Structure of the Labour Force in 53 Countries*, Paris.

Papola, T. S., and Bharadwaj, V. P., 1970, 'Dynamics of Industrial Wage Structure: An Inter Country Analysis', *Economic Journal*, March.

Pigou, A. C., 1924, *The Economics of Welfare*, London: Macmillan.

Podoluk, J. R., 1965, *Earnings and Education*. Canada: Dominion Bureau of Statistics.

Psacharopoulos, G. and Hinchliffe, K., 1972, 'Further Evidence of the Elasticity of Substitution between Different Types of Educated Labour', *Journal of Political Economy*, July/August.

Taira, K., 1966, 'Wage Differentials in Developing Countries: A Survey of Findings', *International Labour Review*, March.

Thias, H. H. and Carnoy, M., 1969, *Cost Benefit Analysis in Education: A Case Study on Kenya*, Washington: International Bank for Reconstruction and Development, Economics Report EC-173.

Selowsky, M., 1968, *The Effect of Unemployment and Growth on the Rate of Return to Education: The Case of Colombia*, Cambridge, Mass.: Harvard University, Center for International Affairs, Report No. 116.

Williamson, J. and Devoretz, D., 1967, 'Education as an Asset in the Phillippine Economy', paper presented to the Second Conference on Population, 27-29 November 1967, Manilla (mimeo).

New Seeds and Income Distribution in Bangladesh

By Douglas V. Smith*

Linear programming models are employed to examine the objective conditions constraining farmer adoption of a new seed-fertilizer-water control technology in Bangladesh. Equal access to the technology and a static set of factor endowments are initially assumed. It is then demonstrated that realistic assumptions of differential access to inputs and a dynamic view of class formation processes illustrate the incompatibility of existing social relations and the new seeds.

The seed-fertilizer-water control technology that is slowly transforming the production of food in Asia had begun to be introduced in Bangladesh before the events of 1971. New varieties of rice and wheat with high response to fertilizer were beginning to make an impact on agriculture in East Bengal; there were serious technical problems of seed availability, disease, and water control to be sure, but the prospect looked bright.

With political independence, the future of food production in Bangladesh looks even more hopeful. No longer are important decisions being made in Islamabad by men interested in markets for low quality foodgrains from West Pakistan. Bengali subsidies to West Pakistan development have stopped, and the resources of Bangladesh can be invested at home.

There are many analysts of the new seed-fertilizer technology, however, who predict difficulties ahead. Some of these difficulties are technical—concerning water control and stable disease resistance—but others are social. These analysts recognize that technologic changes pose challenges to the means by which production is organized. They are apprehensive that these challenges will lead to major upheavals in social relationships.

Technology, however, is not a demon to be feared, but a set of tools to be controlled and used for the betterment of man. It is not technological change which threatens the social stability of countries like Bangladesh, but rather a set of institutions unable to ensure that all citizens reap the benefits of high yielding food crops or of other new, capital-creating activities. Furthermore, the nature of the technology adopted, as determined by existing institutions, may itself have a profound impact on future institutional development.

To analyze the first-round effects of the new seeds on Bangladeshi farmers, it is necessary to know the resources at their disposal, the way in which produce is distributed, and the technical relations of production.

---

*Consultant, Northville, New York.

The first-round distributive effects may then be related to the dynamics of rural change as influenced by differential income movements of various groups in rural society. A village in Comilla District was chosen to explore some of the likely consequences of seeds and fertilizer.

TRADITIONAL TECHNOLOGY AND FARMER CHOICE

Dhaniswar was in 1960 a village of 426 persons located in eastern Comilla District, near the border with the Indian State of Tripura [*Qadir, 1960*]. The village is demographically and agriculturally similar to others in the area of the Academy for Rural Development; an area for which farm management data are available. Of the 77 families in Dhaniswar, the heads of 60 report farming as their main occupation, 5 report service, 3 were washermen, and 8 were labourers. One widow was a beggar.

Rice was the principal crop: grown on an average of 2·32 acres of cultivated land per landed family. (There were 12 landless families.) Milk production provided a supplement to some incomes, however, although there was no grazing land in the village. Some villages in the district have fish-ponds but the ponds of Dhaniswar were used for domestic purposes only. Minor amounts of jute, pulses, chilies, and vegetables were grown, and there were a few betelnut trees and bamboo thickets.

The soil is silty loam and, when dry, is hard and almost impossible to plough. The topography consists of higher land (built up to protect from flooding) on which is situated the homestead; *viti* land, which is high enough nearly always to remain above water and which is used for vegetables or rice seedlings; intermediate land, which is closest to the village and thus naturally fertilized by village wastes; and low land along the river. The low land is single-cropped because the early floods make the cultivation of *aus* (spring) rice difficult. The intermediate land is double-cropped for the most part, generally with *aus* rice followed by *aman* (autumn) rice.

To determine the likely effects of change a model was formulated to represent farmer choice in the presence of resource constraints. The model results were compared with actual data for traditional production activities; after minor adjustment, the model was used to examine the potential impacts of new production possibilities on farmer choice, and to identify probable future resource bottlenecks.

The model was of linear programming form. It was based on single-farm resource availabilities (for each of 8 different 'representative' farms as defined in Table 1), 1 year of operation (investment activities were not modelled), and deterministic hydrologic and economic parameters. The farmer was assumed to maximize his net revenues from agricultural production provided adequate foodgrains (see Table 1) were grown to feed his family in at least x years out of 100, where x was normally taken to be 90.

Resource constraints were included on land of two types (intermediate and low), monthly labour, monthly animal power, and monthly working capital. (Monthly water constraints were added for irrigated conditions.) Model options permitted hire of labour, draft animals, and water lifting devices, and borrowing of working capital. Model algebra and further details have been presented elsewhere [*Smith, 1971*].

Since this study's interest lies in estimating the impact of technological change on different groups of farmers, 'representative' or model farms are selected to reflect their group's resource position [*Lee, 1966, pp.58-61*]. It is assumed that all farms face the same prices and that all farms have identical technical coefficients; aggregation theory, therefore, focuses on resource availabilities as the determinants of aggregation group definition. Thus, for exact aggregation there must be proportional variation in resource availabilities between farms [*Day, 1963, pp.797-813*]. Examination of the data led to the conclusion that land of two types is available to all farms in fixed proportions, as is animal power and water. Labour, working capital and subsistence requirements, however, are functions of family size: therefore farms must be classified both by total cultivated acreage and by family size. For Bangladesh, classification of farm types was made according to Table 1.[1]

TABLE 1
RESOURCE POSITION OF 'REPRESENTATIVE' FARMERS[a]

Cultivable Land (acres)	Tenure Form	Work Animals (nos.)	Family Size (nos.)	Consumption Units (nos.)	Work Units (nos.)
·75	owner-operated	·5	5	4	$1\frac{3}{4}$
1·5	,,	1	6	$4\frac{1}{2}$	2
3·0	,,	2	6	$4\frac{1}{2}$	2
4·5	,,	3	7	$5\frac{1}{2}$	$2\frac{1}{4}$
1·5	,,	1	3	$2\frac{1}{2}$	1
1·5	,,	1	10	8	3
1·5	rent	1	6	$4\frac{1}{2}$	2
1·5	sharecrop	1	6	$4\frac{1}{2}$	2

Year end assets = Rs. 275/acre = average returns from aman harvest (available January 1), assuming no debt.

Monthly   = (1 pound per day per consumption unit) × (30 days per month) ×
subsistence   (1/80 maunds per pound) × (22 Rs./maund retail price).
[a] All numbers in this table are based on the 1960 agricultural census and the 'Master Survey of Agriculture'.

Production activities used in the linear programming model were simply defined by crop: few distinctions were made on the basis of alternative cultivation techniques. Data for activity coefficient definition were composite values from farm surveys and minor differences in technique are thus not reflected.[2] It is a basic assumption of this model that farmers currently try to optimize their allocation of resources. Revenue response is insensitive to the minor changes in technique observed in Bangladesh, however; so that even though individual farmers will use what appear (because of differences in microclimatology, whim, etc.) to be different means of crop production from our viewpoint the differences are of curiosity value only because they involve near-identical uses of scarce resources. It is only when new technologies (or institutions) are introduced into a region that farmers must learn again what techniques are best for them. We thus say that under traditional agriculture there are many near-optimal production decisions but that with technological change peasants learn (slowly or rapidly depending on individuals and propaganda) and try to optimize their incomes. Thus, although these models are termed 'farm models' they reflect not the decisions of a farm but rather the modal decisions of farms in a particular aggregation group; generally speaking, therefore, we assume that no one does appreciably better than anyone else who is in the same resource position once static technologic and institutional conditions prevail.

A series of 8 basic farm-type models was run with the fixed to the farm resource assumptions outlined in Table 1 and with a set of traditional crop production activities deemed suitable for eastern Comilla District. The cropping activities on intermediate land are: transplanted *aman* paddy, broadcast *aus* paddy, jute, gram or other winter pulse, summer til, winter

TABLE 2
OPTIMAL CROPPING PATTERNS AND SHADOW PRICES OF FIXED RESOURCES UNDER TRADITIONAL TECHNOLOGY†

		units	(a)	(b)	(c)	(d)	(e)	(f)	(g)
	Cultivable Land	Acres	·78	1·5	3·0	4·5	1·5	1·5	1·79
	Family size	no.	5	6	6	7	3	9	6
	Share of crop kept by family	%	100	100	100	100	100	100	50
land type 1	Transp. aman 1	acres	·57	·76	1·59	2·38	·73	1·10	1·24
land type 1	Broadcast Aus 1	,,	·38	·22	—	—	·23	·61	·91
land type 1	Jute	,,	—	·72	1·85	2·77	·58	·14	·03
land type 1	Gram	,,	·04	—	—	—	—	·08	—
land type 1	Til	,,	·27	·29	·64	·95	·44	·52	·57
land type 1	Mustard	,,	·09	·54	1·02	1·53	·56	·17	·36
land type 2	Broadcast Aus 2	,,	·16	·20	·52	·78	·30	·30	·36
land type 2	Transp. aman 2	,,	·16	·30	·60	·90	·30	·30	·36
	Net Revenue	Rs.	352	743	1491	2133	724	698	376
shadow prices	Maximum type 1-land shadow price	Rs./acre	181	174	174	174	174	181	173
shadow prices	Maximum type 2-land shadow price	,,	259	19	64	73	42	237	168
shadow prices	April bullock	Rs./animal team-day	3	10	*	*	3	3	6
shadow prices	July bullock	,,	3	24	*	*	7	3	6
shadow prices	Nov. capital	Rs./Rs.	—	—	—	—	—	—	1
shadow prices	Subsistence	Rs./maund	8	14	—	—	—	8	19

*not recorded
†prices are 1970 level

til, mustard, and sugar. The low land (which is subject to flooding and is more remote from homesteads) can grow broadcast uas and transplanted aman paddy, both with reduced average yields and adjusted planting and harvesting dates.

Table 2 summarizes those model solutions of most interest here. It is assumed that no borrowing of working capital is permitted to any farm unit (for traditional farming activities in Comilla District such capital is of minor import) and that all farms can hire labour. (We speak of net hiring on a monthly basis). Three farm types, namely those with 0·75 acre and 5 family members, 1·5 acres and 9 family members, and 1·5 acres held on a crop-share basis and 6 family members, were unable to meet subsistence requirements with these assumptions. In order to develop a cropping pattern to meet subsistence it was decided (1) to allow limited hiring of bullocks during April and July, and (2) to increase the cultivable land area slightly, as shown in row I of Table 2. Actual adjustments would also in reality be made by peasants by (3) the sale of family labour; (4) engagement in petty trade or handicrafts, and (5) a higher than average fraction of cash crops in the cropping pattern. [3]

Comparison of the cropping patterns shown in Table 2 with information available from the agricultural census and sample surveys shows good agreement (for the area around Dhaniswar) except for oilseeds (til and mustard). The high acreages devoted to these crops by our models may reflect more animal power rigidity than is present in practice: since oilseeds have low animal power requirements, or it may arise from agronomic restrictions involving soil moisture needs that are not well understood by agriculturalists but are understood by farmers.

The sharecroppers' difficult position is shown dramatically in the last column of Table 2. With the district average of one bullock per 1·5 acre farm, but with the possibility of renting another, and assuming an even split of costs and returns with the landlord, a cultivator needs a minimum of 1·8 acres to meet his family's subsistence requirements. He does this by owning one bullock and teaming him with a neighbour, relative, or landlord's bullock in a bullock or labour exchange relationship, *and* by hiring outright additional animal power during April and July. A separate column for a tenant paying a fixed annual rent has not been given, since resource allocations are only affected in the unlikely event that working capital reserves are unduly depleted at planting time by rent payments due. Working capital requirements for traditional agriculture are small in any event and therefore we ignore this case here. (The sharecropper of column (g), Table 2, does have a binding working capital constraint in November, but this is in fact a subsistence effect caused by exceedingly low foodgrain reserves just prior to the aman harvest. If he is allowed to borrow in November on a short-term basis, he will be able to shift his cropping pattern slightly to reflect greater freedom of choice, and he will plant more aman paddy and less aus paddy as the pre-harvest food crisis diminishes in importance.)

These farm analyses indicate the minimum size of farm for self-sufficiency. For an average size family of five members headed by an owner-cultivator, ·8 acre is the minimum if some hiring of bullocks to supplement the assumed institutionalized bullock exchange is permitted, and if we assume no debt repayment, replacement of equipment or animals, or consumption beyond subsistence. For a sharecropper with family of six, an absolute minimum of 1·8 acres on half shares is needed. Again, some flexibility in bullock hire arrangements is assumed.

WATER PROJECT AND IMPROVED SEEDS

The second set of farm models includes new activities (crop varieties), revised resource availabilities (water and working capital), and modified expected returns from crop production activities (due to altered input requirements and crop yields).[4] It is assumed that a tubewell irrigation scheme distributes priced water on an acreage-held basis to all farmers in a given area and that small embankments provide flood protection to lower-lying land. These state provided projects with *equal access to all*, and the availability of chemical fertilizer, produce one basic land type in the village of Dhaniswar. (This is exclusive of garden and homestead lands which are considered separately.)

Each farmer has open not only the traditional cropping activities, but also a new set of improved varieties and of irrigation demanding cash crops. For example, Mexi-Pak wheat, IR8 rice, IR20 rice, IRRI aus rice, improved jute, potatoes, and irrigated sugar cane are added to the traditional crops and varieties.

TABLE 3

OPTIMAL CROPPING PATTERNS UNDER MODERN TECHNOLOGY IN COMILLA DISTRICT

Cultivable Land	units acres	(a) ·75	(b) 1·5	(c) 4·5	(d) 1·5	(e) 1·5	(f) 1·5
Family size	no.	5	6	7	3	10	6
Share of crop kept by family	%	100	100	100	100	100	50
Potato	acres	·24	·53	1·82	·69	·48	·47
Wheat	,,	—	—	—	·27	—	—
Transp. aman	,,	—	—	—	—	—	—
IR20	,,	·54	1·04	2·92	·67	1·08	1·09
Baus	,,	—	—	—	—	—	—
IRRI aus	,,	·50	·99	3·20	·85	1·01	1·01
Jute	,,	—	—	—	·21	—	—
Boro (IR8)	,,	·33	·68	1·64	—	·66	·65
Gram	,,	—	—	—	—	—	—
Til	,,	·15	·30	·90	·50	·30	·30
Mustard	,,	—	—	—	—	—	—
Sugar (irrig.)	,,	—	—	—	—	—	—
Net revenue	Rs.	1212	2462	6250	2158	2425	1207
Largest monthly land shadow price	Rs./acre	628	628	445	245	628	314

Table 3 presents results for six representative farms. There is no hiring of draft animals, nor is there any borrowing of working capital; but labour hire is permitted. If the same prices are used as before, but if water and

TABLE 4

OPTIMAL CROPPING PATTERNS, LEVEL OF HIRING AND SHADOW PRICES OF FIXED RESOURCES UNDER MODERN TECHNOLOGY IN COMILLA DISTRICT: SUPPLEMENTAL RESULTS WITH HIRING PERMITTED, CHANGED PRICES, AND WATER SHORTAGES

	units	(a) 4·5	(b) 4·5	(c) 4·5	(d) 4·5	(e) 1·5	(f) 1·5	(g) 1·5	(h) 1·5
Cultivable Land	acres								
Family size	no.	7	7	7	7	6	6	6	6
Share of crop kept by family	%	100	100	100	100	100	100	100	100
Hiring activities allowed		no	labour	labour and bullock	labour, bull. and capital	none	water scarce in April	higher jute price	higher sugar cane price
Potato	acres	1·31	1·82	1·71	3·98	·53	·53	·53	·44
Wheat	,,	1·63	—	—	—	—	—	—	—
IR20	,,	1·41	2·92	3·01	1·04	1·04	1·04	1·04	·79
IRRI aus	,,	1·78	3·20	2·90	2·71	·99	·62	·10	·75
Jute	,,	·57	—	1·08	1·79	—	·35	·82	·29
IR8	,,	—	1·64	2·07	—	·68	·68	·68	·54
Til	,,	2·46	·90	—	—	·30	·32	·36	·54
Sugar	,,	—	—	—	—	—	—	—	·32
Net revenue	Rs.	5078	6520	6773	7333	2462	2432	2667	2571
Max. land shadow price	Rs./acre	92	445	439	773	628	604	407	615

		Level of hiring			Shadow Prices (Rs.) Rs./Unit			
		11	8	64				
Feb. labour	man days	—	—	—	—	—	—	—
April labour	"	78	97	42	—	—	—	—
May labour	"	—	—	5	—	—	—	—
July labour	"	36	34	19	—	—	8	—
Aug. labour	"	30	69	34	—	—	—	—
Oct. labour	"	15	13	17	—	—	—	—
Nov. labour	"	—	—	83	—	—	—	—
Dec. labour	"	88	102	23	—	—	—	—
April bullocks	animal team-days	—	12	6	46	36	44	12
Oct. bullocks	"	—	—	19	8	12	5	10
Dec. bullocks	"	—	—	—	1·3	1·3	1·6	1·3
Jan. capital	Rs.	—	—	958	—	5	—	3
April water	acre feet	—	—	—	—	—	—	—

labour are non-binding resources, the new cropping patterns show a marked proclivity for rice. (If either water or labour are scarce, however, wheat and jute enter the cropping patterns—see Table 4.) Potatoes are a profitable crop in Comilla District (since there are cold storage facilities for seed potatoes), but potato planting is limited by a shortage of working capital or credit availability for purchase of seed potatoes and fertilizer. (The shadow price on working capital in farming varies from 1·3 to 1·6 rupees per rupee borrowed for 1·5 acre farms.)

For the small farm the absence of a full team of draft animals is a major impediment to increased production. Since all farms of 1·5 acres or less are assumed to share draft animals with others, the situation during the busiest periods in April and December becomes very constricting to farmer choice. In fact, for the 1·5 acre farm the shadow price on animal power during April is Rs. 46 per animal-team day. (We assumed teams hire for Rs. 3-4 per animal-team day.)[5]

The solutions for the larger farms change markedly as assumptions are altered regarding the types of hiring and borrowing permitted. Table 4 shows the effects on a 4·5 acre farm of (a) no hiring, (b) labour hire only, (c) labour and bullock hire, and (d) labour and bullock hire and short-term borrowing. The 4·5 acre farm with labour hire chooses to force both wheat and jute out of the model cropping pattern and to replace both crops with rice. (Remember: water is not a limiting resource.) During December this farm requires 88 man-days, or approximately 3 man-months, of hired labour.

A comparison of Tables 2 and 4 shows that modern technology results in a revenue increase for the 4·5 acre farm of Rs. (6520-2133) or approxiimately Rs. 4400. Since fixed costs are about the same in each case (irrigation and flood control investments are government made), the revenue increase nearly equals the income increase. It should be noted that if this farmer's land were not fragmented, a fractional tubewell could be paid for in 2 or 3 years from this economic surplus. On the other hand, if the tube-wells are government supplied, as we assumed here, then this economic surplus could go for other farm investments, consumption, transfer out of agriculture, or the purchase of additional land. Since none of the technologies being used in this analysis are undeveloped and untested, these dramatic increases in farm incomes are quite possible.

If draft animal hire is also open to this farmer with 4·5 acres of land, he will choose to hire during April and will go back into jute cultivation. (His labour hire requirements during December now go up to 102 man-days.) If, in addition, the farmer can borrow on a short-term basis, he will do so during January (in the amount of Rs. 958 assumed payable at 12 per cent annual interest at the end of potato harvest in April). This flexibility produces another dramatic jump in expected revenues to Rs. 7333 and an equally dramatic jump in the marginal value of land: from Rs. 92 for no hiring, to Rs. 445 for labour hire only, to Rs. 773 for labour, animal power, and capital hiring. Short-term borrowing also simplifies the cropping pattern significantly, as would be expected, causing a concentration in potatoes, IR20, IR *aus*, and jute.

Water has been considered a non-binding resource under the modern technology assumption, but if water were scarce during the dry month of April (because of inability of centrifugal pumps to lift water from wells affected by drawdown, for example), then a comparison of columns (e) and (f) indicates some of the effects. The primary result of a foreseeable shortage of irrigation water is a shift out of water consuming IRRI rice and into jute.

A similar shift in favour of jute occurs if the aus/jute price ratio is decreased. Columns (e) and (g) compare optimal cropping patterns based on the same rice prices and an increase in jute price (to the farmer) from Rs. 24 to Rs. 36 per maund. This shift probably represents a better valuation of foreign exchange (in 1970)[6], but it does not reflect current farm-gate price ratios.[7]

A similar analysis was performed to examine cropping pattern sensitivity to changes in sugar cane price. No run made using Rs. 1·2 per maund produced any sugar under any conditions. The more reasonable social price of Rs. 2·2 per maund also failed to produce a shift to sugar for our 1·5 acre farm. As increase to Rs. 3 per maund (above both the private price and likely social value), however, brought sugar into the solution at the expense of all the oilseeds, two-thirds of the jute, and minor amounts of IRRI boro paddy, IRRI aman paddy, IRRI aus paddy, and potatoes. (It also caused a shift into some jute because of water shortage during April.)

LAND, TECHNOLOGY, AND INCOME DISTRIBUTION

Fundamental patterns of rural income distribution are set by the ownership of land. Traditional technologies affect these distribution patterns, as the fixed costs of indivisible inputs (for example, bullocks) have a greater relative impact on incomes of small farms than on incomes of large farms. In Bangladesh, however, draft animal teams are rarely owned outright by the poorer farm families, and effective divisibility of this input is nearly achieved under traditional conditions by animal sharing, animal-labour exchange, and a market for draft animal hire. Although the details of these mechanisms await future description, the effects are to produce an income distribution pattern among landed cultivators roughly equivalent to the land distribution pattern among the same groups. Table 5 shows the computation of farm incomes using the previously-generated 'farm revenues' and a set of assumptions regarding farm fixed costs. (Modal family sizes according to census data are assumed for each farm size.) These incomes are used in Table 6 to show the effects of technology on the distribution of farm incomes. Under traditional technology the distribution of incomes is slightly better than the distribution of land, but only because we are forced to assume all farm families survive and that therefore families with the least amount of land must seek outside employment to raise their incomes to subsistence level.

The distribution of incomes under modern technology depends greatly on resource access assumptions. Since we assume unlimited access to hired labour at a daily wage rate of Rs. 3, the larger farms will employ labour until its marginal productivity equals Rs. 3. On the other hand, small, self sufficient farms will exhaust the supply of family labour or employ it until its marginal productivity is zero and will thus utilize modern, labour-using technologies more productively. Fixed resources of animal power, on the other hand, favour the larger farmer because of a greater access to work animals (with modern technology there will be a shortage of draft animals in many areas) and because of relatively lower fixed costs. (For all farms, we assume equal access to water, seeds, and fertilizer at given costs.) These conflicting trends produce little change in the distribution of incomes, as can be seen by an examination of the last three columns of Table 6.

These computations of income distribution have been done for one village where details of *each* family's size, composition, and land tenure status are known. It should be noted, however, that Village Dhaniswar has few sharecroppers—a result presumably due to a relative lack of many intermediate tenure holders during the Zamindari period.[8] Using 'Master

TABLE 5
FARM INCOMES UNDER TRADITIONAL AND MODERN TECHNOLOGY

Land Area[a]	Net Revenue[b]	Traditional Technology				Net Income
		Bullocks[c]	Fixed Costs			
			Equip.	Bldg.	Total	
(Acres)	(Rs.)	(Rs.)	(Rs.)	(Rs.)	(Rs.)	(Rs.)
·5	360	30	25	50	105	255
1·5	740	60	25	50	135	605
2·5	1250	120	25	50	195	1055
3·5	1750	150	25	50	225	1525
4·5	2130	180	25	50	255	1875
5·5	2590	210	25	50	285	2305
6·5	3050	240	25	50	315	2735
7·5	3520	240	25	50	315	3205
8·5	3990	240	25	50	315	3675
9·5	4460	240	25	50	315	4145
		Modern Technology				
·5	810	30	40	50	120	690
1·5	2460	60	40	50	150	2310
2·5	3880	120	40	50	210	3670
3·5	5430	150	40	50	240	5190
4·5	6520	180	40	50	270	6250
5·5	8080	210	40	50	300	7780
6·5	9550	240	40	50	330	9220
7·5	11,010	240	40	50	330	10,680
8·5	12,490	240	40	50	330	12,160
9·5	13,960	240	40	50	330	13,630

[a]*De facto* status land area includes all land held by village residents that is actually cultivated under the supervision of the family. It includes owned and operated land as well as other's land held by the family on mortgage, rent, or share-cropping.
[b]See Table 2, col. (a) for 0·5 acre farm; Table 2, col. (b) for 1·5 acre; Table 2, cols. (c) and (d) for larger farms under traditional technology. For modern technology, see Table 3, cols. (a) and (b) for smaller farms and Table 4, col. (b) for larger farms.
[c]Assume one bullock costs Rs. 300 and works 5 years.

TABLE 6

DISTRIBUTION OF LAND AND FARM INCOMES IN VILLAGE DHANISWAR

Range Acres	Farm Size			Area		Traditional Tech. Income			Modern Tech. Income			Cum. Income Increase (x/y)
	Mean Acre	No.	Cum. %	Acres	Cum. %	(y) Rs./farm	Total	Cum. %	(x) Rs./farm	Total	Cum. %	
·01—1·00	·5	20	31	10	7	255	5,100	8	690	13,800	7	2·7
1·01—2·00	1·5	17	57	25·5	25	605	10,285	26	2,310	39,270	25	3·8
2·01—3·00	2·5	14	78·5	35	50	1055	14,770	50	3,880	54,320	51	3·7
3·01—4·00	3·5	6	87·8	21	65	1525	9,150	65	5,430	32,580	67	3·5
4·01—5·00	4·5	3	92·5	13·5	75	1875	5,625	75	6,250	18,750	76	3·3
5·01—6·00	5·5	2	95·4	11	83	2305	4,610	82	7,780	15,560	83	3·3
6·01—7·00	6·5	1	97	6·5	87	2735	2,735	87	9,220	9,220	88	3·4
7·01—8·00	7·5	0	97	0	87	3205	0	87	10,680	0	88	3·3
8·01—9·00	8·5	1	98·5	8·5	93	3675	3,675	93	12,160	12,160	93	3·3
9·01—10·00	9·5	1	100·0	9·5	100	4145	4,145	100	13,630	13,630	100	3·3
		65		140·5			60,095			209,290		

Figure 1. Distribution of Land and Incomes for a Village and a
Sample of Farmers in Rural Bangladesh.

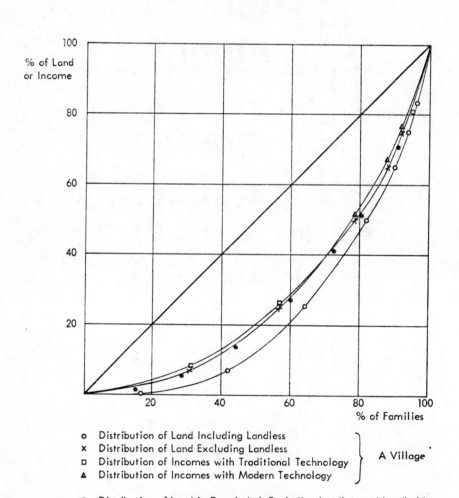

- o Distribution of Land Including Landless
- x Distribution of Land Excluding Landless
- □ Distribution of Incomes with Traditional Technology
- ▲ Distribution of Incomes with Modern Technology

A Village

- • Distribution of Land in Bangladesh Excluding Landless and Landholders
  with less than .25 – from "Master Survey of Agriculture – Round 6"

Survey of Agriculture' results and excluding all rural households with fewer than ·25 acres (that is, excluding 32 per cent of rural households), the distribution of land is less equitable for Bangladesh as a whole than it is for Dhaniswar, where only the landless (16 per cent of households) are excluded.[9] Figure 1 shows this comparison together with the effects of technology on Dhaniswar income distribution.

It is impossible, however, to understand either the statics or the dynamics of rural society in Bangladesh by an analysis of relative differences in income (or wealth) alone. Class and status group relations must form the basis of any non-arbitrary analysis. As Myrdal has reminded us:

> Low average income, income inequality, and social stratification are causally interrelated. But social stratification is itself an aspect of inequality, one that need not uniquely correlate with income distribution . . . . Thus it may well be the case that the upper strata in a poor village in India do not have a significantly higher income than sharecropping tenants or landless peasants. Yet there is an important difference between these groups: the former often receive incomes without working while the latter not. A distribution of income by social strata would therefore indicate a high degree of equality when in fact the social structure is harshly inegalitarian. (*Myrdal, 1969, p. 569*).

CLASS IN RURAL BANGLADESH

To fathom the dynamic implications of technological change in rural Bangladesh it is necessary to analyze the processes of inequality formation and their enhancement by patterns of social stratification and state-enforced legal measures.[10]

In contemporary Bangladesh an important determinant of political behaviour is the faction.[11] Factions are vertically integrated groups of rural residents dominated by 'rich' peasants (or a landlord); poor peasants and landless labourers, who are in an economically dependent position vis-a-vis faction leadership, follow the political guidance of that leadership. Political conflict thus takes place primarily between factions and not between classes, although sometimes factions of self sufficient peasants have a faction-class nature in relation to factions spanning a wider spectrum of classes. One of the implications of 'modernization', of course, is to weaken the power of traditional faction leadership and to substitute new bases for group cohesion. The slow introduction of the market principle to govern many relations has thus led to a series of fundamental changes affecting the functions of faction groups.

Feudal relations in Bengal have been in a process of decline at least since the onset of British rule. Social reorganization promoted by the introduction of free trade tied changes in village life to the vagaries of international markets. The opium trade, the great famine, the forced cultivation of indigo, and the disastrous decline of the hand-woven cloth industry, all represent facets of the profound convulsions introduced into Bengali society by the intrusion of imperialism. But through much of this time of change peasants faced a system of feudal relationships that harnessed many to the demands of landlords (more correctly, rent collectors) while sheltering them from the worst buffetings of a system under severe strain.

Partition, in 1947, brought an exodus of the zamindars from East Bengal to India: they were primarily all Hindu. This removal of the major part of the feudal landlord class was followed by the East Bengal State Acquisition and Tenancy Act of 1950 which allowed the concentrated (but subinfeudated) zamindari lands to come under control of the tiller. Tenancy and sharecropping still exist in Bangladesh, to be sure, and sharecroppers remain without legal protection of their position, but the severe concentration of land control so prevalent in other parts of South Asia is absent. It would, however, be folly indeed to conclude from this that village life is equalitarian in nature, or that the seeds of profound class differentiation are not present.

Knowledge of the current situation with regard to the relative importance of economic classes will permit assessment of the major technological forces influencing trends in rural Bangladesh. The statistics are sufficient for only an outline of class structure, but this outline is revealing. The attempt will be made to classify farmers according to our assessment of the probable alliances of interests that will form over the following key issues of rural policy: taxation, nature of rural works, prices of foodstuffs and jute, land reform, introduction of labour-saving machinery and herbicides, wage level determination, interest rate levels, co-operative formation, and type of water resource development (whether public or private). Thus groups of farmers defined by economic criteria will be termed a 'class' if they may be expected to be in general agreement regarding resolution of the above set of issues. 'Class' members, however, are not assumed to be in mutual intercourse; in fact, being peasants, they are assumed to normally be isolated from one another.

The model-based analyses reported above indicate that, under traditional agriculture in Comilla District, a farm size of from 3·0 to 4·5 acres requires utilization of hired labour.[12] Using 4·0 acres as the cutoff between self-sufficient and labour-hiring peasants, 9-10 per cent of households in Comilla District must hire labour for a part of their income. Perhaps half of these households make a substantial part of their income from exploitation if land rent and moneylending are included with labour hire. Other regions of Bangladesh have a larger fraction of households in possession of land in excess of 4 acres. The 'Master Survey of Agriculture-Round 6' indicates 18 per cent of households in the country have more than 4 acres. Because of rainfall patterns and soil conditions, however, Comilla District is particularly well suited to traditional forms of agriculture, and therefore 4 acres in Comilla is worth somewhat more than 4 acres in, for example, Dinajpur.[13]

A self-sufficient owner-cultivator in Comilla District might have between 1 and 4 acres of land. Clearly, there is a substantial difference in economic position across this range, with the owner of one acre likely to bear a substantial debt burden (substantial in terms relative to income); but such peasants would hire small amounts of labour and would not work as hired labourers themselves. These peasants also own nearly all their farmed land. In the villages studied by Bertocci and Qadir, about 48 per cent of households fell in this category. The proportion in other districts is considerably less than this, due to the greater prevalence of sharecropping and the more pronounced inequalities of land distribution.

The poorest peasants are semi-tenants, tenants with less than 2 acres, or cultivators with less than 1 acre of land. (These divisions arise from our previous analyses based on requirements for subsistence.) Bertocci reports 34 per cent of landed households in his sample had less than 1·15 acres; Qadir found 23 per cent with less than 1·00 acre in Dhaniswar.

On a country-wide basis, about 11 per cent of agriculturalists are bargadars (share-croppers), and 4 per cent are bargaders-cum-labourers or owner-cum-bargadar-cum-labourers. The 'Master Survey of Agriculture' also indicated that 48 per cent of land-owning cultivators have less than 1·25 acres. There is, however, some overlap in categories.

The landless comprise 10 per cent in Bertocci's sample, 16 per cent in Qadir's, and 4 per cent in the 'Master Survey of Agriculture–Round 6'. Although a few of these landless are members of the rural petty bourgeoisie most are farm labourers or handicraftsmen.

To summarize, we estimate the class composition of rural Bangladesh to be roughly as follows, with the ranges indicating regional variations from greater equality in the East to less in North Bengal:

landlords	1 per cent
'rich' peasants	8-10 per cent
self-sufficient peasants	35-50 per cent
poorest peasants	25-45 per cent
proletariat (rural)	15-22 per cent

All fishermen, boatmen, and rural handicraftsmen (weavers, pottery makers, etc.) are excluded from this classification. They should probably all be classified in the two lowest categories, depending upon whether or not they own their equipment.

It should be emphasized, however, that there is a considerable amount of overlap between these classes as far as class attitudes are concerned. For example, how does one determine how little land a poor peasant has to have before he identifies with the landless? Furthermore, some 'rich' peasants are moneylenders or traders as well and derive a substantial income from those occupations while other 'rich' peasants are in debt and receive little or no income from land rent. Aggregated statistics do not illuminate these subleties, although the village studies of Bertocci and Qadir are useful for this purpose.

MODERN TECHNOLOGY AND CLASS DIFFERENTIATION

As can be seen from the above data, Bangladesh has at present a rural society influenced by capitalist relations. This is in comparison with areas like pre-1945 China, of course, and not relative to the USA. Consider that one-third of all farms in East Bengal in 1960 grew jute for sale, one-half reported indebtedness, and two-thirds reported using some wage labour. [*Agricultural Census Organization, 1960*]. While legacies of feudal relations remain, they have had difficulty surviving the abolition of zamindari. Modern technology will enhance the trend toward market control. Return to Table 2, column (d), and Table 3, column (c), to see the potential impact of the seed-water-fertilizer revolution on the 4·5 acre 'rich' peasant. His revenues increase by approximately Rs. 4400 per year under the conservative assumption that no additions to draft animal or mechanization availability are made and that no borrowing of working capital occurs. (At the same time his labour hire requirements increase from 66 to 258 man-days per year.) We assume no substantial increase in fixed costs, since it has been (1971) government policy to supply irrigation water at nominal, if not zero, rates.[14] Thus, this Rs. 4400 per year is an increase in income.

This remarkable increase in income, achievable today with irrigation, will lead the 'rich' farm family (1) to consume; (2) to invest, or (3) to purchase land with the surplus. Since the high rates of return possible from agriculture will be obvious to the farmer, he will be likely to regard investment in unimproved land as wise for himself and his children. Thus land agglomeration seems inevitable unless (a) urban investments suddenly become attractive; (b) he owns land unimproved by government projects which he can improve by investments of his own; (c) new technologic possibilities appear faster than he can keep up with (e.g., livestock business opportunities), or (d) he consumes the entire economic surplus. None of these events is likely, not even in combination, although (b) and (d) may provide a short-term delay; and the process of land agglomeration now being seen in the Punjab (India) will occur, *ceteris paribus*: the dynamic implications of this are clear.

It is necessary, however, to consider the poorest and self-sufficient peasants. A struggling self-sufficient peasant with 1·5 acres has a net revenue of Rs. 740 under traditional technology—barely sufficient to provide a slight buffer against variations in output from year to year. With advanced technology his net revenue triples to Rs. 2460. Since fixed costs are assumed approximately constant, this amounts to an income increase of about Rs. 1720. Clearly such a cultivator has choices open to him that are similar to those of the expanding, capitalist farmer—with the provision that consumption might be expected to take a larger proportion of this surplus, considering the miserable conditions in which a 1·5 acre peasant lives at present. In addition, such a peasant is almost certain to have a not-insignificant debt whose repayment may have priority: especially if his land is held in mortgage. Thus the farmer with 1·5 acres is much better off with the new technology and can be expected to re-invest modestly, but his capacity for land expansion without considerable luck or drive is limited. In a situation like that now prevailing in Comilla Kotwali Thana where land prices are rising, it is the better-off farmer who can outbid others in purchase of land.

THE PROSPECTS FOR AN EQUITABLE DISTRIBUTION OF BENEFITS

Up to this point it has been assumed that everyone has equal access to the new technology. Clearly, even with this assumption and a *static* view of technologic impact, many residents of rural Bangladesh (those who presently own no land or less than 1 acre) will benefit only modestly—but their absolute position should improve. The new seeds have a remarkable possibility to improve the lot of all: even the landless who will find demand for their labour increasing. As we saw earlier, if, under equal access, land ownership and tenure patterns remain static, income distribution will improve slightly. Retention of the equal access assumption but adoption of a more *dynamic* view of technologic impact (a view obscured by Figure 1), uncovers the spectre of drastic changes in relative well-being, however, and hints at the threat of a worsening in the situation of many. All who rent or sharecrop land may find that their former access to land has terminated as owners find cultivation with hired labour more profitable.[15] Under current land law, sharecroppers have no more rights to land than landless labourers [*Ahmed and Timmens, 1971*]. In Comilla District, from where our examples are taken, this will not be as important as in North Bengal—where 50 per cent of all farms are at least partially tenant farms—but it must hit a marginal group everywhere in Bangladesh as it has in India [*Narain and Joshi, 1969*]. The ranks of the effectively landless could be swelled significantly as the new value of land affects renting decisions: and an imbalance in local adoption rates will accelerate the trend.

Differential access to resources (especially water and credit, but also draft animals) will increase the pressure on farmers who are denied, or who neglect to take advantage of, the new seeds; usufructuary mortgage may become an even more important means of land transfer, outright purchase of land from those left out will increase, and eviction of tenants and sharecroppers is not unlikely. These events have occurred elsewhere in Asia with the introduction of new techniques of production, and Bangladesh is not that unique. Thus, Ladejinsky notes in discussing India that:

> The green revolution affects the few rather than the many, not only because of environmental conditions, but because the majority of the farmers lack resources, or are 'institutionally' precluded from taking advantage of the new agricultural trends. (*Ladejinsky, 1970, p. 763*).

In government policies in East Pakistan there was a long record of favouritism toward the 'rich' peasant-moneylender.[16] There has also, however, been a modest movement through the Comilla-based co-operatives to organize poor and self-sufficient farmers to improve their relative lots. These co-operatives arose because of Akhter Hameed Khan's contention that rural credit on fair terms was available only to the wealthy and that mobilization of rural savings (and initiative) would be best achieved through disciplined co-operatives.

East Bengal has had a long history of agricultural co-operatives [*Ghose and Sinha, 1945, pp.189–203*] and these have evolved into a variety of forms, including those serving specialized groups such as sericulturists and fishermen, those involving different degrees of commitment by the agriculturist, and those providing different services to members. The 'Multi-purpose Co-operative Societies' had the primary function of channeling credit from the Provincial Co-operative Bank to farmers. These societies are in most instances controlled by the wealthier farmers, and loans are generally not repaid. A closely-related type of co-operative that has grown rapidly with the expansion of portable pump irrigation is the 'pump group co-operative'. These co-operatives are, in fact, formed merely for the purposes of obtaining a pump and of qualifying for sub-sidized credit. They are thus severely limited in their concept of a co-operative, and their impact on class relations may strongly favour the wealthy elements.

The most impressive co-operatives in East Bengal are those arising out of the Academy for Rural Development in Comilla.[17] Although, even in Comilla Kotwali Thana where the programme is concentrated, only 40 per cent of the farm families were organized into 'Comilla-type' co-operatives in 12 years, the success with the organized groups has been impressive and the job of organization is formidable indeed. To most Western intellectuals, the burden of assuring equal access to modern inputs rests with these Comilla-type co-operatives.

The Comilla co-operatives' organizing impetus arises from a belief that a rural society controlled by small farmers is an important social goal. The co-operative effort helps farmers to learn their collective power and to build their economic and political strength. Discipline is stressed and consequently the wealthier farmers have been reluctant to join until recently when they more accurately perceived the threat to their positions as moneylenders and labour exploiters. Professional management (as well as many other services) is provided by the thana-level co-operative association. The Comilla co-operatives are designed for the peasant whose self-sufficiency needs reinforcing. Only 14 per cent of Comilla Kotwali Thana co-operative members have less than 1 acre of land (as compared with 49 per cent of the rural population in Kotwali Thana with less than 1 acre) while 43 per cent of co-operative members have from 1 to 2 acres (compared with 24 per cent of the Thana rural population who have farms of that size). Thus most of the poorest peasants and the rural proletariat are excluded from co operative benefits.[18]

Farmers with from 1 to 2 acres have benefitted perhaps the most from co-operatives, and 68 per cent of the rural residents of Kotwali Thana with farms of this size have joined the co-operatives. It is an ominous sign, however, that 'rich' peasants have begun joining in greater numbers and that primary society defaults have been increasing. An examination of all the Thanas of Comilla District where village co-operatives have been formed shows that moneylenders and traders who have joined have deliberately defaulted to destroy the co-operatives.[19] While they were slow to perceive the danger to their positions in the early years of co-operative development in Kotwali Thana, they soon learned these dangers, and their counterparts in other Thanas are now aware of them. The old 'Multi-Purpose Co-operative Societies' were captured by the powerful classes, and there is every reason to expect these new village co-operatives will also succumb to their greed. This will be especially true in new co-operatives formed on the Comilla model but without the substantial financial commitment lavished on Comilla Kotwali Thana.

Moreover, exclusion from a village co-operative in Comilla Kotwali Thana has been a serious handicap to adoption of the new technology, because it has made difficult access to the *essential* ingredient: water. Although some non-members do purchase water from co-operative societies, those non-members that do are overwhelmingly the better-off. Thus surveys in the Thana in 1970 have shown that while over 65 per cent of co-operative non-members have less than 1 acre of land or are landless, only 31 per cent of non-members have been able to get access to winter irrigation water.[20] When it is also realized that farmers with less than 1 acre rarely are eligible for government loans—whether co-operative members or not—it is seen how unsatisfactory are the dynamic implications of these co-operatives. The margin of survival as a cultivator in Bangladesh is too thin for imbalances in development rates not to have a profound impact.

Thus the equal access assumptions, even under the best of existing conditions (that is, the Comilla co-operatives), are subject to serious question. Moreover, the dynamics of the generation and utilization of the economic surplus from adoption of new varieties makes the situation even less favourable to equity. If the more advantaged groups use their surplus to increase their consumption fraction, potential reinvestable surplus is lost and economic growth is slowed. If they buy unimproved land, income distribution is immediately worsened.

Of even more significance may be the actions of the somewhat better-off 'middle' peasants. If they privately reinvest their incremental economic surplus, their condition must improve faster than that of other groups forced to increase their consumption fraction and pay off debts. The process compounds and leads almost invariably to a widening gap, exacerbated by land-buying on the part of the expanding capitalist class. (Unless, of course, investment possibilities outside of agriculture look favourable: and they do not.)

Thus we can foresee the provision of irrigation, for example, leading the 'richer' beneficiaries to bring their newly purchased, non-irrigated lands under irrigation; poor peasants are excluded from access to credit, and often water, and many cultivators find animal power constraints, increasing consumption desires, and debt repayment pressures to be overwhelming. If to this scenario is added the dominant force of 'rich' peasant-landlord-moneylender-trader interests preserving their privilege in co-operatives, tax structures, agrarian reform laws, and price policies, the outlook is grim indeed. While we have emphasized the shortcomings of the approach with the most favourable prognostications—that based on the Comilla experiments—we are cognizant of the implications of the much more prevalent types of agricultural input delivery systems where credit goes to the wealthy, extension advice is lavished on the rich, and water control is vested in interests with power. Since the present Awami League government derives its governing impetus from precisely those 'local influential people' who currently control the direction of government resource flow, prospects for government-sponsored institutional changes of a meaningful sort are slim indeed. While some tinkering with land ceilings can be expected, substantive moves to protect the rights of sharecroppers (and simultaneously to increase their share from the one-half it is almost everywhere), to provide extension and research attention to all, and to guarantee equal access of all (even the farmers with less than an acre of land) to government-supplied resources, would be surprising indeed.

CONCLUSION

The much-heralded seed-fertilizer-water control revolution has the potential to increase dramatically the welfare of nearly all residents of rural Bangladesh. The new technology sets in motion, however, forces of change that will strain current institutional structures to their utmost: inevitable imbalances in class and regional access to scarce inputs will accelerate on-going processes of land agglomeration and add to the vast pool of the landless proletariat. Even the much-heralded Comilla experiments seem incapable of halting the forces unleashed by the incompatibility of a new technology and an old system of social relations. The ranks of the landless and dispossessed will increase even as they have in other non-socialist countries experiencing a development surge on the land.

NOTES

1. The basic sources of information on agricultural and socio-economic conditions in East Pakistan are Agricultural Census Organization [*1962*] and East Pakistan Bureau of Statistics [*1964–1968*]. Table 1 is based on these sources and on Qadir [*1960*] to relate estimates to a specific village. Note, in Table 1, the exceptionally low labour availability for East Bengal compared with most of the rest of the world due to prohibitions against women working. For an interesting discussion, see Myrdal [*1969, pp. 1083–1091*].

2. Coefficient estimation for agriculture used results of farm management studies conducted by the United Nations Food and Agriculture Organization, the East Pakistan Agricultural University (Mymensingh), the Academy for Rural Development (Comilla), the Bureau of Economic Research (Dacca), the Pakistan Ministry of Agriculture, and the East Pakistan Water and Power Development Authority. For traditional agriculture see Ong [*1955*], N. Islam [*1967*], Ministry of Agriculure [*1970*], Farouk and Rahim [*1967*], Academy for Rural Development [*1964–1970*], and East Pakistan Water and Power Development Authority [*1968*]. Yields were drawn from Bureau of Agricultural Statistics [*1969*].

3. This phenomenon is reported in R. Ahmed [*1963, p.43*].

4. Coefficients are reported in Smith [*1971*], and were estimated from the sources given in note 2 and from Kaonime [*1967*], A. Islam [*1967*], Masud and Underwood [*1970*] and Rahman and Hoque [*1967–69*]. Water requirements were estimated from Center for Population Studies [*1968, chap. II c*]. Prices used were 1970 farmgate prices.

5. Note that we assume the modal ·75 acre farm owns half-shares in one draft animal and the 1·5 acre farm owns outright a draft animal: but 2 are needed for a team so that nearly all cultivators must share, borrow, or rent animals during the busiest seasons. For example, in Comilla District in 1960, out of 118,950 farm holdings between 0·5 and 1·0 acre, only 23,930 reported a total of 37,840 work animals, and of these 19,540 were cows. The figures for all of East Pakistan were similar. See Agricultural Census Organization [*1960, pp.272 and 278*]. In Comilla Kotwali Thana, only about 8 per cent of farmers with less than 1 acre and 26 per cent with 1 to 2 acres owned a pair of bullocks in 1963 [*Pakistan Academy for Rural Development, 1964*]. Unfortunately Qadir does not report bullock ownership for Village Dhaniswar. Apparently there exists labour/ bullock exchange of the type once common in parts of China and institutionalized into Mutual Aid Teams, but no systematic study of this has been performed.

6. For a discussion of appropriate prices to use in evaluating water projects see Mulder [*1970*].

7. To summarize our results regarding the sensitivity of jute to resource searcity and prices, we have seen that with current *aus*/jute farmgate price ratios the decision to grow jute is sensitive to resource scarcities. It water is available for purchase in essen-

tially unlimited quantities and if modern rice varieties are available, a scarcity of labour and working capital on a 4·5 acre farm produces mixtures of IR *aus* and jute, wheat, and til to level out labour peaks. If labour can be freely hired when needed, jute and wheat leave the cropping pattern and the labour intensive IRRI varieties of rice enter in large amounts. Draft animal restrictions then become binding. If bullocks can be hired, jute re-enters the cropping pattern (primarily to utilize otherwise fallow land during the spring). If working capital is available for borrowing (at 12 per cent annual interest), production of potatoes increases dramatically—driving out all IR 8. The production of jute is also increased modestly. Not surprisingly, the effect of water scarcity during the driest month of April is to favour a switch from IR *aus* to jute: a similar result manifests itself if the *aus*/jute price ratio reflects the correct (1970) foreign exchange values of rice and jute rather than (1970) prices to the farmer. For studies which deal with farmers' response to prices in East Bengal see Hussain [*1969*] and the list of references therein.

8. For a description of land tenure changes in East Pakistan see Ahmed and Timmens [*1971, pp.55–64*]. Also see Qadir [*1960*] for a description of the historical situation in eastern Comilla District.

9. For Dhaniswar we have used throughout this section the *de facto* land-holdings, that is, mortgaged land is considered the property of the mortgagee. Dhanishwar has a low incidence of sharecropping and renting of land, and thus we are spared the complications arising from these phenomena. For distribution of land-holdings for East Pakistan in 1964-65, see East Pakistan Bureau of Statistics, 'Round 6' [*1966, p.34*]. Somewhat different results may be found in the 1960 Census of Agriculture. For a sanguine view of rural income distribution and some interesting farm budget data, see Jack [*1927*], who writes that: 'It is clear that the agricultural wealth of the district is divided with considerable fairness in such a way that the great majority of the cultivators have a reasonable share. This is no country of capitalist farmers with bloated farms and an army of parasitic and penurious labourers'. Several more recent studies support the contention that the socio-economic structure of rural East Pakistan is relatively egalitarian. See, for example, Bertocci [*1970 b, p.114*]. He postulated that this egalitarian social system is partially due to families' constantly shifting fortunes, and the consequent dynamism causing moderated shifts in land ownership in a cyclical pattern. For a contrasting view, see R. Mukherjea and M. M. Mukherjee [*1946, pp.327–328*], where they compute the Gini ratio as 0·51 for 12 villages near Sriniketan and 0·44 for 6 villages in Bogra District. For a discussion and review of the literature relating to income distribution in South Asia and the world see Myrdal [*1969, pp. 563–579*].

10. For historical analyses of class structure in Bengal see Marx [*1853*], Mukherjea [*1948, pp.660–672; 1957*].

11. For descriptions of faction politics in Bengal see Bertocci [*1970a, pp.150–178*], Nicholas [*1968, pp.243–254*], and Zaidi [*1970, pp.73–89*].

12. Statistics [*Agricultural Census Organization, 1960, Table 49*] show a considerable fraction of cultivators 'hiring' labour; in our opinion, however, most of the smaller cultivators who do this are in reality exchanging labour. Our interest is with those who must hire a net amount of labour from outside the family. The cutoff at 4 acres is only valid for current conditions—traditional technology. For modern technology the cutoff is between 1·5 and 3·0 acres, but our interest now is on the present-day situation.

13. For useful regional analyses with an agricultural foundation see Rashid [*1967*], and Brammer [*1969*]. The fundamental work on agricultural statistics for the area is Ishaque [*1946*]. An excellent summary of regional land-use and land-capability differences is contained in IBRD [*1972*].

14. Stated policy in early 1973 is to increase water charges for low-lift pump, tubewell, and large-scale irrigation schemes but no concrete actions have been taken.

15. It is instructive to note the work of Ghosh [*1948, pp.425–442*], who illustrated on the basis of data collected from 1931 to 1945 some of the insidious effects of sharecropping. His work helps to understand the position of the rural proletariat in Bengal and to appreciate the complexities of labour hire. The 'Tebhaga' revolt among peasants in North Bengal over the fraction of the crop to be paid to the landowner is also interesting for the light it throws on peasant stratification, Alavi [*1965, pp.273–274*].

16. One government programme ostensibly developed to assist the poorest members of rural society but in fact used to bolster the positions of the 'rich', local cronies of

Ayub Khan was the Rural Works Programme [*Sobhan, 1968*]. For descriptions of the workings of the traditional credit system, see M. I. Khan [*1963, pp. 66–97*], Shahjahan [*1968*], Rahman [*1973*] and Registrar of Co-operative Societies [*1967*]. The latter report indicates that loans are obtained from well-to-do people and friends and relatives in the proportions of 52 per cent and 26 per cent of total loans. Institutional loans are given primarily to the larger landholders. Multi-purpose Co-operative Societies (primary) default regularly as their relatively wealthier members observe the almost complete lack of sanctions against their failure to repay loans.

17. A general description of the work of the Academy is contained in Raper [*1970*]. More detailed summaries of the co-operatives' progress are contained in the annual reports. See, for example, B.U. Ahmed [*1970*]. Government policy is apparently to foster the creation of co-operatives in many areas of Bangladesh. See Planning and Development Department [*1970*], and 'PM urges people to organise co-operatives', *Bangladesh Observer*, April 26, 1972. Just what form these co-operatives will take is impossible to predict now, but the generally conservative cast of the Awami League government leaves little doubt that they will be unlikely to threaten the interests of the more prosperous cultivators.

18. Many of the data reported here are from Faidley and Esmay [*1970*]. The conclusions are my own.

19. Ali Akhter Khan of the Academy for Rural Development, Comilla, in 1970 surveyed 6 of the 30 village societies that had defaulted to that time. Among other things, he found that 60 per cent of loans went to 25 per cent of the members—the managing committee of 'influential leaders'. It was these wealthier men who stopped repaying! Also see the highly informative account of Akhter Hameed Khan, 'Tour of Twenty Thanas', [*Khan, 1971*]. Concerning Chandina Thana: 'The village mahajans have carried on unceasing propaganda. They have tried to undermine confidence . . . Some powerful defaulters have banded together . . .' In Daudkandi Thana: 'In the case of Patuikanda society a loan of Rs. 25,000 was taken by the manager, but only Rs. 15,000 were distributed to the members . . . there are several other rich and influential managers like the manager of Patuikanda. Not only have they defaulted their loans, they are agitating for the issue of pumps without loan repayment.' There are many other similar stories, but also an ever -present faith on the part of Akhter Hameed Khan that peasant organization can overcome these difficulties.

20. These data are reported by Faidley and Esmay [*1970, p.14*] and are based on analysis by Dr. Faidley of surveys of the Comilla Academy for Rural Development.

REFERENCES

Agricultural Census Organization, Ministry of Food and Agriculture, 1962, *Census of Agriculture: East Pakistan, 1960,* Karachi: Government of Pakistan.

Ahmed, Badar Uddin, 1970, *A New Rural Co-operative System for Comilla Thana— Rural Co-operative Pilot Experiment Ninth Annual Report, 1968–69,* Comilla: Pakistan Academy for Rural Development.

Ahmed, I. and J. F. Timmens, 1971, 'Current Land Reforms in East Pakistan', *Land Economics,* 47: 1.

Ahmed, Raisuddin, 1963, *Farm Income in an East Pakistan District,* Dacca: Agriculture Information Service, Department of Agriculture, Government of East Pakistan.

Alavi, Hamza, 1965, 'Peasants and Revolution', in R. Miliband and J. Saville (eds.), *The Socialist Register 1965,* New York: Monthly Review Press.

Bertocci, P. J., 1970a, 'Elusive Villages: Social Structure and Community Organization in Rural East Pakistan', Ph.D. thesis, East Lansing, Michigan State University.

Bertocci, P. J., 1970b, 'Patterns of Social Organization in Rural East Bengal', in A. Lipski, (ed.), *Bengal East and West,* East Lansing: Asian Studies Centre, Michigan State University.

Brammer, Hugh, 1969, *East Pakistan Summary of Agricultural Development Possibilities,* Dacca: Soil Survey Project of Pakistan.

Bureau of Agricultural Statistics, 1969, *Agricultural Production Levels in East Pakistan (1947–1969),* Dacca: Directorate of Agriculture, Government of East Pakistan.

Centre for Population Studies, 1968, *Progress Report—Ganges-Brahmaputra Basin Studies,* Cambridge, Mass.: Harvard University.

Day, H., 1963, 'On Aggregating Linear Programming Models of Production', *Journal of Farm Economics*, 45: 4.

East Pakistan Bureau of Statistics, 1964-1968, *Master Survey of Agriculture in East Pakistan*, seven rounds, Dacca: Government of East Pakistan.

East Pakistan Water and Power Development Authority, 1968, *Farm Management Survey Report of Irrigation Projects under EPWAPDA for the year 1965–66*, Dacca: Director-ate of Land and Water Use.

Faidley, LeVern W. and Esmay, 1970, *Introduction and Use of Improved Rice Varieties: Who Benefits?* East Lansing: Department of Agricultural Engineering, Michigan State University.

Farouk, A. and S. A. Rahim, 1967, *Modernizing Subsistence Agriculture*, Dacca: Bureau of Economic Research.

Ghose, T. and H. Sinha, 1945, 'Agricultural Co-operation in Bengal and Rest of British India (1918-19 to 1938-39)', *Sankhya-Indian Journal of Statistics*, 7: 2.

Ghosh, Ambica, 1948, 'Agricultural Labour in Bengal', *Indian Journal of Economics*, 28: 110.

Hussain, S. M., 1969, 'The Effect of the Growing Constraint of Subsistence Farming on Farmer Response to Price: A Case Study of Jute in Pakistan', *Pakistan Development Review*, 9: 3.

International Bank for Reconstruction and Development, 1972, *Bangladesh Land and Water Resources Sector Study*, Washington.

Ishaque, H. M., 1946, *Agricultural Statistics by Plot to Plot Enumeration in Bengal, 1944 and 1945*, Alipore.

Islam, Aminul, 1967, 'An Investigation into the Production Including Costs and Returns in the Production of Potatoes, in Comilla Kotwali Thana in 1966–67 Rabi Season', M.S. thesis, Mymensingh: East Pakistan Agricultural University.

Islam, Nazrul, 1967, 'Impact of Irrigation on Cropping Pattern and Production Practices in Two Villages under Comilla Kotwali Thana', M.S. thesis, Mymensingh: East Pakistan Agricultural University.

Jack, J. C., 1927, *The Economic Life of a Bengal District*, London: Oxford University Press.

Kaonime, I., 1967, 'An Economic Study of Farms Introducing Boro Rice Production at Kalyanpur, Mymensingh', M.S. thesis, Mymensingh, East Pakistan Agricultural University.

Khan, Akhter Hameed, 1971, *Tour of Twenty Thanas*, Comilla: Pakistan Academy for Rural Development.

Khan, Mohammad Irshad, 1963, 'The Development of Institutional Agricultural Credit in Pakistan', *Pakistan Development Review*, 3: 1.

Ladejinsky, Wolf, 1970, 'Ironies of India's Green Revolution', *Foreign Affairs*.

Lee, J. E., 1966, 'Exact Aggregation—A Discussion of Miller's Theorem', *Agricultural Economics Research*, 17: 2.

Marx, K., 1853, 'India', *New York Daily Tribune*, August 5, No. 3838.

Masud, Sharif and F. L. Underwood, 1970, 'Gumai Bil Boro Paddy Profits and Losses, 1967-68 Season', *Farm Management Research Report 5*, Mymensingh: East Pakistan Agricultural University.

Ministry of Agriculture and Works, 1970, *Schedule for Farm Management Research in Pakistan*, Islamabad: Planning Unit, Government of Pakistan.

Mukherjea, R. and M. M. Mukherjee, 1946, 'A Note on Concentration of Income in Bengal Villages', *Sankhya—Indian Journal of Statistics*, 7: 3.

Mukherjea, R., 1948, 'Economic Structure of Rural Bengal: A Survey of Six Villages', *American Sociological Review*, 13: 6.

Mukherjea, R., 1957, *The Dynamics of a Rural Society: A Study of the Economic Struct-ure in Bengal Villages*, Berlin: Akademir-Verlag.

Mulder, P., 1970, 'The Valuation of Agricultural Commodities in East Pakistan', in *Thakurgaon Tubewell Project Extension (Modified Feasability Report)*, annexe IV, Dacca: East Pakistan Water and Power Development Authority.

Myrdal, Gunnar, 1969, *Asian Drama*, New York: Pantheon Press.

Narain, D. and P. C. Joshi, 1969, 'Magnitude of Agricultural Tennacy', *Economic and Political Weekly*, 4: 39.

Nicholas, Ralph, 1968, 'Structures of Politics in the Villages of Southern Asia', in M. Singer and B. S. Cohn (eds.), *Structure and Change in Indian Society*, Chicago: Aldine Publishing Company.

Ong, Shao-or, 1955, *Interim Report to the Government of Pakistan on Farming Systems and Suggested Changes in the Ganges-Kobadak Irrigation Project Unit*, Rome: Food and Agriculture Organization of the United Nations.

Pakistan Academy for Rural Development, 1964, *Livestock Population in Comilla Thana*, Comilla.

Pakistan Academy for Rural Development, 1965–1969, *Crop Cutting Surveys, Comilla Kotwali Thana*, Comilla.

Planning and Development Department, 1970, *Integrated Rural Development Programme, 1970–1979*, Dacca: Government of East Pakistan.

Qadir, S. A., 1960, *Village Dhaniswar—Three Generations of Man—Land Adjustment in an East Pakistan Village*, Comilla: Pakistan Academy for Rural Development.

Rahman, M. and A. Hoque, 1967-1969, *Costs and Returns for Irrigated Winter Crops*, Comilla: Pakistan Academy for Rural Development.

Rahman, Mujibur, 1973, *Farm Credit Situation in Bangladesh: A Survey*, Dacca: Agriculture Economics Section, Planning Commission.

Raper, A. F., 1970, *Rural Development in Action: The Comprehensive Experiment at Comilla, East Pakistan*, Ithaca: Cornell University Press.

Rashid, Haroun er, 1967, second edition, *East Pakistan—A Systematic Regional Geography and its Development Planning Aspects*, Lahore: Sh. Ghulam Ali and Sons.

Registrar of Co-operative Societies, 1967, *Agricultural Credit in East Pakistan*, Dacca.

Shahjahan, Mirza, 1968, *Agricultural Finance in East Pakistan*, Dacca: Bureau of Economic Research.

Smith, Douglas V., 1971, *Technology and Dynamics of Rural Class Differentiation in East Bengal*, Cambridge, Mass.: Harvard University Center for Population Studies.

Sobhan, Rehman, 1968, *Basic Democracies Works Programme and Rural Development in East Pakistan*, Dacca: Bureau of Economic Research.

Zaidi, S. M. Hafeen, 1970, *The Village Culture in Transition: A Study of East Pakistan Rural Society*, Honolulu: East-West Center Press.